SEXUALITY
AND THE
RELIGIOUS
IMAGINATION

SEXUALITY
and the
RELIGIOUS
IMAGINATION

Bradley A. TePaske

Spring Journal Books
New Orleans, Louisiana

Published by
Spring Journal, Inc.;
627 Ursulines Street #7
New Orleans, Louisiana 70116
Tel.: (504) 524-5117
Website: www.springjournalandbooks.com

Cover design by
Michael Mendis
24 Blackfriars Street
London, Ont. N6H 1K6, Canada
e-mail: mmendis@rogers.com

Cover art:
Bradley A. TePaske

Printed in Canada
Text printed on acid-free paper

Library of Congress Cataloging-in-Publication Data Pending

Dedication

Donald F. Sandner
(1928 - 1997)

Arlene TePaske Landau

For many are the pleasant forms which exist in
  numerous sins,
  and incontinencies,
  and disgraceful passions,
  and fleeting pleasures,
    which (men) embrace until they become sober
  and go up to their resting place.
And they will find me there,
    and they will live,
    and they will not die again.

—"The Thunder, Perfect Mind"
The Nag Hammadi Library

Contents

Acknowledgments

Right acknowledgement of the individuals supportive of this book must begin with my expression of gratitude to Nancy Cater of Spring Journal Books for the respect she has shown for my original text, as well as to my gifted editor, Sylvia Ruud, for her expert contributions.

My regards extend also to three remarkable souls, gratefully remembered, who contributed immeasurably to my studies and to my religious understanding over many years: Prof. Gilles Quispel; the Tantric scholar and art collector Ajit Mookerjee; and my beloved mentor and friend, Donald F. Sandner, whose passion for the Spirit was indeed wondrous to behold! To these I must add James Hillman, whose differentiated archetypal perspective, aesthetic discipline, and sheer creative tenacity have long inspired me, and influenced both this writing and my work as a psychotherapist.

I also wish to express special appreciation and thanks to two other distinguished scholars: Larry J. Alderink, Professor Emeritus of Comparative Religion at Concordia College (Moorhead), who presented me with a signed copy of his fascinating Ph.D. dissertation on the Eleusinian and Orphic Mysteries, and Birger A. Pearson, Professor Emeritus of the University of California (Santa Barbara), a contributing translator of *The Nag Hammadi Library in English*, whose lectures on Mystery Religions of the Graeco-Roman World and Origins of Christianity I was privileged to audit, and who has graciously responded to my topical queries over the years. The intellectual rigor of these devoted teachers has challenged me and assisted me in assessing my limitations.

I express my appreciation also to Lyn Cowan, Nancy Qualls-Corbett, Murray Stein, and Rosamonde Miller for their rich affirmations. To the many people who allowed me to use their dreams in this book, I owe thanks. To Carolyn Radlo, Elizabeth Kay, Marcus and Jonas TePaske, and my extraordinary wife and fellow Jungian analyst, Arlene TePaske Landau, I express my love and gratitude for their constructive comments, for "getting me," and for all the reasons to believe that they bring to my life. My indebtedness to my lively and courageous mother, Vera, and to the living mystery I call "Sophia!" may simply abide in silence.

Bradley A. TePaske
January 2008

Image Credits

Everything comes to be out of One and is resolved into One.

— Musaios, pupil of Orpheus

Preface

C arl G. Jung observes that "anything psychic is Janus-faced—
it looks both backwards and forwards. Because it is evolving,
it is also preparing the future."[1] The present moment, like
any present moment in the expanse of history—or in your reading of
this work, inevitably arises within the parameters indicated in the
following dream. With both silent profundity and wry critique, it once
voiced its demand for an individual response to the timeless questions:
Where do we come from? What are we? Where are we going?

*I find myself standing on a vast arid plain stretching in every direction to
distant mountains on the horizon. Before me stand two ancient
monumental, seemingly Roman structures constructed of rough limestone
blocks. On each is mounted a beautifully wrought bronze plate covered with
mysterious diagrams and hieroglyphs. The tablet to the left is inscribed with
the record of the origins of the universe and all creation, while that on the
right bears ritual and alchemical formulae by which everything indicated
on the first may be realized, a reversal of the process but very different.
Suddenly, war is about to break out! I am frightened off by a wild duck,
jump in the car with my mother, and drive off.*

Awe inspiring, portentous, and now twenty-five years in the past, the
emergence of such a dream would rightly arouse caution in any
attending analyst or duck hunter! For the patient and his mother
complex, practical emphasis on tenacity in the plodding alchemy of
everyday life was strongly indicated, and so it has been. But beyond
any personal case history, our dream is one of those striking instances
wherein Psyche simply displays her ingenious inner workings—the
dream's vast plain a stage where the preconditions and irrepressible
anticipations of humankind are set. The absence of actual massing
armies emphatically indicates creative struggles of a different order in
the psychic interior, necessitating the sharp eye of a birdwatcher for
whatever may arise in the dream's tense ambit. But intimidation from

a wild duck and that getaway with mom? Clearly, dreamers must learn to work psychologically—and laugh at themselves, at their infantile fears and eccentricities, even in the face of war and cosmic mysteries. How like the effeminate Encolpio of Fellini's *Satyricon* crying out at the feet of the Minotaur: "Please, please don't kill me. I'm not a trained gladiator. I'm only a student!" Prior to mother's rescue, the wild duck is actually the only other living creature in the dream. It is saving and essential to value, like Giacometti's cat crouching amidst the Rembrandts in a burning museum. Panic too has its virtue here, prompting a healthy response of flight from things too large to address prematurely, though now the backdrop of all that follows. A moment's hearty laughter, then—and a prayer for the versatility of a duck in moving through air, water, earth, and perhaps fire.

With the biological rhythm of Birth-Sex-Death so fundamental to our very existence on this plane of becoming, with body and biosphere so palpably the medium of spirit, and both sex and the dichotomy of gender utterly pervasive in the human imagination, how can it possibly be that the numinosity and sacral significance of sex has been officially ignored through two thousand years of Christian tradition? This is the germinal question of this study.

In the face of today's pornographic sprawl and the frenzied commodification of our world, the recognition and reintegration of the forgotten dimensions of sex as it is actually lived and experienced ("sexuality") arises for me as nothing less than a moral imperative, though by no means in any patriarchal sense of that expression. Jung tells us that "a particularly fruitful source of religious symbolism is the instinct to which most importance is attached in a given epoch or culture," and likens the sexual instinct to an "injured deity" returning to claim its due.[2] Such provocative words immediately place the "Sex" in our biological equation in quite another light. For just as timelessness and immortality are qualities ascribed to deity, so psyche possesses its own ambiguous relation to calendar time. Furthermore, the psyche seems both to attend carefully, and to ignore the body's death. It speaks rather of a transoceanic flight for which the black-clad stewardess says no luggage is required, a luminous tunnel to a reunion with long dead family members, the engineer passed away but back at college to major in music, a night drive to the remote villa of a wealthy but unknown husband. The denial of death is not simply a defense, like sex or inspiration—it is the divine gift of penetrating discernment!

A second question arises here: If sexual and bodily enactment plays so central a role in religious complexes such as Hindu Tantra (our prime non-Western example), what historical experiences within the broader Christian or our Western pagan religious tradition approximate or epitomize the confluence of sexuality and the religious imagination? In Christian history we see the "injured deity" most clearly in erratic and distorted forms on the heretical fringe, welling up monstrously within *Ecclesia* herself in recurring inquisitions or even in the sadomasochistic display of the crucifixion. Noting the root of "heresy" in the Latin *haeresis*, "an action of taking, a choice," we promptly set course for materials more fruitful for the imagination. This work draws upon many archetypal images, myths, and practices, from ancient Mediterranean cults, such as those of Cybele and Attis, Aphrodite and Eros, and Dionysus and Hermes, to those of Shiva and Kali in India, but ultimately returns to the advent of the current era. For like rediscovering the fair and youthful body of a lover long lost to glacial ice, a collection of Gnostic documents discovered at Nag Hammadi, Egypt, in 1945 will bring us full circle in contemplating the individual experience of the psyche with the aid of the images of Mary Magdalen and Sophia in ancient Gnosticism.

Grounded in myth, variously crude or refined, each of these religious complexes sought in its own way to articulate and answer the most fundamental emotional needs and existential concerns of its devotees. Accordingly, a depth psychological study must reflect and serve the passion, suffering, and imagination of the individual soul. Intimate experiences of sexual and psychic life are fundamental to this entire undertaking, concerned as it is with the nascent images of behavior, dreams, fantasy, and visionary states. The individual human being lives in history and in the moment simultaneously, and with the fact of mortality. Historical and cultural perspective is an essential part of depth psychological inquiry. It would, however, be both banal and obvious to speak of our actually very mysterious "history and moment" without specific qualifications, each related to the interweaving of the personal and archetypal unconscious. I do not see the archetypes and the collective unconscious as either eternal or as a simple repository of abstract Platonic forms, but rather as resonant living patterns, even habits, inseparable from the flow of Life (*zoe*).

Jung's original expression, "collective unconscious," remains congenial to me, not least because it has prompted such frequent accusations that Jung was a mystic. The alternate expression, "objective psyche," coined by Jung in 1929, often strikes me as a philosophical nuance—clean, politically correct, a far cry from the complications of Jung's dream of a row of tombs in *Memories, Dreams, Reflections,* where the mummified bodies of knights, each from a preceding century, revivify as Jung moves back in time.[3] The practical function of the archetypes is most immediately comparable to the holistic phenomena of speciation and environment on one hand, and to the image-based behavioral language of ethology (the branch of zoology concerned with image-based interactions) on the other. Drastically limited in our ability to ascertain the inner experience of even a child—let alone the sentience of birds, animals, or plants—the body of childhood is readily forgotten as one embraces other bodies in the attempt to retrieve its elusive totality. Amidst all this, the personality awaits initiation into the matrix of its origin and the birth of an expanded psychic consciousness. The poetry of Octavio Paz captures the essential mystery of the body and its psychic imagery very beautifully:

> The body is imaginary, not because it lacks reality, but because it is the most real reality: an image that is palpable yet ever-changing, and doomed to disappear. To dominate the body is to suppress the images it emits ....[4]

The clarity of the Greek language unified the ancient world. Discernible already in the "prephilosophic insights" of early Greek, life as *bios* indicates both biography, "the limited life of one man," and the life of any creature. It does not exclude *thanatos.* Contrasting with the "life-death" of *bios* is the unconditioned *zoe* that animates *bios. Zoe* thus represents an essential quality of "indestructible life," personified by Dionysus, the dying but ever resurgent Lord of Souls. The mythologist Carl Kerényi observes:

> What resounds surely and clearly in *zoe* is "non-death." It is something that does not even let death approach it. For this reason the possibility of equating *psyche* with *zoe,* the "soul" with "life," and of saying *psyche* for *zoe,* as Homer did.[5]

Zoe and *psyche,* life and soul, are entwined so intimately together! This stated, words revert back into the living images, the living body of fantasy and imagination, the basis of our specific human capacity for reflective consciousness. The degree to which the living body—*any* "living body"—is seen either as a concrete transient object or as an imaginal process and presentation remains central to the whole question of sexuality and the religious imagination.

For anyone acquainted with religious phenomenology it is an open secret that although physical and spiritual passion are deadly enemies, they are nevertheless brothers-in-arms for which reason it often needs the merest touch to convert one into the other.

—C. G. Jung

CHAPTER ONE

Religion and Sexuality, Psyche and Imagination

O n a bluff overlooking the capital city the domed cathedral of St. Paul stands in full classical Renaissance decorum, mother church of its Archdiocese and an impressive regional landmark. Researching this book in Minnesota in the late 1980s, I was deeply struck by the ostensibly perverse, but extremely telling parallels and comparisons forced upon me by the fact that directly across the freeway from this cathedral stood an old erotic haunt for men called the Faust Complex. For anyone familiar with C. G. Jung's writings or the dramatic works by Goethe or Marlowe, the very name Faust resonates with connotations germane to that intimately personal path of desire, inevitable duplicity, and ambivalent light and darkness along which any individual's moral equation is calculated and lived out.

Encountering Faust coupled with "complex" in that part of town was no less striking, given the specific nature of that term in its psychological meaning. Indeed, the most fundamental psychological factor to which Jung directs his attention, the complex, consists of a personal constellation of emotionally charged psychic images, endowed with its own memory, living an autonomous life outside the ego, given to spontaneous self-representation (so conspicuous in dreams), and ceaselessly challenging us to deepen our consciousness beyond our personal conflicts and towards their archetypal roots. The author's mother complex is a ready case in point, the *prima materia* of this work. In a comparable manner, the Faust Complex is collectively emblematic of corresponding emotionally charged contents that have been moralized and obliquely rejected by collective Christian consciousness—their images, memories, and enduring vitality banished from any officially sanctioned Christian notion of the sacred. The cathedral stands on its hill in triumphant affirmation of all things spiritual and ethical, while the numinosity of desire, the body, sexuality, nature, as well as the forgotten stuff of our pagan religious heritage languish in the Christian psyche on the level of a shabby sex club with private booths for a nocturnal congregation. Thus the church and the men's club betray their dubious symmetry. At the Faust Complex the particulars of ritual confession for the shortcomings of the flesh appear grotesquely inverted in the ritual of the peep show booth with its closed door and parting-curtained window, its coin box, iconographic candles, postcard racks, and devotional literature. In closets in secret at the cathedral or across the freeway, the soul *in extremis* may unburden itself in a kindred issue of word and seed— one confessional tended by a ceremonially clad priest, the other by mechanically unveiled interactive handmaidens of the forgotten goddesses and sexual gods to whom so much of this writing will be devoted.

An initial vignette of a ritual process from the far side of earth serves as a ready response to this tawdry Western parody and the dilemma it reveals. Ponder the auspicious, or perhaps the suspicious role of a young female celebrant entering the precinct of a Hindu tantric ritual:

> The girl may be seated on a low altar, with legs spread wide apart to display the hallowed symbol of adoration, the yoni, which, like the yonis of all the women present, must be unshaven. Or she may lie spread-eagle on the floor in the pentacle position, her head and outstretched arms and legs forming the five points of a star. She is sprinkled with wine and rendered sacred by the rite of applying *(nyasa)*, the priest ritually implanting upon her limbs the power of the goddess. This he does by lightly touching her forehead, eyes, nostrils, nose, ear lobes, throat, breasts, arms, hands, navel, thighs, knees and feet, with his hands, while intoning the appropriate mantras.
>
> Special homage is paid to the yoni, which the priest touches with his lips and anoints with sandalwood paste, and to which he symbolically offers libations from a yoni-shaped vessel. ...

> The girl is thus transfigured into Shakti and becomes a deity
> incarnate. She is adored and worshipped like a goddess and
> treated as one. The whole congregation now forms a living
> mandala within the ritual chamber.[1]

The proposition that every conceivable variation of human sexual behavior, from its most life-enhancing to its most destructive, carries concealed within it a powerful religious impulse is at once a provocation, an evocation, and an invocation. While inescapably antagonistic to excessively rigid patriarchal establishments—Catholic, Christian fundamentalist, or otherwise—the insights our proposition reveals will speak to the individual priest struggling with his secret pedophilia; the rabbi agitated by serious questions about Adam's first consort, Lilith; the evangelist compulsively cruising for prostitutes; or the sexually starved pastor trapped in an exemplary public marriage. For tragically enough, the patriarchies of Christianity or Judaism—in blatant disregard for the deep connection between religion and sexuality—have failed to provide adequate images, symbols, mythologies, or rituals through which the full range of sexual instincts might be accepted, positively valued, reflected upon, and imaginatively cultivated.

As a clinical psychologist, Jungian analyst, and religious historian seasoned in the treatment of both survivors and perpetrators of sexual abuse, I have been granted a unique window on the deeper dimensions of sexuality. The sheer magnitude and ubiquity of solitary suffering experienced by countless individuals in relation to sex, erotic love, and traditional religious perspectives only deepens upon looking beyond the consulting room to the culture at large. Though collective in its reflections and archetypal in its scope, this work will maintain a central concern for the life and experience of the individual soul, though hardly only those with professed religious creeds and interests.

Of no less concern in setting forth is an anticipated provocation, which is sensed with responsibility but considered both inescapable and crucial. It pertains to the uncertain emotions of people who have suffered deep sexual injury, those whose personal experiences of "every conceivable variation of human sexual behavior" have amounted to a lifetime of emotional turmoil, relational ambivalence, or worse. It pertains also to the personal reflections, emotions, and dreams of sensitive police investigators, nurses, pediatricians, social workers, psychotherapists, sex workers, and prisoners who stand close witness to the full spectrum of contemporary sexual pathology. These include intelligent and highly committed people who are confronted daily with clinical imperatives, are urgent about legislative and judicial practical remedies for sexual violence, and long since wearied by sudden defendant claims of being "born again" on the way to trial, but who retain such conventional notions about religion that a "religious" approach to diverse sexual phenomena may appear suspicious, baffling, or simply irrelevant.

Immediately the religiously sensitive person will see Christ crucified in the ritually abused child or the sexually humiliated Abu Ghraib prisoner, imagine the demeaned and raped woman in terms of the Biblical woman taken in adultery and threatened with stoning, or empathize with the perennially slandered Mary Magdalen. Associations such as these arise in relation to cultural and historical types. But beyond this, images of sexual pathology, unfamiliar sexual variations, or the sexual customs of peoples remote in locale and time evoke strong responses by activating both personal complexes and the powerful archetypal energies at their core. Thus there is an invitation here to an exploration for which a gift for metaphor and symbolic understanding is an essential asset. Solitary wanderings beyond familiar psychological turf, in uncharted expanses of a glaring desert or the green tangled corridors of the rainforest—mind or body, have proverbially brought one face to face with oneself and the numinous other.

Surely, where the depth psychologist *fails* to persuade that the behavioral style and fantasy patterns associated historically with Aphrodite or Venus are quite alive in the young hooker working the street, or with Pan in the rapist as he discards the missing convenience-store attendant in a ditch, or Persephone in the sad tale of a twelve-year-old abducted from a slumber party and murdered, or again, Dionysus living on in the sex clubs and bathhouses—here a protest of a poetic irrelevance is justified. But this is not our fate. For to consider the deeper dimensions of the sexual instinct and proceed to amplify their images with parallels from ancient religious complexes and mythology is by no means to romanticize or trivialize matters of glaring reality. Our resort to historical materials serves quite simply as an indispensable aid for discerning the soul-stuff of sex in its myriad forms. The preceding examples are only initial hints of the behavioral drama, imaginal specificity, and autonomous power through which the archetypes and the collective psyche create reality every day. From a depth perspective, however, they represent only ready external examples of sexuality in concrete enactment.

As we expand our inquiry to embrace human sexuality generally, a basic principle remains constant: where psychological reflection on inner psychic phenomena is neglected, the dynamics of the sexual instinct simply manifest themselves automatically in behavior or symptom. Here the individual unconsciously *becomes* the image of the instinctual drive by acting it all out in whatever innocuous or distorted form. There is no reflective vessel of containment, for the body has yet to be realized as a temple and a microcosm. The soul value of conscious interdiction and the resulting possibility of an expansion of consciousness within the flow of passionate experience is only realized by taking the instinct's *interior self-representation* in images and symbols as a starting point—by embracing and seriously reflecting upon them.

Constructive means for creatively entering the intrapsychic play of erotic images—for getting involved with Psyche—would presumably fall in the province of either religion or professional psychology. As the greater portion of this exploration is focused on the religious question, we may note here in passing that the word "religion" has in itself little to do with creeds, doctrines, institutions, or popular confessions of faith. It pertains rather to a highly individual quest, born of necessity and founded upon the immediate personal experience of body, soul, and spirit. Regarding professional psychology, more pointed observations are required immediately.

In the last year of his career, Jungian psychiatrist Donald F. Sandner proposed that "the entire field of academic and professional psychology stands guilty of malpractice for cutting off half of the experiential universe and refusing to even acknowledge that it exists."[2] This bold critique is at the very least a commentary on the degree to which the field is intractably bound to the external, objective, concrete, and quantifiable order of things. It is devoid not only of any appreciation of the fact that as self-reflective human beings we are poised between nature's outside and nature's psychic interior, but is incapable of grasping that fact for want of an appropriate philosophical base. Its literalistic purview systematically cuts the universe into exclusive opposites and supports that unspoken agenda of secular science: to hunt down any remaining vestige of the sacred and kill it! The phenomenon of consciousness itself, much less the reality and autonomous archetypal life of the psyche, is rarely addressed by professional psychology.

Consider the familiar *Diagnostic and Statistic Manual of Mental Disorders*, published by the American Psychiatric Association and legally required for any psychologist's official record keeping. Its behavioral and clinical descriptions and formal diagnostic categories remain only that. One may apply these diagnostic guidelines to perfection, but remain utterly clueless in regard to the actual psychic contents or inner landscape of the individual soul. Strictly focused on the externally observable, the manual is based in a root fantasy of objectivity whose *a priori* philosophical assumptions are rarely questioned. At V62.89: Religious or Spiritual Problem, for example, one notes that "the focus of clinical attention" may involve "distressing experiences that involve loss or questioning of faith, problems associated with conversion to a new faith"—though, also, a "questioning of spiritual values that may not necessarily be related to an organized church or religious institution."[3] The inclusion of the latter category is rather refreshing for a psychopathology text, however culturally predictable its correlation of religion with mere faith.

The question of insight (gnosis) vis-à-vis faith is fundamental to the ensuing discussion. Presently, however, that questioning of spiritual values unrelated to church or religious institutions encourages us to point out that the root fantasy of objectivity and its inevitable correlates—*concretism* and *literalism*—are archetypally based on Apollo, the abstract aerial god of Greece (comparable to the solar Helios or the Word in the Gospel of John). Likewise Kronos (Saturn) presides archetypally over the progressive extension of order, which certainly is a prominent feature of the *DSM:IV*. Religiously and depth psychologically a painful irony arises here: the pervasive Apollonian understanding of Jesus Christ as God robs the divine figure of his earthly, incarnate, and emotionally intimate aspects— his equally legitimate relation to Dionysus and Eros—while simultaneously suggesting how and why a nearly seventeen-hundred-year (since the Nicean Council, 325 C.E.) Apollonian trajectory of Christian otherworldliness, abstraction, and institutional dominion can, in our "postmodern" age, end up willy-nilly as the cosiest of bedfellows with "scientific objectivity" in relation to Life, a rapacious consumer economy in relation to the biosphere, and the apocalyptic theocracy of the imperial state in relation to human diversity and the soul.

A decisive step is taken here towards an essential paradigm shift that is simply demanded by the earthly nature of psychic life and necessitated by the contemporary malaise—a shift away from the self-destructive worldview of patriarchy (built on the dissociative and ossified logos of Apollo and Kronos) to the holism and universalism of mythos. We have already begun wrapping myth around the mental tools and crisp rationalistic purview of the behavioral sciences (mistakenly called psychology), whose claim to ultimate authority will repeatedly come to mind in our critique of patriarchy. This shift is immediately pertinent to the generally fruitless attempts of scientific psychology to provide emotionally satisfying insights into the nature of dreams, fantasies, intuitive realizations, visionary experiences, and most all other means of accessing nature's animated psychic interior. These attempts fail for want of mythopoetic understanding.

The very terms with which this writing sets forth, "sex" and "religion," offer reciprocal images and meanings in that the former term traces its root to the Latin *secare*, meaning "to cut," while the latter derives from the Latin *religare*, "to tie back" or "to bend back." The "cut" of sex indicates our division as males and females and as individuals of mixed masculine and feminine psychic endowment, but simultaneously our specific human position as distinct creatures vis-à-vis what the Gnostics would call the All. Be this conceived mystically in the moment or materially and historically on a gradient from genealogy to biology, botany, geology, chemistry, microphysics, we find ourselves psychically imbedded in a seamless universe that expands in every direction without and within. This wrap-around, this vessel of reflection, *is* the All; and its demands tear both linear time and the uninitiated ego's sense of control to shreds, like myth itself. The fundamental sympathy of all created things as well as our deep nostalgia for origins is reflected in diverse myths of human emergence and return like those from the New Hebrides where a tribal Adam and his sister emerge from the dual-chambered nut of a Melmel tree, or from the Asmat people of New Guinea whose new year ritual celebrates the tribe's birth from the wind and trees. Jung accordingly correlates *religare* and *reflexio* as kindred processes that reconnect us with the archetypal foundations of our being. Note that the tenacity of bodily and emotional yearning for satisfaction from some soothing *other* is characteristic of both the religious and the sexual instincts. The extremity of this is indicated by the ancient devotees of the Moabite god Bel-Peor, who ritually display each orifice of their bodies and offer its emissions before the cult icon.[4] Furthermore, both the religious and sexual instincts share a common inclination towards the enactment of rituals.

A profound tension is inherent in the terms sex and religion: the wounds of primordial separation, our immersion in life's endless current of passion as limited gendered beings, and our sustained yearning to salve that primal wound. What remains crucial to the entire process of psychological individuation is a progressive *differentiation* of masculine and feminine psychic elements through the lifelong trials of love. Sex and religion: each with its elusive promise that what has been cut asunder may be bound together again.

Innumerable myths, like those of Gnosticism, speak of the whole of existence in a state of gender and multiplicity as a human, even a cosmic, catastrophe. Consider Adam's wound of separation following Eve's generation from his rib, their combined ejection from Paradise beneath a flaming sword; Christ's separation from Magdalen and the other disciples to suffer his flagellation, pierced chest, and death by crucifixion; the lesser known but aboriginal separation of Sophia from her All-Father to wander blind, afflicted, and bound in matter. All are essentially kindred instances in the greater Judeo-Christian-Gnostic tradition, and recorded respectively in Torah, the New Testament, and the recently recovered "Third Testament"—the Gnostic *Nag Hammadi Library*.

The essential *moment* of cutting and yearning is also reflected in a vignette from Plato's famous myth of the original androgynous human: the overweening creature with two faces, dual private parts, four arms and four legs is cut in twain by the sword of Zeus as it seeks to storm Olympus. The image is immediately suggestive of a lively affinity between whatever primal androgyny may be common to humankind and the very realm of the gods. At the same time, the cutting asunder of male and female marks the threshold between the human and the divine—a dual cutting, as it were, both horizontal and vertical. The deepest mysteries of sexuality and the religious imagination thus arise on that razor's edge.

Plato sees the clamor of severed partners for their correlative body not only as basic to copulation and reproduction, but to the entire erotic quest for beauty and soul. This accords with the fact that depth psychologically, and in religious complexes outside the patriarchal order, biological reproduction is a mere footnote to human sexuality. And here Jung's recognition of a close association between the sexual instinct and the striving for wholeness comes most specifically and powerfully into its own. These motifs of separation, gender, and their dynamics will be variously elaborated. But important to note in passing is that the writings of Plato decisively impacted our entire religious trajectory throughout late antiquity and into the Christian era. His classic visions of the ideal world galvanized Jewish metaphysical speculation, already charged with messianic and apocalyptic anticipations; it informed the ascendancy of Egyptian Gnosticism with its legacy of solar hierophanies, divine kingship, and the cult of Isis. However, the stark carnality of Plato's androgyne and all it implies in earthly terms is clearly no central feature in Christian lore. Such imagery persevered rather in the Christian underground of alchemy and hermetism, as it does in the personal and collective underground of sexuality to this day. The androgyne of the *Symposium,* merely one image of Eros, emerges in an ambiance ruled by Dionysus and Aphrodite, a drinking party of upper-class homosexual Athenian men where Socrates, the great devotee of Eros, is himself described as resembling a satyr!

The mythic androgyne hangs in uncertain time and space, in what religious historian Mircea Eliade is forced to describe as *in illo tempore* or *ab origine*—in an "illusive time," an "original time," once upon a time. Like all mythic images, it is a creation of the archetypal imagination, pertinent to the pinnacle of religious ideation and to the object relations of the mother-child dyad, but defined by neither. Michelangelo's Adam reaches to touch the hand of God even as Harlow or Bowlby remind us that the "cling response" is a human instinct even more immediate than feeding.

A substantial portion of Sigmund Freud's contribution to depth psychology is devoted to the differentiation of our understanding of sex. His notion of religion, however, is nearly as limited as the "patently

infantile" religious beliefs he critiques in *The Future of an Illusion* (1927).
His conceptualization reduces god-imagos to personal parental images,
and splits the personality into a punitive (notably, castrating) superego
and the ostensibly chaotic drives of the id (*das Es,* "the it"), while
leaving the ego transfixed in stoic isolation. Freud himself resorts to
Plato's androgyne as reason and science fail him. He clearly rediscovered
the sexual gods (his *libido sexualis* a veritable god-imago), but reduces
the numinosity of sex to an ultimately materialistic substrate, depriving
it of its natural affinity with the religious instinct by rationalistically
rejecting religion as an illusion. Jung's attention to sex is deeply
insightful. He reacted to Freud's theoretical reductionism by fighting
for a general recognition of psyche's right to speak its own language,
free of any theory. At the same time, Jung's original give-and-take with
Freud is clearly evident in the following remarks:

> If man's striving for a spiritual goal is not a genuine instinct
> but merely the result of a particular social development,
> then an explanation according to sexual principles is the
> most appropriate and the most acceptable to reason. But
> even if we grant the striving for wholeness and unity the
> character of a genuine instinct, and base our explanation
> mainly on this principle, the fact still remains that there is
> a close association between the sexual instinct and the
> striving for wholeness.[5]

This striving for wholeness is an essential feature of Jung's religious
instinct manifested in the individuation process of the maturing
personality, its "psychic energy" now detached from Freud's sexual
libido. Reducible neither to spirit nor matter, mind nor body, the
essential *tertium non datur* appears in Jung's epistemological assertion
of 1936, his embrace of a psychology with soul in accord with the
ancient etymological roots of that word, i.e., *psyche* ("soul") and *logos*
("meaning"). Jung observes that

> ... only an insignificant minority regards the psychic
> phenomenon as a category of existence *per se* and draws the necessary
> conclusions. It is indeed paradoxical that *the* category of
> existence, the indispensable *sin qua non* of all existence, namely
> the psyche, should be treated as if it were only semi-existent.
> Psychic existence is the only category of existence of which we

have *immediate* knowledge, since nothing can be known unless it first appears as a psychic image.[6]

Jung's words are echoed by those of an ancient Gnostic text from the 2nd century C.E. that is similarly bold in regard to the primacy of the image as the psyche's fundamental language. The *Gospel of Philip* states, "Truth did not come into the world naked, but it came in types and images. The world will not receive truth in any other way."[7]

A comment on the proverbial fantasy of a spiritual departure from the world is in order here. The entire Western ecclesiastical and philosophical history of the Spirit in its *masculine* nuance tends to seek its exclusive ends by objectifying, denying, transcending, "essentializing," or otherwise demeaning the created world. An historical compulsion, to be sure, but surely the most dangerous of any archetypal fantasy to ever be taken literally, the "transcendence complex" characteristically surfaces in psychic trauma. But it also arises in hysterical fundamentalist prayer meetings, as the inevitable correlate of excessively concrete interpretations of Scripture, in any marriage of religion and the state, in the collective pathology of a rapturous apocalypse—or in suicide. Tersely put in light of the appalling irresponsibility of patriarchal faiths today in relation to sex, body, and biosphere, a simple credo, "Be true to the earth" (*Sei Erde treu!*) and an explosive commentary from Friedrich Nietzsche's *The Birth of Tragedy* (1872), sufficiently cautions us, while surrendering none of its original pique:

> Christianity was from the start essentially and thoroughly disgust and weariness with life, which only dressed itself up, only hid itself in, only decorated itself with the belief in an "other" or "better" life. The hatred of the "world," the curse against the emotions, the fear of beauty and sensuality, a world beyond created so that the world on this side might be more easily slandered, at bottom a longing for nothingness, for extinction, for rest, until the "Sabbath of all Sabbaths"—all that, as well as the absolute desire of Christianity to value only moral worth, has always seemed to me the most dangerous and most eerie form of all possible manifestations of a "Will to Destruction," at least a sign of the deepest illness, weariness, bad temper, exhaustion, and impoverishment in living.[8]

Life and earth might cry out in harmony: emotion, sensuality, passion, fantasy, imagination, joy in the aesthetic presentations of the natural world, the very possibility of Becoming (*werden*), right here, where the *feminine* nuance of spirit as anima, psyche, or soul hovers close to living and embodied things—here where a little girl ponders the orangutan nursing its child and whispers to her mother, "That was a holy thing!" Is this not the appointed province of our soul?

An additional and paradigmatic response to the "absolute desire of Christianity to value only moral worth" may be found in Rudolf Otto's classic steps beyond the *idea* of the holy to a quality of immediate experience. A Protestant scholar of comparative religion of the late 1920s, Otto affirms many worthy ideas and rational concepts in the Christian tradition. These respects paid, however, he dispels any expectation that religious experience might be comprehended by the intellect alone. Concerned rather with a "unique feeling-response," he observes:

> The fact is we have come to use the words "holy," and "sacred" (*heilig*) in an entirely derivative sense, quite different from what they originally bore. We generally take "holy" as meaning "completely good"; it is the absolute moral attribute, denoting the consummation of moral goodness.[9]

Otto proceeds to discern a crucial "overplus," which at the very least arises upon asking what might stand over against such consummate goodness. He explains that rather than representing a merely acquired meaning, "'holy,' or at least the equivalent words in Latin and Greek, in Semitic and other ancient languages, denotes first and foremost *only* this overplus," adding that, "if the ethical element was present at all, at any rate it was not original and never constituted the whole meaning of the word."[10] Psychologically minded people will not find this all that surprising. But, with religious fundamentalism so pervasive today, especially in America and the Middle East, one need not underestimate the provocation represented by every step Otto takes, even simply beyond rationalism—the Biblical "peace that passeth all understanding" notwithstanding. Responses to such a consignment of the "ethical element" to so relative a position vis-à-vis sudden unknown forces will surely range from utter noncomprehension to moral uneasiness to panic or righteous rage. For people reared with little trust in the body, long schooled in the belief that the religious quality is purely good, or whose notion of the sacred is restricted to its ethical and moral meaning, the mere thought of a religious dimension to sexuality will inevitably arise as something akin to the Calvinists' "total depravity," with all the unconscious fascination of sensuality inherent in that term.

Accordingly, the prospect of personally being called upon to truly exercise one's moral faculty may prove even more unnerving than any confrontation with Eros. This innate moral capacity is not instilled by fear-based religious disciplines. If so, it is only superficial. Rather, it is cultivated by a sustained and personalized attitude of recognition for a child's unique emotional being and imagination. Otto's step beyond the moral aspect of the religious element (his "overplus") must accordingly be understood as *prior* to good and evil, not in terms of some lurid leap beyond it. However decisive its moral or ethical implication and consequences, the "religious element" must be sought close to nature, a mother scarcely inclined to negate her own creation without the punitive action of "righteous men." Jung speaks to the effect that any real moral decision begins where the penal code leaves off. Likewise the possibility of numinous experience of one's own.

A vast gulf exists between any doctrine abstracted from life and the individual's immediate response to the "just so" quality of *mana* and the disturbing object. I once placed a big yellow circus balloon with a smiling clown in front of my easygoing one-year-old son with a measure of papa-pride. A stiff copper wire attached to it made it bounce unpredictably. To my amazement, Marcus responded with instant anxiety and panic—an unfamiliar object and the immediate evaluation of it as "the bad object." Seconds after typing that sentence, the butt of my palms weary from typing, I reached round a blind corner for a towel to cushion them at the keyboard, only to pull out a yellow towel with clown faces on it! Even so mundane an example affords a fleeting glimpse of the essential quality of soul-stuff, the synchronicity of the moment where image and meaning coincide on their own, this time prompting surprised laughter. The old literature of folklore and anthropology, like Sir James George Frazer's "Taboo and the Perils of the Soul," cites countless examples of this phenomenon at increasing levels of emotional intensity and significance. The feeling-tone of "taboo" or *mana* may attach to objects, strangers, locations, birth, death, variously ranked persons, or any of the bodily organs and their products; also things weird, out of bounds, forbidden, ill-omened, calamitous, sins against natural law, incest, etc. Eliade notes that "even latrines have a certain *mana* in that they are 'receptacles of power'— for human bodies and their excretions have it."[11] The Romans, too, knew their *Venus cloacina*, goddess of toilets, just as Mercury may live in sewers.

The pertinence of all this to an entire range of human erotic fascinations, fixations, and sexual games is obvious whether or not object-relational distortions lie at their roots. Freud once remarked that the infant's vision of the maternal breast was the primal experience of Beauty. In contrast, the Marquis de Sade's famous remark that the greater part of pleasure is the overcoming of disgust is no less suggestive. First and foremost, the characteristic human response of simultaneous fascination and revulsion for things charged with *mana* indicates that which is psychically and imaginally *alive*—Janus-faced, at once developmentally retrograde and anticipatory, the consummately good and all we might call profanity.

Expressions such as taboo or *mana* are but localized equivalents of what Jung understood as psychic energy, which when manifested in fantasy and imagination represents "the direct expression of psychic life."[12] "The manifest meaning is found in the actual 'look' of the fantasy image."[13] Otto's "overplus" and Jung's "psyche" express a single mystery. The *mana* of both is inseparable from the actual appearance of and relationship between created things. Like consciousness itself, it is a field phenomenon. Now an instructive *in vivo* example:

Placed in an orphanage as a child with no explanation from a mother "overwhelmed" by the care of two older sisters, Candice was twenty-two, deeply needy, and quietly enraged. She was also the first lesbian I had ever worked with, adding an additional unknown to the analysis. An initial dream featured an actual roadblock at which tigers and lions rend one another outside the car. In the face of such intense affectivity, I found myself inclined towards the classic intellectual defense of excessive interpretation. Following one difficult early session this dream came to me:

I am sitting in my chair, but rather than Candice or her chair, a huge glistening blue lion lies in her place, composed of some subtle matter and staring at me intently with its one milky-blue eye. Only secondarily do I notice the beast has an extraordinarily long tail, ringing round its body and disappearing down its throat. The lion's face then becomes a dark circular wood-carved mask radiating black rays, with large bumps like penises or breasts protruding from each cheek. It suddenly arcs through the space and clamps itself onto my throat.

Awakening the next morning with a sore throat, I had developed my first-ever case of laryngitis by nightfall. After assistance in supervision, the memory of a surrealist painting in which a human figure had ears on its knees, and a week of whispering, I just *listened*—as it were, with ears on my belly. The tension eased. Only after my patient departed did I realize my voice had fully returned. Want of a proper body-mother, who could mediate the primal energies of this girl's soul in childhood, had left them reeling autonomously within her, unconscious, powerful, but not without their imagery. Like the energy that physicists postulate prior to the big bang and thus beyond known laws (prior even to matter), a starved will-to-manifest burst forth from Candice, telling this therapist what she needed in the most palpable way. The old anthropological expression, *participation mystique,* describes this instance of therapist-patient identification in mutual unconsciousness very precisely. It remains the bottom line in any psychological relationship, never completely done away with, like an adventurer's path hacked through jungle vines that quickly reclaim it. Fantasy and imagination are prime avenues through which unconscious elements submerged in a *participation mystique* emerge into consciousness.

Few passages in Jung grant such priority and primacy to fantasy and imagination as those in his *Psychological Types*, where we read, "A fantasm is an *idée-force*. Fantasy as imaginative activity is identical with the flow of psychic energy,"[14] or again, fantasy is

> the creative activity from which the answers to all unanswerable
> questions come; it is the mother of all possibilities, where, like
> all psychological opposites, *the inner and outer worlds are joined
> together in living union.*[15]

"Fantasm," or "phantasm" (preferred by Freud, the "phantasy" of early psychoanalysis) is intriguing both for its antique patina in the Latin and Greek *phantasma*, "the object presented to the mind," and for approximating the name of a god! Subtle of flesh, the blue lion with its milk-blue eye is encircled by and swallows its own tail. I once owned a pet Texas indigo snake whose eyes always grew milky before it shed its skin, peeling it off inside out like a woman shedding fancy hose. Naturally suspicious, the one-eyed snake indicates a cyclopic instinctual consciousness, reflexive in its responses and remote from human categories. Merged with the long-tailed blue lion in the *monstrum compositum* of the dream, the serpentine might presumably begin to warm its blood, sprout hair, and grow the leonine mane of its glistening subtle body. Curiously, Candice also once dreamt of pulling out her left eye, only to find myriad tiny eyes, like a cluster of frog's eggs in the water.

Wood is material and sensual, just as carving wood is both a functional and aesthetic fashioning of mother material. The wooden mask of the dream flies forth from a simultaneously zoomorphic and "astral" matrix as a creative god of revelation and initiation might emerge from a cosmic egg. Archaic in its aspect, androgynous in its erect, indistinguishable breasts and phalli, wreathed with black rays, and fanged for blood; this is the mask of a dark being who is stern and rueful, but laden with possibilities. At a similarly fateful juncture in Goethe's *Faust I*, a dramatic hush ensues with the abysmal descent of a magic key into the "Realm of the Mothers." But suddenly, the sprightly puer Euphorion arises in the open air. A Dionysian emissary of indestructible life, Euphorion is neither human nor bound to time or place. Likewise, the dream and the therapeutic experience display the dynamic soul-stuff of individuation transiently in retrograde, then progressively—but also as the deep experiential foundations of *creation mythology* and the emergence of a new vision of the world.

James Hillman tells us:

> Initiation as a transformation of consciousness about life involves necessarily a transformation of consciousness about sexuality.[16]

Here a most mysterious revelatory and initiatory god, who figures recurrently throughout our study, may accordingly be introduced:

Phanes. Phanes is an ancient and specialized form of Eros who, most simply, refers to the "coming of light." He appears in an archaic form in the Orphic creation myth recorded by Robert Graves, though he is variously elaborated in other mythologies of this pagan Greek gnostic tradition:

> The Orphics say that black-winged Night, a goddess of whom even Zeus stands in awe, was courted by the Wind and laid a silver egg in the womb of Darkness; and that Eros, whom some call Phanes, was hatched from this egg and set the world in motion. Eros was double-sexed and golden-winged and, having four heads, sometimes roared like a bull or a lion, sometimes hissed like a serpent or bleated like a ram. Night ... lived in a cave with him, displaying herself in triad: Night, Order, and Justice. Before this cave Rhea played on a brazen drum, compelling man's attention to the oracles of the goddess. Phanes created earth, sky, sun, and moon, but the triple-goddess ruled the universe, until her sceptre passed to Uranus.[17]

Crucial to bear in mind here is a drastic *relativity of dimension* in myth and psyche: smaller than small, larger than large, localized and cosmic, fractal and hologram—the same imagery pertinent to "self" and "world."

Variations within the mythology of the Orphic tradition also describe Phanes as "marvelously beautiful," "shining," four-eyed or covered with multiple eyes; "a monstrous serpent, appearing with all manner of forms of beasts" and, most strikingly, "bearing within himself the honored seed of the gods."[18] The extreme unnaturalness and protean appearance of Phanes mark him as a *living visionary image,* immediately pertinent to creative imagination and the transformation of consciousness, even as he remains wrapped here in zoomorphic forms. Marie-Louise von Franz emphasizes that creation mythology in general does not describe a literal or material creation of the world (however uncanny certain of its intuitions), but rather a human *coming to consciousness of the world.*[19]

Recognition must immediately be granted to the fact that the Phanes of the above description displays only the heads of animals. Intentionally introduced first in his most creaturely form, we will encounter Phanes again, both in relation to the human infant and as a brilliant solar puer akin to Goethe's appropriately named Euphorion.

In any case, the archetypal imagery of Phanes simply resonates in the psyche, displaying archetypal contents deeply akin to the soul-stuff of our dream—the author's bout of laryngitis only accenting its psychosomatic significance in living experience.

Nietzsche's furious critique of Christianity's curse upon emotion and sensuality and its scandalous attitude towards the created world served only as an icebreaker. Otto demonstrates the drastic relativity of thinking (reason, intellect) and feeling (good, evil) in approaching the "religious element." So does Jung, while focusing his attention on intuition (fantasy, imagination). But particularly in an exploration of sexuality and the body, any neglect of the sensation function would constitute an unpardonable oversight. Thus always delighting in the onomatopoeia of the Greek word (*aisthesis*) for our quick inhalation of breath at beauty's sudden appearance, James Hillman recognizes the necessity that psychology embrace the "aesthetic." Indeed the word is an ancient expression for the sensible and perceptible world as such. What need of a spirit or world exterior to it? Christian artists paint even the apocalypse in living color. Buddhists focus on illusion and mindfulness, or may engage in Vipasana meditations on body parts piled in a heap, but it is the artistic creations of Buddhist tradition that celebrate the aesthetic and the anima. Ramakrishna, the saint of Calcutta, is rescued from the metaphysical "Ultimate" by Mother Kali's bewitching gaze. And Catholics anticipate their own sublime *visio beatifica* in a virgin rose. The sensory aspects of anima and soul remain ever present.

Alternate religious perspectives may rightly regard the neglect or disparagement of sensuality and beauty as a sacrilege in itself. Beauty is simply given with creation—as Aphrodite:

> Beauty is the manifest anima mundi—and do notice here it is neither transcendent to the manifest or hiddenly immanent within, but refers to the appearances as such, created as they are, in the forms with which they are given, sense data, bare facts, Venus Nudata. Aphrodite's beauty refers to the luster of each particular event; its clarity, its particular brightness; that particular things appear at all and in the form in which they appear.[20]

The aesthetic discipline and precision of Hillman's vision finds its poetic counterpart in the deft words of Paz and Stevens: "The reality of the body is a shifting image pinned down by desire."[21] Eros is all eyes: "Beauty is momentary in the mind— / the fitful tracing of a portal; / But in the flesh it is immortal. / The body dies; the body's beauty lives."[22]

Our prospectus now complete, its guiding visions lustrous, the undertaking of the coming four chapters recalls that of Virgil's *Aeneid*: "Easy is the descent to Avernus: night and day the door of gloomy Dis stands open; but to recall thy steps and pass out to the upper air, this is the task, this the toil!"[23] Shining Phanes, like bright Aphrodite, each find their mythic contours in the cave of Night, where the Earth Goddess (Rhea) plays on a brazen drum for the triple goddess of Fate —the proverbial counterpoint to every patriarchal order.

Live by the Spirit, I say, and do not gratify the desires of the flesh. For what the flesh desires is opposed to the Spirit, and what the Spirit desires is opposed to the flesh; for these are opposed to each other, to prevent you from doing what you want.

—Letter of Paul to the Galatians 5:16

CHAPTER TWO

The Patriarchal Sexual Legacy

I am in a Lutheran church carrying a very tall lance or victory standard. There with me is my "wife," a stately, powerful, and beautiful Scandinavian woman in a white gown. We carry the lance together in a procession out of the church to some celebration or reception out in the streets. But I find myself turning, strangely turning … moving along at dusk through the streets of Jerusalem. All the earth of the streets is being turned over, like a field being plowed. It is as if I am at my old church college, but also like Rome. But the streets of Rome are like the streets of Jerusalem. The atmosphere grows altogether uncanny. I see the marble façades of white palaces in the city crumbling and falling along the dirt streets. Then suddenly behind me to my left are black men in antique breechcloths with drug-filled pipes. They are laughing, physically powerful, free.

The opening dream displays the authentic religious impulse of a passionate, culturally educated thirty-four-year-old man in relational crisis. A highly supportive personal anima, an internal revolt against the religion of his upbringing, and the initiatory possibilities of both the Great Goddess and her dark-skinned sons are prominent in its sequence. The crumbling buildings of Rome and Jerusalem vis-à-vis the emergence of such powerful Earth energies bracket the dreamer's internal upheaval and emotional transit, just as the collapsing facades of the Holy Cities bespeak the decline of patriarchal Christianity. As if by arranged marriage, the dreamer meets a spirited new wife in the quickly changing religious sanctuary of the dream. As always, personal associations are pertinent here, for the dreamer thought of Penthesileia, Queen of the Amazons, of whose battlefield conflict with Achilles he knew from *The Fall of Troy* by Quintus Smyrnaeus (4th century C.E.). Beautiful and strong in battle, Penthesileia was nonetheless killed and sexually desecrated by the famous puerile necrophile, Achilles, Western paradigm of martial glory.

The presented image of the dream wife portrays her as adroit, self-possessed, radiant, and in harmonious relation with the dreamer as the pair leads a congregation forth from the church. The wife figure is also reminiscent of Nike-Athena, the daughter of Zeus, who is always strongly for the Father in all things spare marriage. She clearly smiles favorably on the dreamer's heroic quest. In the wake of their triumphant departure, however, things grow uncanny. One may recall here that Athena wears the snake-fringed face of the Medusa on her buckler!

The dreamer's momentary disorientation and rotating movement is one with the turning of earth. The abysmal maternal aspect of the feminine is activated; the dream a fine example of the personal anima working in harmony with Mother Earth. Hillman observes that

> the more successful a religion, the more psychopathology can be sheltered under its aegis, given rationale in its dogma, and allowed operation in its ritual. But once one is outside the sphere of a religion, the psychopathology within it stands out.[1]

That the Black men show no sign of such confinement underscores their ambivalent archetypal power.

The dream raises questions about what may come in the aftershock of the patient's recent divorce, especially given his pain of separation and those drug-filled pipes. But psychopathology, that which "moves the psyche," requires imaginal language rather than the moralistic and descriptive terminology of religion or psychopathology. The dark men in their archaic breechcloths are conspicuously Dionysian personages. Their laugher and physical freedom are an intimate part of the Dionysian cosmos, their appearance the assertion of sensation, feeling, and a pristine joy in body and soul. Christianity offers nothing but damnation for any embrace of such dark and soulful characters, with the intriguing exception of the black Shulamite of the *Song of Songs*. That great moment of American literature in *The Adventures of Huckleberry Finn* is pertinent here—where Huck decides not to turn in black runaway Joe, saying, "Alright then, I'll go to hell." Black men *have* been enslaved and betrayed, personally and institutionally. But it is essential to realize that dream images must not be taken literally, neither as the "morally repressed shadow" nor concretely as actual men of color, but as spontaneous *phantasma*. They are creatures of the black sun, body metaphors with an underworld context. The perspective serves soul in one and all—clean boundaries, at least; an excising of the insidious White Man's Burden; and a move from sociology and politics to psychic depth.

Only sixteen hundred years ago initiates of the Eleusinian mysteries still gave up the ritual cry, "Cross the bridge, O Kore, before it is time to begin the three-fold plowing!" in their procession from Athens to Eleusis. The plowing of the fields is an analogue of the mysteries, the oldest and last ritual cycles of Demeter and her daughter Persephone in the history of Greece. The events open with a ritual spreading of rumor that "the maiden" (Kore-Persephone) is missing. The rites cycle through an entire range of human emotion: the wandering in grief of bereavement for the loss of *zoe* (the Kore), the sacrifice of piglets to the Earth, welling anticipation for the maiden's return with the crossing of the bridge; girls then dancing at the sacred well where they once gave sorrowing Demeter to drink. Each celebrant is finally ushered into the Telesterion by torch-bearing boys, to await their personal vision of the resurgent goddess Persephone in a brilliant fire, a repetition of Demeter's ability to confer immortality by burning away mortal dross. The Eleusinian cycle is suffused with secrets of Dionysus and Hades, whose Plutonion—an overarching cave entry, world axis, and conduit to the lower realm— is a natural feature of the low cliffs. Our dreamer finds himself in a similar ambiance of feminine mysteries. His transit from grief to renewal, however, has yet to be played out in relation to the dazzling mystery of his own dark body.

The words of the men who forged the patriarchal sexual morality are fearfully rigid, demeaning, and cold as marble in their critique of the body and its energies, an entire spectrum of sexual behaviors, women, and the natural world—a list readily extended. But fashionable though it may be to attack Christianity, the patriarchal tradition at issue is by no means only Christian. Influences on Christian sexual morality derive from traditions of divine kingship stretching back six thousand years to Mesopotamia, Egypt, and Palestine. But the yearly ritual consummation of *hieros gamos,* the sacred marriage of the solar King and his Queen, a representative of Earth in Babylon and Sumer, has long since ended in hostile divorce.

Historian of sex Vern Bullough cites the most fundamental of all patriarchal laws:

> In sum, the Western tradition as established in the Ancient Near East was a mixed one, but increasingly, it came to be more restrictive, more hostile to *all forms of sex not leading to procreation.* With the Persians, a restrictive sexual life came to be regarded as necessary for salvation and the good life, and the Persian correlation of sexual morality with religious salvation came to have great influence on the West, first its effects on the Jews and the Greeks and ultimately through the adoption of similar ideas by the early Christians.[2]

The Jewish attitude towards sexuality was male dominated, based on obligation to the Father's commandment, "Be ye fruitful and multiply" (Genesis 1:28), and restricted to the covenant of marriage. The Pentateuch is replete with rules and regulations sharply limiting all forms of sexuality not intent on procreation. Leviticus includes wise prohibition on incest with kin, parents, siblings, while sexual relations with neighbors, homosexuality, or bestiality remained grounds for expulsion from the community or even death. The vagina was legislated as the proper goal of seminal emission (an early psychoanalytic prejudice as well) as part of a strategy of control of bodily spontaneity, which obviously deprived masturbation and its attendant fantasy of any worthy individual significance. Menstruation was accordingly feared and concealed. An initial glimpse of the important correlation between variant sexuality and alternate religious devotions appears in the twentieth chapter of Leviticus, with its injunction against the offering of semen to Moloch, the bullish father-god of the Canaanites, whose cult celebrations involved same-sex enactments. Broader indication of patriarchal intolerance for many "just-so" facts of biology and sex (apparently sparing even God from the sight of nature's anomalies) is a ban on participation in religious ritual by anyone blind, lame, blemished, anyone with scabs or running sores, with a crooked back, a flat nose, or those castrated, whores, and dwarves.

The solemn ire of Jewish law bears special contempt for women, which extends to the sexual choices and bodily realities of both women and men:

> If a man lies with a woman having her sickness and uncovers her nakedness, he has laid bare her flow and she has laid bare her flow of blood; both of them shall be cut off from their people. (Lev. 20:18)

Whatever integrity such ancient dictates possessed in their day, they remain integral parts of the patriarchal sexual doctrines. While Eve's gift of fruit to Adam was not associated with sexual knowledge until the Christian period, Hebrew tales of sexually dubious women abound in the Old Testament tradition. Lot is plied with alcohol by two incestuous daughters. Potiphar's wife accuses Joseph of rape after she tries to seduce him. Delilah robs Samson of his strength and sight. The painted Jezebel turns her husband Ahab to the worship of Baal and Ashtoreth. Unruly Lilith refuses to have sex perpetually beneath Adam and is exiled to the desert to watch her children die. Lilith's name appears ever after in discussions of witchcraft as she who steals the male's seed to fashion demons from it by night. This "she who steals" underscores both the autonomy of the "witch complex" and the obvious male fear of possession that it reflects, imbuing nocturnal emission with a distinctly negative *mana*. An agent of a feminine fury akin to Hecate or the Furies of Greek mythology, Lilith strikes terror in the soul of patriarchal men—Exodus 22:18 a blunt confession of that very fact: "Thou shalt not suffer a witch to live." The magico-religious power of the witch, should it be manifested in dreams, in men's fear of women, in cultic contexts like that of Jezebel and Ahab, or with Persephone in her identity as Queen of the Underworld, invariably inclines consciousness towards an alternate dimension of numinous experience.

The same patient brought this second dream, selected for its striking symmetry and far-reaching reciprocity with the central figures of the preceding dream—those black men on the left:

I am beneath Rome, walking through a subterranean museum and contemplating how one can go on for miles through the labyrinthine catacombs and ancient displays. Then I come to the transept of two hallways where a woman lies on a cot. She is extremely erotic, and covered in a light purple dust or powder. She is also lying ill, but I touch her and speak of how very beautiful she is. Then sex begins. As I touch her clitoris and caress her the atmosphere becomes intense, but I am wary that she may have some dreadful venereal disease. Speaking in wild sexual language, I finally climax. "This is a taste of pure paganism!" I think. But then I am suddenly in my father's business office, where seven huge rats run towards me. I beat them to death with a club and try to get the dead rats into a bag.

Facing the fact that one's soul is both sick and very powerful is a sobering proposition. The dream's psychic "stratigraphy," the archaeological term for investigating deeper levels, is nearly as pronounced as the real subterranean Vatican *scavi* tour: down beneath the high altar of St. Peter's Basilica, past the bones of Peter to an ancient crypt-lined, mosaic-floored Roman necropolis with its green frescoed peacocks of rebirth.

Falling together in form, ambiance, and general conflict with that preceding, this dream focuses on a provocative purple-powdered woman. She lies ailing and alone on a simple x-framed canvas cot (with military-medic associations for the dreamer) like a timeless victim of war deep beneath Rome. Wanton and beautiful in the eye of her beholder, tragic but attractive in her aspect, a more ambivalently charged image of the anima could scarcely be found. "With the archetype of the anima we enter the realm of the gods, or rather, the realm that metaphysics has reserved for itself. Everything the anima touches becomes numinous—unconditional, dangerous, taboo, magical."[3] Certainly the case here, the anima's violet color indicates a highly charged emotional situation within the personality of the dreamer. Little wonder that the patient spoke strongly of simply hating a particular pair of dangling magenta-colored earrings often worn by his new lover, a woman afflicted (appropriately enough) with a severe borderline personality disorder. This diagnosis for a woman, or for this man's anima, is commonplace for those touched by incest, sexual abuse, or suffering from object-relational injury.

The purple-powdered woman lies at the transept of intersecting halls in the labyrinth, indicative of the many opposites she may embody. She possesses a subtle-body quality. The fine powder covering her skin combines the red of passionate blood and of the open expanse of blue sky. So fine it is scarcely matter, the powdery substance has an underworldly phosphorescence about it like museum minerals glistening under black light. The unpredictable violet powder is right there between the dreamer's caressing hand and the alluring flesh of the woman. Both material and spiritual, it is "in between," imaginally the very definition of *psychic*—with a *mana* that conditions the entire interactive field. The famous Cretan Palace of Knossos is itself the labyrinth through which Ariadne (Aphrodite) leads Theseus with her thread of gold—at least before he abandons her and she finds her truest love in Dionysus. Beneath the high altar of St. Peter's her sexual power is reduced to a malady, the threat of "venereal" disease—a metaphorical Venus as the classic symptom, the axiomatic blowback of patriarchal sexual values. No more appropriate a study in the fear and loathing of Christian culture for feminine beauty can be referenced than Giuseppe Tornatore's disquieting film, *Malèna* (2000). Tornatore portrays the group mind of provincial Syracusa in Mussolini's Italy with stark realism, a collective consciousness so suffused with patriarchal animus that even local women publicly brutalize Malèna ("evil woman") while their husbands (her patrons in prostitution by fate) enjoy a satisfaction comparable to that of the White racist's pleasure at staging fistfights between black men.

The dreamer is subsequently challenged to understand the invasion of rats, which he has clearly inherited from his father. Any authentic change in a man's relationship with the anima or with women presupposes a deep confrontation with the masculine shadow. No better opportunity could be offered for this responsibility than the dreamer's encounter with the seven rats. Fortunately, the dreamer does manage to withstand their onslaught by beating them to death with the proverbial "blunt instrument." Do note that the anima does not follow him here, for this is *phallus* vs. *phallus*, the masculine side of the equation. For all his sexual urgency, the dreamer is left alone to deal with the deep dynamism of his raw masculine drives, his own gnawing tooth-phallus—if for no other reason, because when a woman experiences the darker aspects of male sexuality, the relationship is over! An additional response to the dream's opening scenes might well include the Faustian invitation: "Sure, go on, take a good look at the legacy of Rome, the alluring games, your dice cast for a favorite gladiator, the whores hot for the breaking crowd." The energies of this primitive level, it is true, may blend right in with "men being men" and a rough-and-tumble night on the town. Entire industries depend on it. But here we encounter the pathological imagery of the dreamer's crippling anxiety, his core psychological issue. The strength of the dreamer's own club is commensurate to the rats' frontal attack, but there is something provisional about it. While anticipating the potential capacity for appropriate sacrifice to these archetypal powers—part of it an acceptance of his own lust, part of it sheer prohibition, more of it emotional maturity and transformation—the clubbing remains defensive. The fecundity, adaptability, and sheer survival power of the rodents must be realized as powerful psychological endowments in the dreamer himself. They possess real significance for consciousness (teeth) on a deep level, and reflect a ceaseless hunger that even Eros cannot escape. To the degree these energies are confronted and disentangled from the negative father complex, they will contribute to the dreamer's expanding masculine stature. Untended, the rats will merely continue skittering along, unconsciously lending their teeth to the wounded, sexualized, anxiety-provoking anima. Shadow and anima might thus work unconsciously and in tandem to cast a perpetual spell of sexy allure, biting animus, sentimentality, and relational treachery that the dreamer (mysteriously enough) keeps encountering in the women he chooses!

The purple-powdered woman and the black men (sinister, "on the left") present themselves as veritable guardians of the descending chthonic vortex whose images we trace. While the gods seem to use other people more often than angels to impact our lives, the threshold where all we desire or expect from other humans fails is the threshold of religion. But how beautifully the living psychic images of that desire move ever forward in tandem. This is the archetypal partnership of the "syzygy" in a timeless state of being "yoked together." It must be remembered that *relationships between masculine and feminine are always presided over by the anima*, as is clear in our two dreams, and furthermore is presupposed by our exemplary pairing of the Black Man and the Purple-Powdered Woman. Of far-reaching significance in this study, one may appreciate this intimate correlation in Jung's observation:

> Anyone ... who does not know the universal distribution and
> significance of the *syzygy* motif in the psychology of primitives,
> in mythology, in comparative religion, and in the history of
> literature, can hardly claim to say anything about the anima.[4]

How then do we understand the "vortex" aforementioned? Not since the ancient and long-enduring Eleusinian mysteries slipped into oblivion at the outset of the 5th century C.E. has anything approximating honest collective ritual relations with the Underworld (the *chthonic* dimension of spirit) even existed. With "chthonic" something well beyond the fertility and the green vegetation of Ge (Gaia, earth) is indicated—an immaterial dark expanse that corresponds to, but extends beyond the body's vital functions and opacity to a field of disparate but self-organizing luminosities about which much more will be revealed. "Chthon" bespeaks the spirit within the body, the manifestations of the spirit in sexuality, in passion, and the emotions, but also a "realm"—the descending reach of the world axis, where hellfire is a mirror image of the sun. Our perilous situation in time, the distortions of our spiritual and erotic culture, and our urgent need to reassure the very continuity of life on this planet simply demand recognition for this sacred reverence. The anima-animus syzygy personified by our Purple-Powdered Woman and Black Man personify most adequately the stuff of Persephone and Dionysus-Hades at the shadowy threshold of the underworld. This syzygy, these two in tandem, are our secret ones. Consider their permutations in all that will follow.

In *Return of the Goddess,* Edward C. Whitmont explores the ways in which patriarchal hierarchies enforce a repression of the feminine and effect a sharp dissociation between the heroic ego and the instinctual shadow. Whitmont sees the Judeo-Christian monotheism of "I Am" not only as emblematic of its God Father, but also as paradigmatic of a heroic ego-consciousness that identifies itself with the *aerial* solar pole of masculine spirit. The opening tenets of the Ten Commandments represent the foundational principles of this monotheistic eccentricity:

> I am the Lord your God, who brought you out of the land of Egypt, out of the house of slavery; you shall have no other gods before me.
>
> You shall not make for yourself an idol, whether in the form of anything that is in heaven above, or that is on the earth beneath, or that is in the water under the earth.
>
> You shall not bow down to them or worship them; for I the Lord your God am a jealous God, punishing children for the

iniquity of parents, to the third and fourth generation of those
who reject me, but showing steadfast love to the thousandth
generation of those who love me and keep my commandments.
(Exodus 20:2-6)

A quick lesson in psychodynamics and archetypal polarity appears
in the Law being vouchsafed to Moses atop Mount Sinai while the
children of Israel set to worshiping a golden calf at the base of the
mountain. The calf may be associated with the indigenous pre-
Yahwistic polytheistic cults of Mother Rite. It is not ours to discuss
the Decalogue in detail, or to detract from the necessity of proper
ordinances in social matters—so long as they actually remain connected
with life. However fundamental to Judaism and Christianity, the
legalistic rigidity and punitive wrath of the patriarchal order casts an
extremely punishing amoral shadow, a cold overplus of Justice.
Whitmont stresses this as being all the more strongly the case where
patriarchy loses its original sanctity and supports a purely secular
power-hierarchy in the modern world. He boldly considers what, in
human and collective terms, may be considered the object-relational
deficit, the borderline condition enforced by the super-ego Father:

> The patriarchal ego is heroic. Its idealized achievement is
> conquest of self and world by sheer will and bravery. Personal
> feelings, desire, pain, and pleasure are disregarded. Failure to do
> so is accounted weakness. The resulting psychological
> achievement is a sense of personal identity vested in a body-
> limited, separate self, answerable to the law of the group and
> God-king. Consciously, it no longer feels organically contained
> in, or one with, group, world, or the divine.[5]

This passage conveys a sense of the heroic ego and its allegiance to the
patriarchal Father. A backward glance at the dream where the ego's
heroism is accented by a "lance or victory standard" and the support
of his anima-wife as he leaves a church indicates a heroic revolt that
Whitmont might well appreciate. For it leads directly to the ritual
celebration of plowing the streets, feminine mysteries, the crumbling
of palace façades, and vivid black body-imagos—a movement towards
reconnection with body, nature, and all things nonhierarchical.

Everything hinges on the complementarity of masculine and
feminine, god and goddess. Jung's observations of monotheism and

polytheism in relation to his psychology are most pertinent here—his reference to Manichaeism an anticipation of our biography of St. Augustine:

> The anima/animus stage is correlated with polytheism, the self with monotheism. The natural archetypal symbolism, describing a totality that includes light and dark, contradicts in some sort the Christian but not the Jewish or Yahwistic viewpoint, or only to a relative degree. The latter seems to be closer to Nature and therefore to be a better reflection of immediate experience. Nevertheless, the Christian heresiarchs tried to sail round the rocks of Manichaean dualism, which was such a danger to the early Church, in a way that took cognizance of the *natural symbol,* and among the symbols for Christ there are some very important ones which he has in common with the devil, *though this had no influence on dogma.*[6]

Prominent in the Ten Commandments, the proscription against the fashioning of graven images (historically an anti-polytheistic stance) is today pointedly anti-psychological. The shadow must be concealed for strategic reasons; the anima held under strict control precisely because she opens the realm of the *gods.* While demonized by patriarchy, their magical field is one with the very fabric of the Great Goddess herself. Here I recall an excursion in India with the colleague to whom this book is dedicated, Don Sandner. Prior to our departure, he dreamt of the Goddess Kali standing black and awesome, some ten or twenty feet tall, in the middle of an expanse of land and crying out repeatedly in a thunderous voice: *"Where are my sons?!"* Weeks later, we arose before dawn in Bhubaneshwar, Orissa, taking a car out to where the fields give over to deep forest, to visit a yogini temple. Instantly enchanted by the circular structure with its nine exterior niches in which the Goddess stands, then marveling at the myriad forms of women ringing the temple interior, we emerged only to be met by a tour group of American women whose leader blurted out brusquely, "What are *you* doing here?!" Like the Goddess herself, patriarchy is scarcely the exclusive province of women or men.

> The Great Goddess represents being and becoming. The Feminine is not concerned with achieving or ideating. It is not heroic, self-willed and bent on battling against opposition. Rather it exists in the here and now and the endless flow. It values the vegetal dimension of growth-decay, the continuity

and conservation of natural orders. It expresses the will of nature and the instinctual forces rather than the self-will of a particular person. The feminine form of consciousness is global, field, and process oriented. It is functional rather than abstract or conceptual. *It is devoid as yet of the strict dichotomy of inner-outer or body-mind.*[7]

How markedly all this contrasts with the God Father's administrative threat of multigenerational retribution for anyone serving other gods—that "visiting the iniquity of the fathers upon the children" of the third commandment.

A vivid illustration of the divine disconnect described comes from the deeply influential Old Testament book of Ezekiel. It is the prophet's account of a visionary experience of Yahweh's jealous indignation at his children's turning to graven images and alternate religious devotions. The text's opening expression regarding "a likeness as the appearance of fire" immediately indicates a visionary plane wherein autonomous *phantasma* simply present themselves to the visionary eye. Seated before the elders of Judah, Ezekiel recounts how Yahweh takes him on a tour of the Temple of Israel, first by lifting him into the air by a lock of his hair:

> Then God said to me, "O mortal, lift up your eyes now in the direction of the north." So I lifted up my eyes toward the north, and there, north of the altar gate, in the entrance, was this image of jealousy.
>
> He said to me, "Mortal, do you see what they are doing, the great abominations that the house of Israel are committing here, to drive me far from my sanctuary? Yet you will still see greater abominations."
>
> And he brought me to the entrance of the court; I looked, and there was a hole in the wall.
>
> Then he said to me, "Mortal, dig through the wall"; and when I dug through the wall, there was an entrance.
>
> He said to me, "Go in, and see the vile abominations that they are committing here."
>
> So I went in and looked: there, portrayed on the wall all around, were all kinds of creeping things, and loathsome animals, and all the idols of the house of Israel.
>
> Before them stood seventy of the elders of the house of Israel. Each had his censer in his hand, and the fragrant cloud of incense was ascending.

> Then he said to me, "Mortal, have you seen what the elders
> of the house of Israel are doing in the dark, each in his room of
> images? For they say, 'The Lord does not see us, the Lord has
> forsaken the land.'"
> He said also to me, "You will see still greater abominations
> that they are committing."
> Then he brought me to the entrance of the north gate of the
> house of the Lord; women were sitting there weeping for
> Tammuz. (Ezekiel 8:4-14)

Specific to its historical moment, the text documents a time when theological battles over Mother Rite and polytheism raged. The many animal forms in the vision reflect a range of devotions that extend to the natural symbols of earth. The prophet and his god view all this as an abomination. Whatever the integrity of Ezekiel's visionary experience in its ancient context, today, nearly twenty-six hundred years later, the situation is essentially the reverse. Goddess religion has always recognized the religious dimensions of life itself, as well as the sacred qualities of bodily instinct. Thus our concern for the sacred dimensions of sex, body, nature, and earth, and for what individuals behold in their own inner "room of images." But what might the women weeping for Tammuz tell us?

The ancient ritual context of weeping women in that damnable chamber in the Hebrew psyche harkens back to the old Babylonian cult of Tammuz and goddess Ashtoreth, and to an even earlier Sumerian myth of the two goddesses Inanna and Ereshkigal, where Tammuz is called "Dummuzi." In Ezekiel's vision, the women ritually weep for the dying and resurgent god in accord with the nigh universal myth of the Great Goddess (the "image of jealousy") and her "son-lover," to be met again in the biography of St. Augustine. These devotions were given a place in Jerusalem, even amidst the protestations of Yahwists such as Ezekiel:

> This custom of lamenting the dead god on the threshold of
> Yahweh's sanctuary shows that the women who practiced it
> must have regarded it, not as something which would abolish
> the worship of Yahweh, but rather as something
> supplementary to it. ... [F]rom the prophet it is clear that the
> intrusion of such creaturely features into the realm of Yahweh
> ... was an act of apostasy.[8]

The dream of the crumbling towers of Jerusalem and Rome already leads us to the Demeter-Kore dyad in whose rites Dionysus (Hades) plays a crucial role, just as Dummuzi does in the pervasively feminine context of the Inanna-Ereshkigal myth. In her classic book, *Descent to the Goddess,* Sylvia Brinton Perera brings a uniquely feminine realism and beauty to the exploration of Inanna's descent to Ereshkigal's grievously emotional and imaginal depths. Portrayed in the myth is a sequential shedding of seven rainbow-colored garments, each associated with planets, gems, etc., but indicative of a psychic journey that is no simple stroll to pick flowers. Star goddess Inanna, an equivalent of "the maiden" Persephone (or radiant Aphrodite), must suffer a progressive unveiling on her passage below. While especially pertinent to daughters of the Father, this descent to levels of "lower consciousness" (the chthonic realm) is no less pertinent for men through their inner experience of the anima:

> This motive suggests the removal of old illusions and false identities that may have served in the upper world, but which count for nothing in the Netherworld. There one stands naked before the all-seeing eyes of the dark goddess. The unveiling means being stripped bare, the unveiling of the goddess to herself—the original striptease. It suggests a need to be utterly exposed, undefended, open to have one's soul searched by the eye of death, the dark eye of the Self.[9]

Christianity was born following the spread of Greek culture through the Mediterranean world and well after Rome came to its ascendancy in the region. Among the Greeks there was a tolerant attitude towards sexual variance. They demonstrate how this is fully compatible with a high level of culture. It is evident that a male-worshipping and generally misogynous culture does not mean a sex-negative one. But however famous the women of Lesbos, or the institution of the hetaera (the cultured female companions of some upper class Greeks), and however many female figures appear in Greek mythology—women were second-class citizens. Maidens and mothers (the dual goddesses of Eleusis and women's participation in that ritual cycle notwithstanding) were kept away from the public arena while male commerce and male affections were dominant. Greek men generally married wives substantially younger than themselves, and the maintenance of female virginity as well as girls' preparation for childbearing were unquestioned civic obligations. Vern L. Bullough points out that Greek writers caution their readers against having oversexed wives for "fear that a sexually demanding wife could curtail the extracurricular activities of her husband or also that she might be more inclined to commit adultery, female adultery being a threat to the survival of the family."[10] A classic refrain even today, an extension of these fears is indicated by the fact that mature, maternal women frequently figure in Greek tragedy as dangerous. We need only think of Jocasta, Clytemnestra, or the raving women of Dionysus in the *Bacchae* of Euripides—including Agave, the mother of Pentheus—who tear him to pieces.

Correlated with such apprehensions regarding the feminine is the Greek cultivation of homosexual love and the institution of pedagogical eros. Greek homoeroticism was celebrated in academic and civil contexts, as in the image of the naked young athlete on whom only male eyes were allowed to fall. These aspects of Greek culture were a matter of disgust not only for Jews, and later Christians, but for Romans as well, who, despite the impression created by Christian slander or a few lurid passages from Petronius (*Satyricon*) or Suetonius (*Lives of the Caesars*), considered homosexuality to be unmanly. As we move towards Augustine's Christian critique of polytheism and the imagination of various erotic affections, recall that the Greek theater was traditionally a Dionysian religious institution—Dionysus a dying and resurgent god and child of the Goddess in many ways comparable to Tammuz or Dummuzi.

Greek philosophical tradition was far and away the chief influence on the formation of Christian sexual dogma. And exemplary of the syncretism of traditional Judaism and the Greek philosophical milieu in the late 1st century B.C.E. was Philo Judaeus of Alexandria. Philo is familiar to students of Jung for his original elaboration of the doctrine of the Logos. He was neither a rabbi, a Christian, or other sectarian, but an inspired philosopher with a distinct ascetic inclination who was interested in adapting Old Testament values to his milieu. But however refined his speculations, Philo quickly betrays the characteristic exclusivity of Logos towards its own spiritual ends—an archetypal force that lends its compelling power to moral doctrines like the Jewish command to procreate and replenish the earth. He not only holds that sex should be restricted to marriage, but should be resorted to only where there is hope of legitimate offspring. He readily compares pleasure lovers to pigs and goats. For Philo, Man in his purest essence is not only a creature of Logos, but asexual (though certainly an asexual male). He views the very category of gender as belonging to an inferior order within the perennial fantasy that men are rational and rationality equals superiority:

> [M]ale was superior to the female … because he represented the more rational parts of the soul while the female represented the less rational. For him progress meant giving up the female gender, the material, passive, corporeal, and sense-perceptive world, and taking the active, rational male world of mind and thought.[11]

Despite his complete familiarity with Greek cultural values, Philo sees homosexual love as an abomination. Consider his stark evaluation of homosexual relations:

> In former days the very mention of it was a great disgrace, but now it is a matter of boasting not only to the active but to the passive partners, who habituate themselves to endure the disease of effemination, let both body and soul run to waste, and leave no ember of their male sex-nature to smolder. … These persons are rightly judged worthy of death by those who obey the law, which ordains that man-woman who debases the sterling coin of nature should perish.[12]

It is ironic that "nature" is suddenly described as a "sterling coin" when sodomites and ancient she-males are at issue, or where lovers indifferent to procreation are compared to "pigs and goats," when nature itself is so suspicious. Anticipating the "natural use" fantasy of St. Paul, both examples already constitute a "variant" sexuality. Such people are diminished as mere pleasure lovers, demeaned like animals, and threatened with death. Philo's avenue to God is thus reminiscent of the Indian yogin's *Neti Neti* ("not this, not this") in a systematic elimination of bisexuality, passion, matter, femininity, the receptive, the corporeal body, nature, sensation, and everything nonrational or imaginal. From any depth-psychological perspective, this leaves virtually nothing (with the natural exception of the mighty male sex-nature!) of which the soul could be imagined to consist.

In a brilliant and far-reaching analysis of "Solar Hierophanies" (appearances of the sun as divinity), Eliade offers valuable assistance for understanding and coming to terms with the solar Spirit concealed behind the hierophanies, hierarchies, theologies, rituals, and tenacious sexual laws of patriarchy. Philo's lofty but distinctly shadowed devotion to the Logos may be critiqued in these terms:

> The final result of giving absolute supremacy to solar hierophanies as developed in one sense only, can be seen in the excesses of ascetic Indian sects whose members go on staring at the sun until they become completely blind. This is a case of the "dryness" and "sterility" of a purely solar order of things, which carries its limited logic to extremes. The counterpart of it is a species of "decay from damp," the turning of men into "seeds," which occurs in those sects which give the same sort of total acceptance to the nocturnal, lunar or earthly order of things. It is almost the automatic fate of those who accept only one aspect of the sun hierophanies to be driven to a state of "blindness" and "dryness," while those who fix themselves exclusively upon the "nocturnal sphere of the mind" are led into a state of permanent orgy and dissolution—a return to a sort of larval state.[13]

Philo Judaeus understood his speculative philosophy as a kind of mystery religion. Twenty years of age at the turn of the millennium (*circa* three years before the birth of Jesus), he personifies the unique intermingling of Jewish and Greek speculative currents in Alexandrian Egypt. The sheer power and exultation of his pneumatic vision is beyond question. But like his patriarchal brethren, Philo also displays the stuff of a potentially rending dissociation of consciousness, however disguised. For as the masculine mind finds itself drawn ever more irresistibly, then thoughtlessly into the aerial vortex of Spirit an *extremely ambivalent* situation develops. It requires ritual control and discipline even in the strongest individuals. A mere hint of that autonomous power is provided by the dream of a detached and self-absorbed humanities scholar, sitting in a single-room cabin absorbed in his studies. Suddenly something rips the roof off—a Tyrannosaurus Rex composed entirely of gold, glaring in the brilliant noonday sun!

In its extremity, a provocative statement by former covert U.S. Army commando, Stan Goff, comes to represent an appropriate comment on the perennial dilemma: "Perfect masculinity is psychopathic." The same propensity is unmasked whenever earth's gravity and the mediating influence of the feminine have been lost. Eliade's perspective on solar hierophanies is pertinent to the split between the virgin and the whore, but even more to that between the ascetic and the libertine.

No more perfect example of the intellectual and institutional dryness and sterility of the solar order could be found than Roman Stoicism, the prevailing philosophy of the Empire in which both Augustine and Catholic Christianity came of age. By then the solar radiation that Philo exemplifies (Logos, Apollo, or Helios) has degenerated into the depleted uranium of lead (Saturn). The supremacy of reason its hallmark, Stoicism was utterly normative, devoid of the still rich transcendental intuitions of mystical Judaism or those of Philo, whose writings remain illuminating for all their sexism, homophobia, and punitive shadow. The key feature of patriarchal sexual morality remains: all forms of sexuality not devoted to marriage and procreation are unnatural, while nature is perpetually defined in the most concrete and literal terms. The fact that Joseph Ratzinger (Pope Benedict XVI) could so stridently impose a new ban upon even the most committed celibate gay aspirants for the Catholic priesthood in 2005 only underscores the point. Like unto it are the sinister ecological implications of the Catholic establishment's insistence that even basic contraceptive methods constitute a moral issue.

With patriarchy, responsibility for evil as well as a special imperative for remedial spiritualization is projected onto women, the feminine, and everything touching their realm. Gender is, after all, *the* most fundamental of all opportunities for prejudice. That archetypal tension is suggestive in itself of the powerful dynamism and challenge represented by the *inner marriage* of masculine and feminine for the whole personality. This union is pervasively ruled by the feminine with the help of Eros. It was Philo who associated irrationality and forbidden sexual knowledge with Eve and Eden, even before Augustine. Philo believed that

> ... the easiest way for women to approach the male level of
> rationality was for them to deny their sexuality, to remain virgins,
> and the words virgin, virginal, ever-virginal occur continually
> in Philo's reference to the best kind of women.[14]

Consider then the presumptuous and banal progression from Philo to St. Jerome: "I praise marriage and wedlock, but I do so because they produce virgins for me," or again with St. Ambrose, mentor of Augustine:

> She who does not believe is a woman and should be designated by the name of her sex, whereas she who progresses to the perfect manhood, to the measure of the adulthood of Christ ... then dispenses with the name of her sex, the seductiveness of her youth, the garrulousness of old age.[15]

It is little wonder that Christian history includes the appearance of a number of transvestite saints, such as St. Pelagia, virtually all of them cross-dressing as men in approximation of the "perfect manhood" of Christ. In any case, the fantasy of this spiritual progress, of masculine adulthood and perfection, casts a glaring shadow, one with which the Catholics and also the Gnostics continued to grapple through the centuries.

The confluence of variant sexuality and alternate religious inclination appears in select scriptural references of the New Testament in surprising ways, even in the most familiar of Bible verses. And no better representative of the now familiar patriarchal values of sexism, homophobia, the spirituality of detachment, and the resulting concrete view of nature could be found than the psychically inflated and emotionally ambivalent Apostle Paul. Our entire history of patriarchal sexual morality resonates repeatedly in his words:

> Let a woman learn in silence with full submission.
> I permit no woman to teach or to have authority over a man; she is to keep silent.
> For Adam was formed first, then Eve; and Adam was not deceived, but the woman was deceived and became a transgressor.
> Yet she will be saved through childbearing, provided they continue in faith and love and holiness, with modesty. (I Timothy 2:11-15)

Woman is again redeemed through her passivity and her maternal function. This sets the characteristic tone. Generally viewed as a mere prophylactic measure against moral weakness and lust, Paul's attitude towards marriage remains ambiguous overall. He opens the seventh chapter of I Corinthians with the statement, "It is well for a man not to touch a woman," and then goes on to display some mutuality of "conjugal rights," albeit in a distinctly legislative tone, cautioning "that Satan may not tempt you because of your lack of self-control." Finally, championing his own celibacy, he concludes:

> To the unmarried and the widows I say it is well for them to remain unmarried as I am. But if they are not practicing self-control, they should marry. For it is better to marry than to be aflame with passion. (I Corinthians 7: 8-9)

Paul's patronizing and lurid style comes most clearly into its own when warning the Romans about homosexual affections:

> Claiming to be wise, they became fools; and they exchanged the glory of the immortal God for images resembling a mortal human being or birds or four-footed animals or reptiles.
>
> Therefore God gave them up in the lusts of their hearts to impurity, to the degrading of their bodies among themselves, because they exchanged the truth about God for a lie and worshiped and served the creature rather than the Creator, who is blessed forever! Amen.
>
> For this reason God gave them up to degrading passions. Their women exchanged natural intercourse for unnatural, and in the same way also the men, giving up natural intercourse with women, were consumed with passion for one another.
>
> Men committed shameless acts with men and received in their own persons the due penalty for their error. (Romans 1:22-27)

Paul's disparagement of zoomorphic (polytheistic) images recalls the creeping things, abominable beasts, and the idols that Ezekiel beholds in the Temple and in his brethren's "room of images." Few things are more common in psychotherapy than dreams of frenzied, starved, or neglected animals in need of care. The individual is thereby given notice of an instinctually impoverished condition, and hopefully prompted to intuit, sense, and feel their way to a new connection with the body and its animal fabric.

The problem is dramatized by the dilemma of a divorced, emotionally starved, and despairing Catholic woman who came to analysis. After recounting a childhood history filled with punitive parental discipline and their repeated expressions of contempt for her adolescent sexual curiosities, she hesitantly disclosed a series of "sick" and "disgusting" fantasies she had been drinking to escape. Assuming she would once again be written off as "a worthless whore," she recounted fantasies and dreams of making love with her father, engaging in lesbian affairs, and having sex with various animals. A woman thus burdened with the ostensible monsters of her human nature is a sad but altogether typical product of object-relational distortions backed by traditional Christian sexual prejudices.

Paul's sharp contrast between the incorruptible God and corruptible man, aforementioned, is the very chasm over which historical and contemporary arguments concerning the human or divine nature of Christ rage. This is the mystery of all the "dying gods" (Dionysus, Tammuz, Attis, Adonis), whose somatic and creaturely qualities contrast with the purely spiritual god, as does the corporeal body of Christ. Naturally, this again points to an intermediary place—*psyche* (a word rarely mentioned in the New Testament)—as a ligament between body and spirit. Sufficient opportunity will be afforded in a coming chapter to reflect psychologically on "degrading passions" and "shameless acts" from outside the moralistic patriarchal box. What strikes one regarding Paul's lustful ones is the line, "Therefore God gave them up to" impurity and degradation because of their idolatry. Paul's suggestion that God allows, or even participates in, their degradation, as well as offering "the truth," has a rich Old Testament ring to it—like Yahweh and Satan sitting together and testing the stamina of Job's righteousness in the Old Testament book bearing his name.

This holistic *experience* of God long preceded the crisp, ostensibly reassuring, but in fact extremely dangerous Christian split between God as the sum of all goodness (*summum bonum*) and evil as the *mere absence* of good (*privatio boni*). Evil thus denied is an evil robbed of palpable reality, left undisciplined and unmonitored. The doctrine is a defensive theological attempt, like many before and many since, to preserve the God imago from any moral stain. Fundamental emotional imperatives give rise to such notions, like the "higher power" of Alcoholics Anonymous or the sheer need of an individual to remain hopeful in a time of deep psychological crisis. But the doctrinal and institutional failure to recognize the amoral and abysmal aspect of God results only in a perpetual lack of religious imagination and personal moral differentiation—it places the full responsibility for evil on the back of humankind.

The contemporary proposition of humankind's original blessedness vs. its original sin merely begs the question. These are two sides of the same coin, like the perennial tension between monism and dualism, the one and the many. Every religious system negotiates and navigates between these universals, with monotheism vs. polytheism representing one more parameter. Patriarchal sexual morality champions dualism. Clear-cut, black and white, split in twain, this distended dualism supports the collective power hierarchy with rules of obedience. Christian and Islamic fundamentalism are perfect examples. The fundamentalist's hatred of depth psychology rests in the disturbing questions it raises: the dark side of God as intimate with God, and the exploration and sufficient *integration* of the personal shadow its starting point. Here in a life lived and deeply examined is that frightening "moral relativism" that the body, psyche, and Fate herself do inevitably demand of an individual, however defended by religious doctrine he or she may be.

Sex, like human nature itself, has *never* been merely "natural." How else could humankind have intuited, much less claimed kinship with the gods from the very outset of our conscious emergence as *Homo religiosus*? A classic alchemical dictum from Ostanes captures this concisely, even as it responds to both Paul and the general patriarchal notion of "natural use": "Nature rejoices in nature. Nature subdues nature. Nature rules over nature." Corresponding perceptions of an animate and transformative "light of nature" (*lumen naturae*) appear in European alchemy, in the *prakrti* concept of Hinduism, in Gnostic myth and, most palpably, in somatic psychotherapies. All point to a spiritual substance, a dispersed consciousness concealed within the body and all created things. But more immediate perspective is required: What is the frequency of sexual interactions in the adult global population that are specifically focused on procreation compared to those that are not? In the actual process of engaging in heterosexual intercourse (particularly at the moment of orgasm), how specifically are the participants focused on the child that they may produce? Presumably a substantial overplus lies on the side of non-procreative sex, even without reference to fantasy, imagination, or religion. The facts of life are more powerful and uniform than any localized notion of sexual morality.

The very notion of *personality* as well as any *positive* concern for the actual content, dynamism, and play of sexual fantasies lie altogether outside the purview of the Father archetype. Its external orientation, concretism, and literalism simply preclude it. Likewise the Great Mother knows nothing of the individual as such, but simply procreates. I recall once driving a narrow stretch of Minnesota highway between two sprawling marshes as hundreds of salamanders sought to cross the road, most of them unsuccessfully. Mother casts life forth in abundance and in myriad forms only to propagate and recycle endlessly (we pray). Going forward, it is not the Father *or* Mother archetypes, but the anima and the animus, the specifically consciousness-making and individuating endowments of the personality, with which we are centrally concerned psychologically.

The patriarchal Father described thus far represents only the *aerial* dimension of spirit, what Eliade most clearly describes in his characterization of Solar Hierophanies. But Eliade also indicates the lower, descending pole of this spectrum—its confluence with Mother Earth and chthonic underworld. Safely embedded in the body of this text, we may speak of this vertical axis stretching from the highest to the lowest, passing through the biological Birth-Sex-Death equation at every point. Gnostic scholar Gilles Quispel once inscribed my copy of his book, *The Secret Book of Revelation*, with a broad five-lettered cross (+) in ancient Greek. Its three horizontal letters spell ZOE (life), while the vertical spells PHOS (light), a recapitulation of Eliade's solar-lunar spectrum in miniature. Worth mentioning is the equivalence of this pairing to Eve (life) and Adam (light). In relation to sexuality and the religious imagination, this cross, these intersections—this syzygy—is absolutely fundamental to the psychological fact that there is simply no such thing as sex *per se* or an "abnormal sexual fantasy." Human beings, not even men, can have sex without it being intimately related to the condition of their souls.

Our epistemology asserts that every experience, including our experience of the corporeal body, is psychically mediated. Psyche (+) is the essential organ of perception and the *sine qua non* of all knowledge. Just as one's moods and mental states may vary from exhilaration and clarity to sobriety, perplexity, or terror, and just as souls ascend and descend in countless religious systems, so the dynamism of life and spirit engenders fantasy and imagination at every turn. The "average person" would be quite amazed, and likely scandalized, by the sheer range, novelty, and extremity of the sexual fantasies that surface from the unconscious of even the most conventional person. While the natural-use fantasy of Paul and patriarchy generally has always been deeply engrained in Christianity, it is a construction of the Father archetype and the Mother archetype *as defined by the former*—pervasively external, normative, concrete, and literally understood. Psychologically one outgrows one's parents only to realize the *parental* (their equivalent qualities) as a living function within oneself and with it the assumption of responsibility for one's own soul-work. With this individual discovery of psyche, the erotic and imaginal sphere opens to a new vision of creation—one in which the anima and animus play the central role.

Beginning with Paul's formulation of the classic split in the Christian worldview, consider the following jumble of alternate sexual and religious inclinations (italicized) that Paul excludes from the realm of positive religious significance. Note how both sexual and religious tendencies are laced with a host of shadowy evils, like the dross with which unprocessed mineral ore binds its treasure:

> Live by the Spirit, I say, and do not gratify the desires of the flesh.
> For what the flesh desires is opposed to the Spirit, and what the Spirit desires is opposed to the flesh; for these are opposed to each other, to prevent you from doing what you want.
> But if you are led by the Spirit, you are not subject to the law.
> Now the works of the flesh are obvious: *fornication*, impurity, *licentiousness, idolatry, sorcery*, enmities, strife, jealousy, anger, quarrels, dissensions, factions, envy, drunkenness, carousing, and things like these. (Galatians 5:16-21)

Other translations of the Bible employ "heresy" in the place of dissensions, and "variance" in place of factions. The same rhetoric recurs repeatedly through Paul's letters and beyond, always with precisely the same lack of differentiation:

> Do you not know that wrong-doers will not inherit the kingdom of God? Do not be deceived! *Fornicators, idolaters, adulterers, male prostitutes, sodomites*, thieves, the greedy, drunkards, revilers, robbers—none of these will inherit the kingdom of God. (I Corinthians 6:9-10)

Some forty years after Paul, the same intermingling of alternate sexual behaviors and religious practices appears in the very crescendo of the New Testament teachings. Revelation was written by a visionary prophet known as the Elder John. Like Paul, "John is neither a disciple of Jesus, nor one of his twelve Apostles."[16]

> To the thirsty I will give water as a gift from the spring of the water of life.
>
> Those who conquer will inherit these things, and I will be their God and they will be my children.
>
> But as for the cowardly, the faithless, the polluted, the *fornicators*, the *sorcerers*, the *idolaters*, and all liars, their place will be in the lake that burns with fire and sulfur, which is the second death. (Revelation 21:7-8)

Finally:

> Blessed are those who wash their robes, so that they will have the right to the tree of life and may enter the city by the gates.
>
> Outside are the dogs and *sorcerers* and *fornicators* and murderers and *idolaters,* and everyone who loves and practices falsehood. (Revelation 22:14-15)

It must be understood that in seeking appropriate psychological validation for sexual phenomena outside the patriarchal order there is no question of seeking to dignify "adulterers," "fornicators," or "sodomites" in the customary sense of these terms. They typify a type of Biblical language for which we have little use. Rather, what concern us are the psychic images and substances that such crass moralistic terminology seeks to conceal. For example, there is indication that the confluence of sexuality and alternate religious currents touches upon a reservoir of fiery brimstone—an analogue of alchemical sulfur (hellfire) that is an essential image of sexual and aggressive libidinal drives. To this, patriarchal Christianity is completely ill equipped to respond in any imaginative psychological fashion. The primitive anima-driven bombast so prominent throughout these passages (and so characteristic of the hysteria and exhibitionism of the modern evangelist) points directly to the undifferentiated feminine dimension of the evangelical psyche, just as the homophobic and erotophobic shadow of patriarchy is conspicuous throughout. The language of our scriptural quotes is extraordinarily pejorative. Precluding reflection or differentiation, the obsessive affectivity that drives it blurs countless specific behavioral and imaginal elements moralistically together—its concretism the typical result of spiritualistic eccentricities, its literalism part and parcel of any patriarchal purview.

Paul and the Elder John, like Philo and Ezekiel before them, were unique personalities whose individuation unfolded within the context of their respective eras. But surveying the institution of the church and the repetition of Scripture today we perceive the same glaring psychological facts: Where an ebullient spiritualistic crescendo hardens into a split, moralistic, and punitive doctrine, the imaginal reality of the body, of sex, and of life itself grows suspicious, darkens, and form a power-driven, morbid, and explosive counter position in the unconscious. This is nothing other than the stuff of Eliade's tense contrast between solar ascetics, who stare at the sun until they are totally blind, and the "decay from damp" characteristic of those fixed on the "nocturnal sphere of the mind." Psychologically, *both* propensities exist in any given soul, which is precisely why Jung can observe that to the degree to which ego-consciousness falls into the grip of the unconscious, there tends to be a reversal of all conscious values. This yields many a dramatic instance in the case of medieval Christian heretical sects. Thus our most important psychological perception of the Biblical text consists in its repeated correlation of variant sexual behaviors with idolatry, witchcraft, sorcery, unbelief, variance (heresy), etc. By replacing these pejorative terms with neutral synonyms, we may understand that opening the imaginal body to the full range of sexual and gender phenomena immediately evokes images, the feminine, alternate magico-religious forces, things nonrational and synchronistic, individual experiential knowledge (gnosis), and individual means of religious self-expression. It might be said that few things are more crucial than the achievement of unbelief (agnosticism is always fertile turf psychologically), for where numinous insight is vouchsafed—where an individual *has a religious experience*—the issue of belief or faith is relative indeed. Gnosis *is* faith. Consider the word "heresy," derived from the Latin *haeresis* and meaning "an action of taking, a choice." Its connotations are clearly individual.

The legacy of no other hero of the Catholic faith comes down to us in such clarity or in such intimate personal detail as does that of Augustine of Hippo (345-430 C.E.), whose biographical *Confessions* have been read by millions of people through the centuries. The man, his writings, and his historical significance are of considerable complexity. His philosophical genius is indisputable, and thus not ours to dispute, for we are concerned with the Augustine of flesh and blood and soul—a sexual man, a man with a dominant mother and minimally described father, a man whose struggles against the extremes of both intellectual and carnal passions led through Plato and Manichaeism as well as through Carthaginian brothels, through a fifteen-year sexual liaison with an anonymous mistress, and a betrothal to a rich Milanese girl, which his mother had finessed. Bequeathed to Catholic tradition by Augustine is an extraordinary weave of sexual myths that reverberate even today. These include the correlation of the fall of man with sexual knowledge and the sins of Sodom with homosexuality, for which no Biblical warrant exists. Augustine was also a major transmitter of tales about libertinistic heretics, naked adamites, and nocturnal orgies. He played a great role in rationalizing and demonizing the Graeco-Roman gods and the rituals associated with them, and wrote extensively on general sexual themes including marriage, procreation, prostitution, and celibacy. His story offers much with which both men and women may evaluate the sort of teacher he was, even as the life of his mother Monica raises questions of its own about the appropriate limits of maternal solicitude as the focus of women's spirituality.

Peter Brown sets out that "what Augustine remembered in the *Confessions* written at 43 years of age was his inner life; and this inner life is dominated by one figure—his mother, Monica."[17] In his early reflections, Augustine displays a keen awareness of the powerful physical and emotional bonds between mother and child. He seems very pleased to say:

> It is the physical weakness of a baby that makes it seem "innocent," not the quality of its inner life. I myself have seen a baby jealous: it was too young to speak, but it was livid with anger as it watched another baby at the breast.[18]

> I was made welcome into this world by the comfort of a woman's milk. ... It was a good experience for them, that I drew so much good from them. ... Later, I began to laugh: first, in my sleep, then, when I was awake.[19]

Even as we see Augustine's delight and emotional insight in these words, we possess a remarkably candid subjective report about the mother who made so indelible an impression upon him. Brown observes:

> Occasionally, we glimpse a genuinely impressive woman—very much what her son would like himself to be, as a bishop: restrained, dignified, above gossip, a firm peacemaker among her acquaintances, capable, like her son, of effective sarcasm. She had been austerely brought up in a Christian family: she clung to traditional practices in the African Church that educated men had always dismissed as "primitive," to Sabbath fasts, and meals at the tombs of the dead. And yet she may not have been an entirely simple soul: she believed, for instance, that a good classical education, though pagan, would eventually make her son a better Christian. Above all, she was a woman of deep inner resources: her certainties were unnerving; the dreams by which she foresaw the course of her son's life were impressive, and she was confident that she could tell, instinctively, which of these dreams was authentic.[20]

Monica was clearly a multifaceted personality. As we consider Augustine's relation with her, one far-reaching observation by Jung may assist us in understanding Monica's power more deeply: that the "mother" is really an imago, a psychic image with many different contents and meanings. Certainly no detraction from the vital role of the personal mother, this realization is in fact a liberating one—for mothers, for children, for fathers, as well as for our experience of the whole psychic process.

The child's experience of the personal mother is a fundamental factor in how archetypal energies emerging from the unconscious are mediated. It is also the matrix from which the more personalized anima image emerges. In this case, Monica's unnerving certainties, her dreams foreseeing the course of her son's life, do possess an uncanny quality. Augustine recalls, "She loved to have me with her, as is the way with mothers, but more than most mothers." Speaking of her reaction to his youthful errors, he reports, "She acted as if she was undergoing again the pangs of childbirth."[21] One rightfully thinks of Oedipus and the Sphinx here—the latter gazing on as a man crawls on all fours, walks upright, then passes into old age with a cane. With the mother in general, and clearly in Monica's influence over her son, we see the mixed stuff of both Providence and Fate. Jung observes that "there are three essential aspects of the mother: her cherishing and nourishing goodness, her orgiastic emotionality, and her Stygian depths."[22] In the life of Augustine these aspects are woven in with Monica's specific maternal style to influence him in at least as many ways. She appears as his champion, as a personification of wistful sentiment and emotional vexation, and as his partner in a shadowy enmeshment filled for Augustine with sexual compulsion, uncertain feeling tones, and eerie intuitions. Still, throughout his *Confessions,* Augustine appears to remain largely unconscious of the shadow side of Monica's personality, though he does note an element of "unspiritual desire" in his mother's possessiveness. Elements of Augustine's biography point ever and again to the chief blind spot in masculine psychology— understanding the role of the mother, the anima, and the greater feminine in his psychic life. The currents cycling within that blind spot are sufficiently powerful to rule a man's emotional life, rendering urgent a son's need to be supported by an equally strong father.

Augustine's earthly father plays as modest a role in the *Confessions* as Joseph, the earthly father of Jesus, plays in traditional portrayals of the Holy Family. Joseph is typically portrayed as a well-nigh expendable appendage to the mother-child dyad, and this was Patricius's fate as well. He was a simple laborer who possessed both considerable temper and noteworthy forbearance. Brown records that "Patricius had been immoderately proud of his son, and was admired by all for the sacrifices he made to complete Augustine's education."[23] He also cites a telling anecdote of father and son: "Augustine records a scene in the baths, in which his father had been delighted to find that his son had reached puberty. All the son will say, in return, is that 'he saw in me only hollow things.'"[24] Apparently Patricius did offer in some measure the dual paternal blessings of pride in and support for the intellectual strivings of his son and this affirmation of the bodily masculinity that Augustine found so hollow.

Augustine thus remains deeply allied with Monica and continues to accept her counsel as the veritable will of God. At midlife he is haunted by the symbiosis between himself and his mother, and describes it in terms both carnal and ghostly:

> I have no words ... to express the love she had for me, and
> with how much more anguish she was now suffering the pangs
> of child-birth for my spiritual birth than when she had given
> birth to me physically. I just cannot see how she could have
> been healed if my death in sin had come to pierce the entrails
> of her love.
>
> If the souls of the dead took part in the affairs of the living, if
> it was really they themselves who spoke to us, when we see them
> in our sleep ... then my pious mother would not fail to visit me
> every night, that mother who followed me over land and sea
> that she might live with me.[25]

Playing her role through Monica, the Mother archetype reveals
significance for both the physical birth (*mater natura*) and spiritual
rebirth (*mater spiritualis*) of her child. Augustine's mother complex is
profound. His statement about "my death in sin" or its coming "to
pierce the entrails of her love," bespeaks not only his perpetual shame
before Monica's admonitions regarding the faith, but betrays a
significant unconscious ambivalence about the emotional entanglement
that surrounds him. He is mystified by her Stygian depths. The
piercing phallicism ("pierce the entrails of her love") is indicative of
an unconscious incestuous bind that carries a subtle sadistic quality,
a frustrated self-determination. This might better have served
Augustine *consciously* as a sacrificial blade with which to finally cut the
umbilical. The closest Augustine ever came to sacrificing his old bond
with Monica was a flight to Rome under cover of darkness without
telling his mother of his departure. The above quotation combines
confidence in Monica's maternal attention with a suggestion that she
powerfully influenced his emotional life with the uncanny subtlety
of dead souls.

Augustine and Monica's disdain for Patricius turned ostensibly on
the issue of his extended postponement in converting to Christianity.
Monica appears dignified, restrained, and above gossip in certain
respects. But we get another vivid sense of her when it comes to the
problem of dealing with a real man in this world. Brown speaks of the
"subterranean tension" in the family relationship and paints a classic
portrait of the kind of maternal animus that has played an incalculable
normative role in human history:

Monica had the measure of Patricius. She would tell her friends, sarcastically, that they were, after all, the "slave-girls" of their husbands: it was not for them to "rise up against their lord and master." Patricius never beat her, as other husbands beat their wives: she would wait, without saying a word to provoke him, until his anger abated. Then she would explain how she had been right. Patricius was unfaithful to her: she again waited, in silence, until, sure enough, he became a Christian. Augustine's childhood Christianity was part of this tension: "I was a believer like all my household, except my father; but he could not cancel in me the rights of my mother's piety. ... For she tried earnestly, my God, that You should be my father, not him.[26]

It takes little imagination to see how the fallibility of this mortal father served the romance between his wife and his son very well. Monica was not only the right and faithful handmaiden of the Heavenly Father, but she also possessed her son Augustine in a classic oedipal bind. This hindered Augustine's access to essential aspects of masculine initiation, allowing him rather to bask in, and suffer, Monica's maternal solicitude well into his years.

Monica's sarcasm, strategic silence, emotional manipulation, excessive maternal solicitude, and her devotion to God may have been her only real way to exercise any power at all. This is a ubiquitous stylistic feature of women in traditional patriarchal contexts. In any case, Augustine's own specific dismissal of his earthly father—"that You should be my father, not him"—betrays the personal coefficient of his contention elsewhere that Jesus didn't have a father at all, only a mother! Augustine's idealization of Monica remains ever in the forefront. It is fascinating to note in Augustine's *Civitas Dei* that virtually everything germane to the shadow side of the Mother: her intimate connection with sex and the body, her intense emotionality, her strange psychic depths, her capacity to bewitch or castrate—aspects that he could never truly see, understand, or articulate in relation to Monica—are all poured out in Augustine's loathing for the Roman cult of the Great Mother!

Augustine finds the most noteworthy aspect of the cult of Cybele and Attis (her son-lover) in the sacrifice of the sex of the *Galli* (devotees) before a sculpted image of Cybele in orgiastic rituals of self-castration. Patricius, like Joseph, is incidental to the sacred syzygy composed of Augustine and Monica on one side, and the Christ Child and his Holy Mother on the other. Both the shadow side of the mother, carried largely by Augustine's anima, and the bodily reality of the earthly man are thus excluded and left to languish in a state of relative nondifferentiation. This is precisely why the traditional portrayals of the Holy Family are so striking. Brown reports that "Patricius died just after he had scraped together enough money to send his brilliant boy to Carthage: Augustine, who will soon experience and express deep grief at the loss of a friend, will mention his father's death only in passing."[27]

Augustine naturally relates that his mother always displays great anxiety regarding his dealings with other women. In descriptions of his new life in the teeming metropolis of Carthage at age seventeen, he impresses one as far more a sensitive, romantic, and needy youth than anything approximating the libertine he is commonly thought to have become. Augustine speaks of being "in love with love," of being repeatedly drawn into love's painful emotional conflicts: "[I] would be lashed with the red-hot iron rods of jealousy, by suspicions and fear, by bursts of anger and quarrels."[28] Concurrent with Augustine's suffering of his first agonies of love, he is drawn to the theater, an institution presided over by Dionysus and devoted to the pagan gods. The theater fanned the fires of young Augustine's erotic imagination and his own propensity for emotional self-dramatization. He records that stage plays were "full of reflections of my own unhappiness, fuel to my raging fire,"[29] and states with all the standard *Weltschmerz* of the puerile lover, "[I], an unhappy young man, loved to weep; and I went out of my way to find something to make me weep."[30] Augustine's maudlin emotionality exemplifies the affective style of a man swamped by his unconscious relationship with the feminine. The unmanageable affectivity—Augustine's jealousy, suspicion, fear, anger, quarrels, misery, tears, and general emotional self-absorption—boils down to a classic picture of the anima in action. Jung speaks of precisely this aspect of men's experience of her.

> They [men] accept her easily enough when she appears in novels or as a film star, but she is not understood at all when it come to seeing the role she plays in their own lives, because she sums up everything that a man can never get the better of and never finishes coping with. Therefore it remains in a perpetual state of

emotionality which must not be touched. The degree of
unconsciousness one meets here in this connection is, to put it
mildly, astounding.[31]

Augustine took in a concubine to serve as his primary bed-woman
for the next fifteen years, in what he termed a second-class marriage.
Nowhere in the entire written work of St. Augustine do we so much
as learn the woman's name, even though it was she who bore
Augustine's only son, Adeodatus. Augustine's attitude towards the
child may be summed up in his own words: "I had no part in that
boy but the sin."[32]

In the face of all his suffering, Augustine exercises an option no
less common today than in former epochs: he attempts to transcend
it all with the aid of a religious conversion. And no more opportune
sect could have presented itself to so troubled a young man than the
new school of Manichaean Christianity that had spread from the
Middle East to North Africa. Augustine became an auditor in the
Carthaginian congregation, but through the eleven years of his
participation never became one of the ascetic elect, owing to his
persistent struggles with the flesh. Today "Manichaean" is loosely used
in the popular press to indicate any radically dualistic spiritual
orientation. It has been used to describe Shiite fundamentalism, and
is a stereotyped adjective often applied to Gnosticism as a whole.
Manichaeism displays a classic Middle Eastern dualistic cosmological
structure, characterized by radically exclusive opposites and, of course,
an equally radical exclusion of the feminine. Gnostic systems based
on what Gilles Quispel calls the "Anthropos model" contrast sharply
with those of the "Sophia model," which includes the feminine from
top to bottom.

Founded by the prophet Mani (216-276/7 C.E.), an evangelical
genius and universalist who drew upon Judaism, Christianity,
Gnosticism, and Zoroastrianism, Manichaeism was widely dispersed,
spreading from the Roman Empire to China and Mongolia in the
second to the fourth centuries of our era. The creation myth of the
system is a classic instance of that ruptured aboriginal sphere of light
described previously. In Manichaeism the resulting shower of
scintillae was imagined as fallen into material darkness. This darkness
was personified as a rival cosmic being, absolutely evil in nature and
co-eternal with the luminous God above, but completely removed

from him. The transcendental God of light was in turn imagined in such aerial extremity that he was completely static and detached from earth. Its Christ-figure was conceived solely in spiritual terms, as a veritable phantom.

It is axiomatic that the worldview of the Manichees is reciprocally concrete. One might say that Manichaeism is the ultimate "piscean" religion: its exclusive opposites are as polarized as the two astrological fish of Pisces. The Manichee could only identify with the "good" but ever more rarified kernel of light within himself. The darker and more affective contents of the psyche were dissociated and banished to a mere shadow existence. This Manichaean attenuation upward in a vertical hierarchy is the archetypal skeleton on which the whole of the patriarchy hangs. It exemplifies the prevailing Western philosophical, theological, and specifically masculine notion of spirit—a transcendental spirit retreating from the material world. Brown describes something of the Manichaean estimation of life:

> [Manichees] avoided the tensions of growth on all levels. Morally, they claimed to do no more than "set free" the good part of themselves, by dissociating themselves from whatever conflicted with their comforting image of a fragment of untarnished perfection lodged within them. The Manichaean discipline therefore, was based on an exceedingly *simpliste* view of the way man acts. ... The complexities of doubt, of ignorance, deep-rooted tensions within the citadel of the will itself, are deliberately ignored in Manichaeism. With all their talk of "setting free," the Manichees had no room, in their religious language, for more subtle processes of growth—for "healing," for "renewal."[33]

Manichaeism clearly provided a convenient mechanism by which Augustine could, for a time, manage his unwieldy emotional life. But unfortunately, the metaphysics of Manichaeism also represent the quintessential example of how an entire religious system may amount to little else than a sanctification of psychic dissociation. Unmediated by the feminine, the setup bears any number of negative implications for our relation with the body, erotic love relationship, emotion, sensuality, and the created world generally. Brown thus discerns Augustine's Manichaean predicament very clearly: "So much of him did not belong to this oasis of purity: the tension of his own passions, his rage, his sexuality, his corrupt body, the vast pullulating world of 'nature's red tooth and claw' outside him."[34] Augustine's lust for light and his parallel lust for the flesh represent twin escapades, proverbial eccentricities—the twin "escape aids" of the ascetic and the libertine.

At age twenty-one, Augustine left Carthage to return to his home in Thagaste (in modern Tunisia) to teach. He took his Manichaeism with him, despite his limited success in the movement. But, as African Catholics considered Manichaeism highly heretical, Monica angrily shut Augustine out of the house until a dream reassured her that her son would eventually return to her religion. With his eye firmly fixed on heaven, Augustine thus fell into a familiar hole. With the powerful influence of Monica upon him once more, Augustine's emotional turbulence continues unabated for more than eight years until he finally slips away to Rome in the middle of the night. His departure calls to mind a legend familiar to Augustine's childhood, that of the abandonment of the beloved Dido by Aeneas, who gazed back to see her funeral pyre on his way to found the Eternal City. In the *Confessions,* Augustine agonizes over Monica's inevitable profusion of tears, and prays for forgiveness for having abandoned her. At the same time, he discerns something of the inheritance of Eve in his mother's affective power, and responds to his own necessity by lying to Monica and escaping. Augustine senses the archetypal power of the mother-anima in this symbiosis, though this is of little consequence for his anonymous mistress, and even less to his discovery of any positive qualities of his sexuality. As for Monica, she was not so easily dissuaded.

Clearly a symptomatic backlash to his attempt to break out of his mother complex, Augustine's first year in Italy brought a bout of severe psychosomatic illness that decisively reoriented his religious life, particularly his understanding of the Incarnation. The intense fantasies that accompany his suffering reflect the dilemma of a man transfixed between a purely spiritual and detached conception of the divine and the claims of bodily reality and the lower world to which the orthodox Jesus Christ had, in greater measure, submitted. Augustine describes his psychological regression, and his Manichaean errors in dense theological language:

> And lo, there was I received by the scourge of bodily sickness, and I was going down to hell, carrying all the sins which I had committed, both against Thee, and myself, and others, many

grievous, over and above that bond of original sin, whereby we
all die in Adam. For thou hadst not forgiven me any of these
things in Christ, nor had he abolished by His Cross the enmity
which by my sins I had incurred with Thee. For how should
He, by the crucifixion of a phantasm, which I believed him
to be? So true, then, was the death of my soul, as that of His
flesh was false; and how true the death of His body, so false
was the life of my soul, which did not believe it.[35]

Augustine continues to speak of his deathly fever, emotional torment,
fears of the fires of hell—and of his mother's sustained prayers for him.
He recovered! Where direct psychological insight eluded him,
Augustine's profound bodily suffering carried him down from the
discarnate and spiritualistic heights to an intense *experience* of the
earthly Adam. Yet even so ardent a repentance as this remains suffused
with sentimentality concerning his mother. The final sentence suggests
that where the body and its emotions are denigrated by excess of
spiritualism, the soul is as good as dead, an inexplicable malady merely.
The archetypal polarity and dissociation represented by the luminous
Manichaean Christ above and the fleshly Adam below resolves itself
in Augustine's new and personal appreciation of the Incarnation.
Christ as the "Second Adam" has become an experiential reality, even
though the *extent* of the Incarnation, for Augustine and all
Christendom, has remained tragically inadequate to this day. What
could demonstrate the limitations of the orthodox notion of the
Incarnation more clearly than the absence of any token or trace of the
Redeemer's earthly sexuality?

    After a difficult year, Augustine moves to Milan to study under
St. Ambrose. The next spring, just as Augustine becomes a Catholic
catechumen, Monica arrives, only to ingratiate herself to Ambrose and
busily undertakes to arrange the marriage of her son to a local Catholic
heiress. Concurrent to this development, Augustine dismisses his
longtime mistress, who returns to Africa alone vowing never to know
a man again. A postponement of the marriage and legal statutes of
the day suggest that Augustine's betrothed was twelve to fourteen years
old. Despite Monica's efforts, the heiress, too, was ultimately dismissed.
Only after Augustine's most famous prayer, "Give me continency and
chastity, only not yet!" and one last affair does Augustine embrace
celibacy. He is baptized in Milan at the age of thirty-three in 387 C.E.

The contemporary dreams we explored early in this chapter suggest a personal quaternio (self-imago) composed of a spirited, White, Scandinavian woman, the dream-ego's Christian (Apollonian) consciousness, the purple-dusted chthonic woman, the black men to the left, and the psychodynamic interaction of all four. Augustine's inner quaternio may similarly be imagined in terms of a luminous maternal anima personified by Monica; his Manichaean phantom-Christ; the orgiastic Cybele, Eve, or his anonymous mistresses; the bodily Adam; and the interaction of all these personifications. Like a template both may in turn be superimposed on the central quaternio of orthodox Christian tradition: the Virgin Mary, the Apollonian Christ, the whore (Magdalene, Jezebel, witch), the inescapable Dionysian devil—and the dynamic interaction between all four. The first feminine and masculine images of each set represent what Jungians call the "upper *coniunctio*," a gendered pair within the psyche that is pertinent to the conscious world of the individual or a pair of lovers interacting on that level. The second pair is accordingly known as the "lower *coniunctio*." Like our exemplary Purple-Powdered Woman and Black Man, this gendered pair personifies and draws its energy from everything generally excluded from consciousness.

The dreams, the biography of Augustine, and the entire patriarchal tradition clearly display how these psychic contents and all they imply of sex, body, emotion, sensuality, nature, life, soul, as well as alternate religious experience, have been rejected and demeaned. The fact remains that it is precisely this lower *coniunctio* that represents the very wellspring of consciousness, the chief agents of initiation, and the driving forces of the individuation process. Thus the dark lower *coniunctio* is the obvious centerpiece for this investigation of sexuality and the religious imagination.

Life is the touchstone for the truth of the spirit. Spirit that drags a man away from life, seeking fulfillment only in itself, is a false spirit—though the man is too to blame, since he can choose whether he will give himself up to this spirit or not.

—C. G. Jung

CHAPTER THREE

Medieval Sexual Heresies

The intermingling of phenomenally discrete archetypal materials in Paul's writing is akin to the implosive dark and baleful dullness of the medieval devil and witch. For devil and witch display sadly degraded vestiges of an entire range of forgotten pagan deities, each with their relation to sexuality, who are altogether familiar in the Graeco-Roman world. Even a brief exploration of the "natural history" of the Christian Devil through his portrayals in art and iconography reveals his morphological similarities to Pan's cloven hooves and horns, Hermes' shape-shifting bisexuality and winged back or feet, Charon's hooked nose and beard, Poseidon's trident, or the protean animal forms of Dionysus. While few people today take devil or witch seriously, the fact remains that this degraded pair reflect a significant impoverishment of the religious imagination. A classic example of this systemic failure appears in an amusing and instructive passage from Goethe's *Faust II*. With the dubious guide Mephistopheles at his side, Faust finds himself gazing beyond the worldview of his medieval Christianity to the animated landscape of Greek polytheism. With characteristic enthusiasm and abandon, Faust himself waxes strong upon his arrival:

> Here! Wondrous portent, here on Grecian land!
> At once I felt the soil where now I stand.
> And I, the sleeper, with new spirit fired,
> Rise up now, like Antaeus, fresh inspired.
> And even if I meet with things most strange
> This fierce labyrinth resolved I'll range.

Mephistopheles, skulking meanwhile around a throng of pagan spirits, is by contrast altogether disoriented:

> Now, as I wandered through the fields of flame,
> I'd much to vex me, much to disconcert:
> Naked the lot, just here and there a shirt,
> The sphinxes brazen, griffins without shame;
> This crowd of creatures, winged and tressed, displays
> No end of back and front views to the gaze…
> We, lewd at heart, can relish the salacious,
> But this antique's too lifelike and vivacious.[1]

Mephistopheles' shadowy (though nonetheless Catholic) imagination is completely ill equipped to enter into or comprehend the visions of antique sensuality that appear before him. This is the historical background of the Faust Complex in St. Paul! Reminding ourselves that Mephistopheles is indeed the Devil, a mythical personification of the Christian shadow, these lines provide additional provocative commentary on the limitations of Christian imagination in relation to sexuality. Despite his ability to deal with Northern witches, Mephistopheles confesses his inadequacy on foreign soil:

> I never saw much value in the Greeks,
> They set the senses free in dazzling freaks.
> The sins they lure men to have light and spark,
> While ours are somber, always in the dark.[2]

The fact that even today such ancient names as Venus, Eros, Dionysus, Adonis, Aphrodite, or even Spartacus may highlight the pornographic newsstand or theater marquees only underscores the tenacity of their continuity, if not their general recognition as *gods*. It is precisely here that the black men at the left and the purple-powdered woman in the dreams of the previous chapter must be recalled. These exemplary archetypal figures emerge respectively with a departure from a church and the collapse of the towers of Jerusalem and Rome, then in the alluring but diseased image of a woman languishing in a labyrinth deep beneath Rome—in the dark, damp, and decayed basement of Christianity. As representatives of the lower *coniunctio* the role of the dark partners parallels that of the Dionysian cult hero in *The Rocky Horror Picture Show* and his flamboyant entourage in that modern film parody. The brassy leather-clad transvestite handily seduces both Janet and Brad in the wake of a proper church wedding to the tune of "Let's do the time warp again," just as he personifies a challenge to their conscious erotic values. Like the devil (incubus) and witch (succubus) of Christian lore, the Black Man and the Purple-Powdered Woman constitute the dark syzygy at the core of this study. Here our perspective shifts dramatically away from patriarchal sexual values to an unprejudiced, phenomenally open, and aesthetic point of view. This indicates no illusions whatsoever about the reality of evil nor a surrender to moral anarchy—but simply the acceptance of deeper instinctual and sexual realities. Outside the confines of patriarchy, it is life's unvarnished reality and the practical demands that serve its vital continuity, as well as sacred Beauty, that figure as pre-eminent moral factors. This conception of Beauty, however, says precious little about a visit to the Louvre, or thrilling to strains of Wagner at Bayreuth, and nothing about a pilgrimage to the Wynn Hotel in Los Vegas! As art therapist Howard McConeghey observes:

> We tend to think of beauty only in terms of pleasure and harmony, but this ignores the presence of the soul. There is great pain and grief in such a paradigm of beauty because it excludes the breadth of human experience. In contrast aesthetic perception sees beauty in the disagreeable and the harsh as well as in the pretty and harmonious. If the presence of psyche suggests a deeper beauty, then beauty must mean participation in the soul of the world, even in the world's grief-filled and wretched moments. Myth does not overlook this: the handmaidens of Aphrodite were Trouble and Sorrow.[3]

Aesthetics pertains to the immediate and unwavering perception of individual created things as they present themselves. Thus, the shadow gets its due even in the sphere of aesthetic perception. Psychologically the personal shadow is a composite of everything that has been morally repressed through culture and training. But as we have seen, the significance of the Black Man, like any archetype that parallels the body's vital processes, extends into the psyche's deeper expanses and represents images and energies far beyond the shadow, moralistically conceived. He personifies the profusion of instincts and emotion we know from Dionysus and his maenads, so exuberant as to overrun itself and descend to Hades, Lord of the Underworld who, with Persephone as his queen, is the keeper of the subterranean realm of psychic essentials.

An especially poignant anecdote, an experience of natural symbolism oft cited by medieval historians, reflects the collective Christian sexual shadow, the heretical imagination, and the archetypal underground of the Late Middle Ages in corresponding fashion. In about 1000, in the French village of Vertus in the district of Chalon, a simple peasant laborer named Leutard came to be regarded as a veritable satanic emissary. His "stubborn insanity" began when:

> [He] was once laboring alone in a field and had just about finished a piece of work when, wearied by his exertions, he fell asleep and it seemed to him that a great swarm of bees entered his body through his privates. These same bees made their way out through his mouth with a loud noise, tormented him by their stings: and after he had been vexed in this fashion for some time, they seemed to speak to him, bidding him to things impossible to men.[4]

Leutard dismisses his wife, vandalizes an image of the Savior in a nearby church, begins preaching but (following a theological dispute with the local bishop) ends up throwing himself to his death in a well. Humble Leutard is completely overwhelmed by the archetypal experience that so suddenly renders him larger that life. Bees enjoy rich archaic association with the Great Goddess and the Cretan origins of Dionysus—also with the fabled beekeeper, Aristaios, a mythic double for the "honeyed" Zeus Meilichios, the god's chthonic form who is Hades himself. Hermes, the phallic messenger of the gods, is also accompanied by three bees who are nymphs—bringing our circle of association directly back to the Great Goddess. Leutard's was an age when the cult of the Virgin was emerging as a popular movement just as early concerns for witchcraft were growing within the church establishment. This remained an era where all sexual behaviors not devoted to procreation were considered heretical. Thus the bees appear as images of the sexual libido that excites Leutard's genitals and imagination and bring iconoclasm and variant religious ideas with them. The colorful career of another lone figure of the early 12th century displays the ritual inclination of heretical sexuality. Claiming special election by God, a certain Tanchelm wandered the region of Utrecht between 1112 and 1114 and attracted many a follower. A contemporary chronicler records:

> [W]hen casting about for a new devise in his search for novelty, he ordered a certain statue of Mary (how the mind is appalled at the mere mention) carried into the midst of the throng. Then he stretched out his hand to that of the statue and by the symbolism of that gesture betrothed St. Mary to himself, sacrilegiously reciting the pledge and all those solemn words of betrothal as is the common custom. "Behold," he said, "I have betrothed the Virgin Mary to myself. Do you furnish the betrothal feast and the expenses of the marriage?"[5]

The fact that Tanchelm with his bride does receive an enormous amount of money suggests that this display of sacred marriage with the Virgin did answer certain emotional needs of the people. In France, Germany, and the Low Countries, wandering spiritualists of this kind became increasingly common in the Late Middle Ages, as Norman Cohn describes in his classic work, *The Pursuit of the Millennium.* Prominent among the more organized networks that adopted a sacramental attitude towards sex were the itinerant mendicant Beghards and Beguines, the Brethren of the Free Spirit in the Rheinland, and related Adamite groups. The ritual and sacramental attitude towards sex, nudity, and sensual license characteristic of all these underground organizations is indicated by one Parisian organization calling itself the *Homines intelligentiae* ("enlightened ones"), who refer to the sex act as "the delight of Paradise" and "the acclivity," an ascension to mystical ecstasy. The leader of the *Homines* "claimed to have a special way of performing the sex act which was that practiced by Adam and Eve in the Garden of Eden." Cohn mentions yet another of these many groups, known as the Thuringian Blood Friends who, as late as 1550, regarded sexual intercourse as a sacrament that they called the *Christerie* ("making like Christ").[6] The anarchic inclination of all these developments anticipated the distant Reformation.

The 10th and 11th centuries saw an enormous upheaval in medieval society. The feudal system was breaking down, concurrent with the growth of mercantile industries as a displaced proletariat flowed into urban centers. Fully established across Europe, the Catholic Church possessed vast holdings and a wealthy clergy, though the spiritual and ecclesiastical power of its hierarchy had grown remote from life and tenuous in its social control. For the vast majority of people hunger, poverty, ill-health, and insecurity were the rule. The *Zeitgeist* of the age was set not only by these human circumstances, but further by the potent mystical prophecies of Joachim of Fiore in the 12th century. Drawing from Jewish apocalyptic literature and mystical Christian letters, Joachim separated all history into three great epochs. The Old Testament was understood as the age of Law, the Christian dispensation of Jesus and the Gospels as the age of Love, and the dawning third age as that of the Holy Spirit—of which Joachim was, of course, the seminal prophet. Such was the New Age of the day, where the knowledge of God would be directly revealed to every human heart. The disenfranchised populations of central Europe were particularly susceptible to the lavish prophecy of Joachim and the prerogative for individual revelations that it excited.

The 13th century was the golden age of mendicant orders of the church, but not all enjoyed papal sanction. Such were the groups of women and men aforementioned as the Beguines and the Beghards. Traditionally, such itinerant holy beggars moved on the edge of orthodoxy and assimilated various heterodox doctrines. Most were poor individuals intent on simply living the *vita apostolica*, a simple, primitive, and inspired Christianity. Some Beguines and Beghards were radically mystical Free Spirits; many were not. Basically members of informal religious orders, the Beguines included many widows and single women who might thus pursue their lives outside of marriage. Noteworthy among their ranks are two women of special interest, Mechthild of Magdeburg and the lesser known author of an important Free Spirit text, Marguerite Porete. Porete was active around 1300 in Hainaut, France. It is coincidental but appropriate that the names of both women harken back to Mary Magdalen.

Mechthild began her career as an orthodox nun, but died among the Beguine sisters of Hefta in Flanders around 1282. She is remembered for her elaboration of *Minnemystik* ("bride mysticism") in which the union of the soul with Christ is detailed as a highly erotic union of bride and groom. Porete, whom Robert E. Lerner identifies as "one of the most important figures in the history of the heresy of the Free Spirit,"[7] had been warned for nearly fifteen years that she was not to disseminate her views. One of her books was burned before her at Valenciennes in 1306 by the Bishop of Cambrai, Guy II. Her major tenets were unanimously declared heretical by twenty-one theological regents of the University of Paris on April 11, 1310. She refused to repent and was subsequently burned to death. Long before the witch craze, the church was thus prepared to act with impunity on the Pauline injunction: "I permit no woman to teach or to have authority over a man; she is to keep silent!"

The proposition that one might attain to so perfect a condition in life as to become incapable of sin and without need of grace is one of Porete's major tenets. Others include an indifference to church law, and liberty for sexual acts when "demanded by nature."[8] Porete maintains that "the soul neither desires nor despises poverty, tribulation, masses, sermons, fasts, or prayer and gives to nature, without remorse, all that it asks." Owing to a miraculous transformation of the soul, "nature is so well ordered that it does not demand anything prohibited."[9] Marguerite's works are singularly mild. While they represent one of the first voices of the Free Spirit heresy, there is no indication that she actively rejected the church or lived what it might call an immoderate sexual life. This can scarcely be said of many of the more radical representatives of the Free Spirit movement. Lerner submits that the proceedings of the inquiry in 1315 of the hooded nuns of Schweidnitz "tells us more about the Free Spirit mentality than any other trial documents we possess."[10] The women of this beguinage practiced an extraordinarily harsh asceticism, renouncing their natural desire for food, drink, and clothing until their complete initiation allowed them complete license:

> One woman said that she beat herself with the hide of a hedgehog and that others did the same to themselves with barbed chains and knotted thongs. Another who had been beaten in the house for eleven months, said that she underwent such brutal exercise that she now was horribly disfigured and could not recover from her injuries even though she had entered as a beautiful girl.[11]

Here we are granted an initial impression of the highly divergent behaviors that may result from the same free spirit, from harsh religious discipline to such thoughtful equivocality as that represented by Porete. Be the beautiful young girl's experience an instance of child abuse within the group or an instance of the flagellation ubiquitous in religious contexts worldwide, it cannot be taken merely as punishment for sin—for such experience ushers in a kind of supernatural consciousness. These are initiatory tortures, which is precisely why religious issues are often intimately related to the dissociative symptoms of victims of sexual abuse and torture. The existential inferiority of the creature before the Creator and the inferiority of the ego before the Self and the archetypes amount to the same thing psychologically. It is the accompanying religious fantasy and the numinous experience of suffering that interests us. One of the sixteen women investigated reported hearing an older member of the order speak of the beautiful young flagellant like this:

> [Just] as God is God, so she was God with God, and just as Christ was never separated from God, neither was she [...] when God created everything [...] I created everything, and I am God with God, and I am Christ, and I am more.[12]

This psychic inflation is a spontaneous but classic description of the shadow side of monism, a rejection of any distinctions between the human and the divine. It displays the "godlikeness" of psychic inflation and accordingly underscores the inherent risks in any breakdown of normative dualism and boundaries. Comparable moments of inflation and confusion may arise for any individual who begins to seriously assimilate contents of the unconscious. Monism and dualism represent archetypal polarities with which any religion or moral system must grapple. The example shows us how asceticism taken to its extreme almost invariably turns to intimately involve the body. The history of the European flagellates or the Mexican *Penitentes* involves severe physical trials that prompt an ecstatic religious consciousness closely akin to intense sexual experience—facts which raise provocative questions for any contemporary sadomasochist for whom sex is imagined as merely a personal and secular affair. Reich would tell us of the masochist's desire to burst from the intolerable muscular constriction of Christian character armor, even as Lyn Cowan would trace Reich's literalistic interpretations more deeply and imaginatively against a background of the dark mysteries of Dionysus in her classic *Masochism: A Jungian View.*

The descent of Inanna, which only resulted in her being hung on a stake before Ereshkigal, is also pertinent to the brutal attitude of the older towards the younger nun of Schweidnitz, to say nothing of the former's personal jealousy of and hatred for the young girl's beauty. Other phases of the Schweidnitz trial reveal that older adepts arrived at a state of perfection sufficient to spare them further austerities—a suggestion also that power hierarchies know no gender. One sister reports that the elders "regaled themselves on butter and lard and drank the best beer, leaving an inferior brew to the neophytes and the worst for the poor."[13] Testimony also emerged that the older women indulged in all manner of sexual license among themselves and with Beghards, who celebrated secret orgies with them:

> One novice claimed that a beghard told her when they were alone that to resist or to have shame at sexual contact was a sign of grossness of spirit, but that she could have the greatest spirituality if she exhibited herself to a man.[14]

Marguerite Porete's *A Mirror for Simple Souls* conveys the basic attitudes of the Free Spirit heresy in the mildest manner, while the starkly contrasting Schweidnitz documents point to an inescapable archetypal problem. The spontaneous formation of any group of ardent visionary seekers may generate the same kind of power hierarchy that we behold in the patriarchal establishments generally. Whereas Porete speaks persuasively of the soul transformed, Cohn characterizes a spiritualistic regime of later Brethren of the Free Spirit that inexorably progresses from the spontaneous prompting of body and soul to hard animus-driven doctrine. Thus, the masculine pronouns that follow are quite appropriate:

> The core of the heresy of the Free Spirit lay in the adept's attitude toward himself: he believed that he had attained perfection so absolute that he was incapable of sin. Although the practical consequences of this belief could vary, one possible consequence was certainly antinomianism or the repudiation of all moral norms. The "perfect man" could always draw the conclusion that it was permissible for him, even incumbent upon him, to do whatever was commonly forbidden. In a Christian civilization, which attached particular value to chastity and regarded sexual intercourse outside marriage as

particularly sinful, such antinomianism commonly took the form of *promiscuity on principle.*[15]

Porete's writings were written for an esoteric audience. They were secret meditations, which were declared heretical owing largely to a conception of the *unio mystica* that differed from that of orthodox mysticism by claiming a *permanent* condition of union with God. The visionary experiences of countless Catholic saints and mystics also exemplify this union, but in transient states of exultation that the church could accept. The difference between the possession of gnosis and a pathological state of possession is a very fine line, often a split decision. One medieval Catholic who did manage to preserve his orthodoxy and, curiously, who fashioned a pair of breeches with in-turned nails in an act of perpetual penitence, was the German mystic Heinrich Suso. He recounts the vision of an autonomous spirit who introduced himself as *das namenlos Wilde* ("the nameless wildness"). This spirit "claimed to come from nowhere, be nothing, and want nothing, and added that his wisdom allowed him complete liberty."[16] Suso clearly retained his capacity to discern the truth or falsehood of the spirit, though his masochistic austerity is noteworthy. One can experience the free spirit as an autonomous agency via reflection, or one may become an elite Free Spirit whose claim to personally embody the divine represents a problematic monism where divine and human categories merge in a psychic inflation.

The dream of an imaginative art historian in her mid-twenties reflects the influx of a nameless masculine spirit of comparable ambivalence. Her initiatory tortures involved addiction to cocaine, captivation by a psychopathic boyfriend, and a series of wild sexual adventures that led her to chemical dependency treatment and on to analysis:

I must leave the place where I am with my sister, mother, and grandmother. This involves opening various doors of a foyer. There is a wild creature of some kind just outside the outer door. I would let my gramma in and the wild creature, but I can only open one door at a time. I open the outer door and go out. Then I am swept out over the country by some crazy spirit-creature, who has four limbs, is all black and hairy, has big shoulders, but is also the wind. I am carried over a huge gorge or canyon, and finally call out "Aphrodite!" as a kind of magic word and call for rescue. We are then suddenly on the ground. I watch as the creature goes through a number of changes. I have an animal shell that falls apart. The creature is taking all kinds of animal shapes.

Sister, mother, grandmother, and a hairy spirit-creature of wind! The appearance of the three women taps into the theme that appears repeatedly in European art, the Three Ages of Women. For all the biographical particulars of sister, mother, and grandmother, the constellation is nothing less than an appearance of the archetypal Triple-Goddess, for which the pervasively feminine Birth-Sex-Death equation mentioned previously represents but one expression: new moon, full moon, and dark moon and their emotional equivalents. Venturing from the maternal container of home, inclined towards grandma (frequently an emotionally safer figure than mother and siblings), but here a Beauty swept away by the Beast, the dreamer makes her fateful choice. The challenge of the spirit-creature, like that of any deep involvement with the archetypal dimension of the psyche, is reflected in the familiar Greek tale of Menelaus's tenacious grasp of Proteus in the *Iliad*. This protean and oracular old man of the sea resists capture with clever transformations of shape: from lion, to serpent, leopard, boar, then flowing water, and finally to a mighty tree. Such shape shifting is germane to countless portrayals of the medieval witches and devil and to Dionysus in his many animal forms—Suso's "nameless wildness" in zoomorphic manifestation. Note the striking similarities between this spirit-creature, Proteus himself, that tail-swallowing lion in this author's countertransference dream, and the double-sexed golden-winged Phanes with his animal heads and appendages.

Recall that Phanes is born from an egg laid when the Wind courted black-winged Night, and furthermore, that Night lives in a cave and displays herself to Phanes *in triad*, and that Phanes creates earth, sky, sun, and moon. This dreamer's black, hairy, four-limbed creature of wind is a conspicuous if formidable initiatory figure! The frightened dreamer is carried out over "a huge gorge or canyon" before her "animal shell" breaks. Then she and the spirit-creature itself are grounded by an emergency call to the Goddess. Does any essential difference exist between this vivid initiatory dream, Night's three-fold appearance to Phanes in a cave, and the Eleusinian Mother (maidenly Kore's grandmother Rhea actually) opening her chasm to facilitate the

maiden's abduction and sojourn in the underworld? Be the agent the
Christian Devil, the Black Man, Jean Cocteau's furry Beast in tears,
Proteus, shining Phanes, or a spirit nameless and strange, the loss of
psychic virginity (for young men, too) remains an essential experience
of indestructible life lying in the bosom of Fate.

As he might caution our dreamer, Cohn observes that Free Spirit
eroticism, "far from springing from a carefree sensuality, possessed above
all a symbolic value as a sign of 'spiritual emancipation.'"[17] One may
ask, emancipation from what? From earth, life, a confusing psychic
situation? Surely not from the dominion of an incipient patriarchy!
But unfortunately, the situation for women among the Free Spirit (or
any other religious hierarchy) calls to mind an old query by Mae West:
"Whenever a man says he wants to protect me, I wonder, from what?"
Where the naïve original prompting of the sexual and religious instincts
gives rise to an elemental sexual-religious ritualism, we behold an
obvious, eminently reasonable, and extremely powerful numinous
development—one through which the historical maladies of patriarchal
sexual morality might be eclipsed. But by the time the Free Spirit
doctrine of "promiscuity on principle" is tied to unbounded eroticism
"as a sign of spiritual emancipation" the bird has definitely flown from
holy lover to slave master—the banality of such repetitions and the
seemingly unquenchable longing of women for father's blessing
notwithstanding.

Cohn discerns the classic arc along which the expansive *puer
aeternus* hardens as the *senex*, the old one—an enantiodromia wherein
the masculine at one extreme begins to constellate its opposite. Here
is Lara's revolutionary boyfriend in *Dr. Zhivago,* rising up against the
Czar's horsemen in youth only to reappear—scar-faced, rigid, and
beyond all enchantment—on an iron Red Army locomotive in winter.
Antinomianism (anarchism) gradually and inexorably produces its
own ideological program, with failure to surrender a sign of "grossness
of spirit." Men tend to personify it, but both women and men are
victims of the negative animus-masculine-spirit that structures and
enforces it. Hermann Hesse addresses the dilemma very concisely
to the effect that the sins of the flesh always retain a certain
biological innocence about them, whereas it is the calculated
perversion of the spirit where the real question of evil begins. Our
remaining examples bear this out quite vividly.

The case of John Hartmann of Ossmann was heard by Catholic authorities on December 26, 1367. Lerner calls him "the most outspoken and unashamed radical Free Spirit of whom we have record."[18] According to Hartmann, "one who is 'truly free' can be subject to no authority because he is king and lord of all creatures."

> John's testimony on sexual matters was so unrestrained that leading questions were not necessary. He maintained that if the nature of a free spirit ("ein frey geist") inclined toward the sexual act he could have intercourse with his sister or his mother in any place, even on the altar, and that it would be "more natural" to have sex with one's sister than with any other woman. Nor would a young girl lose her virginity after sexual intercourse, but if she were robbed of it she would regain it by having relations with one free in spirit. Even if a girl has successive intercourse with ten men, if the last of them was a free spirit she would receive her virginity back. Just as calves and oxen were created for men to eat, so women were created for the use of the free in spirit.[19]

While power has completely overwhelmed sex and sensuality in this overweening theological exercise, Hartmann's extravagant words on incest are provocative psychologically. We remind ourselves, first of all, that these are the words of "ein frey geist" with supernatural sexual powers! He usurps a divine role in claiming to repair virgins and make souls pure and whole. But this is merely a part of the fascination for mother and daughter incest that holds Hartmann in its sway. For the conspicuous regressive pull points directly to the unconscious, to the intrapsychic world of John himself, where both mother and girls figure as images of the anima and the ten men who would copulate with them reflect his own primitive masculinity. All function in complete unconsciousness as aspects of his own power complex, albeit with the convenient proviso that their phallic actions may be counteracted by his own narcissistic appropriation of women.

An heretical outlook would presumably represent the exact opposite of Catholic allegiance to Christ and his Heavenly Father, but patriarchal prerogatives prevail here. Misogyny, however, is a problem even more universal and intimate than racism or bigotry—and this only underscores the core dynamism and challenge of any outer or inner marriage of the male and the female. One amusing footnote to this tale consists of a follow-up question to Hartmann as to whether

Christ had sex with Mary Magdalen after [*sic*] the Resurrection. "John replied, almost coyly, that that was a lofty and profound sentence and said that although he well knew the answer he preferred not to expound on it."[20] His brand of moral anarchism, inflated power drive, and misogyny proceed to sharp crystallized doctrine:

> You shall order all created beings to serve you according to your will, for the glory of God. ... You shall bear all things up to God. If you want to use all created beings, you have the right to do so; for every creature you use, you drive up to its Origin.[21]

Cohn follows the reverberations of such doctrines as these to a 17th-century English sect known as the Ranters. One of their leaders articulates a classic tenet of the libertine, the seductive proposition that "till acted that so-called sin, thou art not delivered from the power of sin."[22] While ardently championing his freedom, the libertine generally remains as dependent on conventional concepts of sin, evil, and outrage as any Free Spirit rebelling against the values of the medieval church. Variations of the attitude appear in the words of exemplary modern libertines, all of whom are highly intellectualizing, disastrous in their human relationships, and extremely negative in relation to their own bodies. The anxious dandy Charles Baudelaire writes: "The supreme and unique pleasure (*volupté*) of love lies in the certainty that one is doing evil."[23] The corpulent Marquis de Sade holds that: "Crime is the soul of lust. What would pleasure be if it were not accompanied by crime? It is not the object of debauchery that excites us, but rather the idea of evil."[24] Similarly, Aleister Crowley, the celebrated occultist and heroin addict, also maintains that the only means of overcoming evil is by exploiting it as an avenue to grace. Despite their respective forms of anarchic furor, each cynically plays on the Christian promise-card of salvation through evil. Curiously, an in-house Catholic version of the same tenet serves to explain the Fall of Man as a requisite, if mild, evil, essential to the process of Redemption itself. For the libertine, this is all simply a question of the extremity of one's means.

No adequate understanding of the sexual shadow of Christian tradition or its content can be had without reference to the witch craze. The most painful distortions of the sexual and religious instincts appear in the witch craze and inquisitions of central Europe, concentrated between the mid-13th and the 15th centuries—the great assault on the Dionysian side of life. The lurid contents and dark propensities of the impoverished patriarchal imagination appear again in projected form. For what the Fathers of the Church saw, the responses they exacted, and the evidence they so ruthlessly achieved in their chambers of interrogation were largely shaped by patriarchal fantasies that had become institutionalized over a period of more than a thousand years. The earliest charge of heresy merged with witchcraft in 1022 was an accusation of devil worship brought by a monk from Chartres. Writing nearly fifty years after the event, the monk records the experience of a priest, Arefast, who went to mass and carefully purified himself before following one of his errant clerics to a gathering of devil worshippers. The monk recounts Arefast's account:

> They gathered, indeed, on certain nights in a designated house, everyone carrying a light in his right hand, and like merry-makers chanted the names of demons until suddenly they saw descend among them a demon in the like of some sort of little beast. As soon the apparition was visible to everyone, all the lights were forthwith extinguished and each, with the least possible delay, seized the woman who first came to hand, to abuse her, without thought of sin. Whether it were mother, sister, nun who they embraced, they deemed it an act of sanctity and piety to lie with her. When a child was born of this most filthy union, on the eighth day thereafter a great fire was lighted and the child was purified by the fire in the manner of the old pagans, and so was cremated. Its ashes were collected and preserved with as great veneration as Christian reverence is wont to give the body of Christ, being given to the sick as a viaticum at the moment of their departing this world.[25]

This "evidence" was sufficient to justify the immolation of ten souls. The details of the report are, however, standard features of a myth of archetypal orgy already known in 186 C.E., when the Roman Senate issued its famous *Senatus Consultum de Bacchanalibus*, condemning the Dionysus cult for its lewd excesses and alleged conspiracy against the state. Surprising, though in full accord with now familiar patriarchal fantasy, contemporary Christian behaviors were also alleged by the Romans to be absolutely promiscuous and to include even incest between brothers and sisters, parents and their children. The charges extended to worshipping the genitals of their leaders, ritually murdering children, and celebrating cannibalistic feasts. The heresy hunters, Irenaeus of Lyon and Clement of Alexandria, carried these classic accusations into Christian literature as polemics against various Gnostic sects. St. Augustine also resorts to the archetypal orgy fantasy in condemning the ascetic Manichaeans with whom he was formerly allied, just as Jews were periodically targeted with similar accusation.

The incidental reality of such ritual behaviors in medieval Europe need not be doubted—nor should the perseveration of historical prejudices and projections be underestimated. Anyone who has studied Tantra or other indigenous sexual practices will recognize the motifs of incest, orgy, and the *lucerna exstincta in loco subterraneo* ("extinguished lamp in an underground place") as widely dispersed features of chthonic and tamasic ("concerned with decay") mystical complexes. This is the spiritual territory of Eliade's "decay from damp." The latter theme even appears in the Doors' unforgettable lyric anthem "When the Music's Over"—turn out the lights! Broader consideration of all we find in our account of medieval witchcraft will be taken up in due course. Note here that incest, orgy, descent, and even cannibalism are invariably related to a deep instinctual yearning for rebirth and the re-creation of Time and World.

The reality of the body is a shifting image pinned down by desire.

—Octavio Paz

CHAPTER FOUR

Conduits of the Body

Jung once remarked that "to see great religious values in the body is a very horrible discovery for a good Christian."[1] It is thus no surprise that the foregoing review of moralistic doctrines and patriarchal prejudices has taught us far less about the nature of original religious experience than about institutional defenses against it. Our attention to dream, to myth, but most of all to the striking confluence of alternate sexuality and alternative religious inclinations comes to focus now on the body and its imaginal dimensions—the psychosomatic nature of religious experience.

Recalling the essential "overplus" in Rudolf Otto's idea of the holy that emerged by stripping away intellect, rationalism, and *a priori* moral definitions of the sacred, we encounter Otto's stunning characterization of naked numinous experience, a broad range of emotions that radiate through the mortal frame that contains them:

> The feeling of it may at times come sweeping like a gentle tide, pervading the mind with a tranquil mood of deepest worship. It may pass over into a more set and lasting attitude of the soul, continuing, as it were, thrillingly vibrant and resonant, until at last it dies away and the soul resumes its "profane," non-religious mood of everyday experience. It may burst in sudden eruption up from the depths of the soul with spasms and convulsions, or lead to the strangest excitements, to intoxicated frenzy, to transport, and to ecstasy. It has its wild and demonic forms and can sink to an almost grisly horror and shuddering. It has its crude, barbaric antecedents and early manifestations, and again it may be developed into something beautiful and pure

and glorious. It may become the hushed, trembling, and speechless humility of the creature in the presence of—whom or what? In the presence of that which is a *mystery* inexpressible and above all creatures.[2]

Amplifying these particular feeling experiences, Otto meticulously gathers synonyms for the numinous, including awe, the uncanny, the portentous, the monstrous, the wholly other, as well as the *mysterium tremendum,* by which an emotional impact sufficient to literally shake one to the bone is implied. Conspicuously bioenergetic in implication, Otto's vision is a holistic embrace of the entire body. Sacred experience of this nature must clearly include the intensity of sexual love or the paroxysm and release of intense orgasm. But let us proceed by reviewing the contribution of various investigators to what we know about the significance of sexuality to the constitution of personality and beyond.

A god-word, some root fantasy, invariably lies at the core of any system that posits a particular energy or dynamism as the root of that system. Anyone capable of reading psychoanalytic literature mythologically will readily perceive the divinity of sex in the extraordinarily global (and fiercely defended) interpretation of the sexual libido and Freud's particular emphasis on the phallus. Given the Newtonian-Cartesian *Weltanschauung* of 19th-century mechanistic science, however, truth for Freud demanded an elimination of any vestige of the sacred, just as it does in the behavioral sciences today. His own confession of faith is exclusive and explicit: "Our science is no illusion, but an illusion it would be to suppose that what science cannot give us we can get elsewhere."[3] How like the retired engineers in my UCLA cosmology class: reading Einstein, Hawking, or Guth into the wee hours, brimming with religious yearning, but wrestling only with the mathematical angels of string theory!

To Freud belongs the distinction of ushering into general Western consciousness an appreciation of the positive psychological significance of sex as it extends beyond procreation to the development of personality and the emotional and mental life of the individual. His "Three Essays on the Theory of Sexuality" begins with the proposition that sexual life is present at birth, before following it through the familiar sequence of oral, anal, and genital somatic zones to the phallic focus of adult sexuality. Actually, studies have shown that periodic erections and evidence of vaginal excitations are present even with the unborn—to whatever degree this suggests "sexuality." The erogenous zones of the child also bear a rudimentary resemblance to the *chakras*, the specific energetically charged bodily zones and symbolic matrices portrayed in the diagrams of Hindu physiology and other systems. Jung once observed that the little word "like" plays an incalculable role in psychology. Psychoanalytic (and Jungian) literature is accordingly replete with perceptions of the chaining of organ simulacra throughout the *psychosoma*: mouth and anus (uroboros), mouth and vagina (*vagina dentata*), penis as breast or tooth (tooth phallus) or umbilical cord (wind phallus), child (dwarf) as penis-phallus, the eye as penis and vagina, etc. Freud's theory has thus been called pansexual. We may assess this expression by considering the organs he cites as erotogenic zones and charged with his *libido sexualis*: the mucous membranes of the lips and mouth including their connection to the digestive tract, the anus with its connection to the innervation of alimentary peristalsis, the genital organs themselves, the skin in its entirety, the eyes, and even the act of seeing derived from touching. Freud sees this extending also to external mechanical excitation as a source of infantile sexual arousal and finally (through sublimation as mind) to the formation of intellectual functions.

I retain this radiating phenomenology as pertinent to sexuality and erotic love, but the proposition that the libido that sustains psychic life is itself essentially sexual must be rejected along with Freud's concretism. Appropriately enough, the intricate field of object relations theory (so indebted to ethology and infant observation) came to challenge Freud's one-sided focus on psychosexual development (the drive-theory), focusing rather on relational factors in the development of personality. I am the breast, I have the breast, mother and I—the long journey from narcissism to world. Freud says that the sexual drives and zones are more or less loosely knit, unorganized, and migratory. This is part of his notion of infant as "polymorphous perverse" child, which is otherwise a highly pejorative expression. This marvelous mythical creature not only represents an eros that possesses *multiple propensities* in childhood, but *remains* a multiple disposition in both self-absorption or relational and mirroring space. Throughout life the divine child plays its role in self-pleasure and masturbation as well as in playful and imaginative lovemaking with a partner. Hiding behind Freud's "polymorphous perverse child" is the archetypal stuff of Phanes (Eros) bearing within himself the honored seeds of the gods! He is also represented by fleet-footed Hermes or even more, by Mercurius, the alchemical son of the philosophers.

A review of memory (anamnesis) is always the first step in the process of looking inward. Biographical details are essential in confronting complexes and the emotional load they carry. A therapist meets patients where they are, steadily drawing forth the personal story. But all memory leads to archetypal *memoria*, which Augustine also discusses in the *Confessions*. Movement back in time is psychologically always a movement inward and down into psychic depth—a breach in linear time, a regression. Reflecting on the implications of this perennial inclination, Jung speaks of startling realities that await adult ego-consciousness when it is gripped by deep emotion and called below for initiation. He observes that "the 'mother' is really an imago, a psychic image merely, which has in it a number of different but very important unconscious contents." And he affirms a view of mother *as anima,* and speaks also of her prodigious archetypal offspring:

> The "mother," as *the first incarnation of the anima archetype*, in fact personifies the whole unconscious. Hence the regression leads back only apparently to the mother; in reality she is the gateway into the unconscious, into the "realm of the Mothers." Whoever sets foot in this realm submits his conscious ego-personality to the controlling influence of the unconscious, or if he feels that he has been caught by mistake or that someone has tricked him into it, he will defend himself desperately, though his resistance will not turn out to his advantage. For regression, if left undisturbed, does not stop short at the "mother" but goes back beyond her to the prenatal realm of the "Eternal Feminine," to the immemorial world of archetypal possibilities where, "thronged round with the images of all creation," slumbers the "divine child," patiently awaiting his conscious realization. This son is the germ of wholeness ....[4]

Jung and Reich both question the fact that Freud, for all his attention to psychosexual development, has little to say about sex beyond paternity or the achievement of adult functioning. Hillman notes that "the Freudian notion of full genitality is, at best, an account of the sexual instinct perceived through the father archetype."[5] Jung's symbolic attitude with its dual emphasis on the mother as birth mother and *mater spiritualis,* and on *rebirth* and the *archetypal* child thus carries many additional implications for sex and Eros beyond midlife— conspicuously, an inner procreativity of soul.

The man who researched human sexuality more painstakingly than any of Freud's original circle was Wilhelm Reich. He affords us many practical experiential observations of sex, the body, and somatic memory that are extremely useful, for instance, in the treatment of victims of sexual abuse. Reich's *Character Analysis* investigates fundamental defense mechanisms, focusing on the individual's blockage of threatening impressions from the environment and from sexual energies and affects emerging internally. These include rage, aggression, pain, grief, and—interestingly enough—pleasure. The notion of "pleasure anxiety" comes from Reich. It is basic to both the fear of psychic expansiveness and the sheer power of Beauty. Therapeutically, Reich concerned himself with the shadow aspects of the analytic relationship, the deeper instinctual energies in the interaction that lie concealed in the unconscious of both parties. This "lower *coniunctio*" (contrasting with the "upper *coniunctio*" of the ongoing therapeutic alliance) may be imagined in terms of our model syzygy—the Black Man and the Purple-Powdered Woman or, by extension, Dionysus-Hades and Persephone. Both pairs personify the raw power of bodily and psychic life.

Reich perceived that mannered politeness, pseudo-happiness, or unpersuasive references to faith or beliefs generally amount to little more than a stratagem for warding off a fear of attack or abandonment. The soft style of the exaggerated male-apologist to strident feminism (or mom) and the passive and seductive *femme à homme* wilting before the demands of her personal self-determination (or dad) are typical examples. Thus mistrustful of the presented persona, Reich devotes particular attention to a patient's facial expression, tone of voice, gestures, and bodily posture. While doubtless overly aggressive in his uncompromising insistence on direct contact, Reich is keenly aware of nonverbal factors in therapeutic interaction—as vividly demonstrated afore by this therapist's laryngitis! He discerned that "character resistance" seeks to maintain control of organismic energies not only through psychological attitude, but through structures of control engrained in the fabric of the body itself. Character attitudes and muscular postures have a common function, for "every psychic impulse is functionally identical with a definite somatic excitation."[6] Complexes are expressed through the body. Reich is accordingly remembered for his view that when one lays one's hands on the body one touches the unconscious.

Reich commenced to apply direct tactile pressure to open his patient's "muscular armor," the body's chronic structural rigidity. He developed stretching exercises and breathing techniques aimed at opening muscular systems to their natural streaming of biological energy. As Reich observes, this brings us beyond psychological defenses to the threshold of psychic content:

> It never ceases to be surprising how the loosening of a muscular spasm not only releases the vegetative energy, but, over and above this, reproduces a memory of that situation in infancy in which the repression of the instinct occurred. It can be said that every muscular rigidity contains the history and meaning of its origin.[7]

Basic practical knowledge for Reichean somatic therapists, and massage therapists as well, these facts are fundamental to any depth psychological approach that respects the body's living reality. Reich drew insights into somatic memory from German biologist, physiologist, and evolutionary theorist Richard Semon, specifically his theory of "mnemonic sensations."

> Semon contended that the involuntary acts of all living creatures consisted in "engrams," i.e., in historical impressions of experience. The eternally self-perpetuating protoplasm is continually absorbing impressions which, in response to corresponding stimuli, are "ecphorized."[8]

Engrams are memory traces, whether actual protoplasmic changes in neural tissue (Semon) or alternately conceived; "ecphorized" indicates the process of memories being activated by a stimulus. Reich understands this mirroring physiologically and very concretely, though he is clearly sensitive to psychic images in a manner comparable to the attention given to critical periods, imprinting, and the disposition of organisms to respond in a specific way—the domain of ethological inquiry. Mythologically it might be said that Echo ("akin") is the nymph who "ecphorized" Narcissus, from whom the clinical term narcissism derives. We'll consider primary narcissism and the "echoes" that stir one from uroboric self-absorption—in childhood and ever after.

Reich responded to Freud's limited speculation on sexuality beyond adult genital functions and procreation by introducing his specific focus on "orgastic potency." He defines this as "the capacity to surrender to the flow of the biological energy, free from any inhibitions; the capacity to discharge completely the dammed-up excitation through involuntary, pleasurable convulsions of the body."[9] The ability to surrender fully to the body's impulses is intimately related to a rich diversity in the emotional life, to the activation of dreams and fantasy, to creative labor, and ultimately to the acceptance of one's mortality with dignity. But the "free-from-any-inhibition" fantasy, so pervasive with Reich, extends something of a red flag, like the flaming sword hung at the gateway to Eden. The shadow is disregarded here. We've visited the Brethren of the Free Spirit, whose demand for absolute freedom brought its own reward. Rousseau's romantic (and colonialist) fantasy of the Noble Savage and his sentimentalized view of Nature are likewise answered by the libertine furor of the Marquis de Sade by the end of their century!

Reich saw the release of the orgasm reflex not only as prophylactic to neurosis but as a natural biological reflex of all creatures. The reflex consists of a wave of excitation and movement that "emerges from the vegetative center" over the head, chest, upper and lower abdomen, to pelvis and legs. In orgasmic crisis the head tends backward, the shoulders curl forward, and legs part spontaneously—as the breath is exhaled. One may ponder the similarity of the orgasm reflex to an entire spectrum of affects that may grip the body (grief, rage, deep laughter), but also the spontaneous, curling cling response of the infant. Reich's observation that men who find such surrender to be feminine are always organistically disturbed is an interesting footnote here, especially given the conspicuous muscular armoring of the macho male.

The study of the orgasm reflex led Reich to deeper reflections on the essential thread of life running through the organic world. At a certain level of penetration, however, Reich's concretism, literalism, and his conceptions of the libido as strictly sexual and the orgasm as primarily biological exact a deeper toll. He maintains that:

In the orgasm, we are nothing but a pulsating mass of plasm. ...
Among more primitive biological organisms, for example,
protozoa, it is found in the form of plasmatic contractions; the
most elementary state at which it can be found is in the division
of single cells.[10]

The proposition of our being nothing but pulsing plasma is indicative
of a one-sidedness that was part of Reich's late-life rebound into psychic
inflation. He posited a mysterious "orgone" energy permeating the
atmosphere as a complement to the cellular "bions" he claims even to
have created. One perceives a psychic splitting and gyrating here, and
a reciprocally rudimentary spirituality—the inevitable consequence
of pushing the materialistic position to its breaking point. It is thus
telling that Reich subsequently concerned himself with a negative
dark orgone. His biographer, Myron Sharaf, titles his work *Fury
on Earth,* but war arose in heaven. Is regular uninhibited bodily
orgasm an end in itself for the second half of life, or is it the harbinger
and complement to a deeper mystery?

Freud and Reich spend their lives exploring sexuality, but cannot
embrace the religious dimensions of sexuality as such. But the daemon
of both men was intimately that of the *spiritus sexualis.* Reich's root
fantasies, the god-words of his system, appear as "biological energy,"
"vegetative energy," "the eternally self-perpetuating protoplasm,"
"vegetotherapy" (an early term for his body work). Once again we see
the archetype behind the theory—Dionysus, the indestructible life:
"the force that through the green fuse drives the flower."[11] Still, the
observation that every muscular rigidity contains history and memory
and the fantasy that plasmatic contractions resembling the orgasm
reflex appear in the division of single cells remain provocative.
Intuitively it leads to the threshold of what Jung called "the psychoid,"
that vanishing point of vanishing points, where matter and spirit, body
and psyche seem to merge. What perspective, what eyes, what organ
of perception is adequate to the task of discerning this dimension?

In "Beyond the Pleasure Principle" Freud devotes fifty pages of
hard reasoning to his search for the origins of sexuality before
capitulating that "not so much as a ray of a scientific hypothesis" can
penetrate so formidable a darkness. We know that the archetype of
sex and gender emerged on this planet 900,000,000 to one billion years
ago, just as we feel the ancient power of sex and gender shifting

momentarily in bodily innervation and fantasy. Freud finally resorts to the image of Plato's androgyne which, like Reich's green force, suggests the inevitability, the sheer necessity of a symbolic approach, of myth and imagination. Freud's deliberative discipline, however, recommends itself as we consider a later psychoanalytic work by Robert Fliess, *Ego and Body Ego*, published in 1961. Fliess's insights into the mysterious relationship between the ego and the body represents a highly differentiated response to parallel observations by Jung that consciousness "issues from a dark body, the ego," and that the latter, while essential for any consciousness at all, consists of "nothing but *the association* of an object or content with the ego." Jung's emphasis on the ego as a mere creature of shifting associations leads to the perplexing summary assertion:

> The ego, ostensibly the thing we know the most about, is in fact a highly complex affair full of unfathomable obscurities. Indeed one could even define it as *a relatively constant personification of the unconscious itself*.[12]

Beginning with Freud's beguilingly simple statement that "the body is, to begin with, a body-ego," Fliess explores the conjunctions and disjunction between the physiology of bodily experience and the way in which ego-consciousness tends to separate itself from the body. The common remark that an infant knows no mind-body problem indicates the former situation, while the latter is pertinent to the mental abstraction we have critiqued all along. Fliess explains that the body-ego could then be spoken of as "the sum total of our organ representations"—all this even while the mundane ego is out about its daily affairs, narrowed in scope and confident in its dominion. The body-ego is the representative, most simply, of how one actually looks and feels to oneself. But how simple is this? Fliess describes three basic avenues of perception by which we arrive at any such evaluation and points towards a subtle, reflective, and specifically psychic core reality that we will meet again in the visionary experiences of no one less than Mary Magdalen. Of the body-ego Fliess states:

> It is perceived *by all the sensory spheres*, i.e., through exteroception, proprioception, and enteroception. Yet the representation of our body in our mind is inaccurate; the body-ego corresponds to

the body not even in the sense in which an object-representation corresponds to the object.[13]

Our conscious experience of the body is imprecise (inaccurate) because our awareness of it arises through these *varied and contrasting means*—clearly one reason why Octavio Paz can speak of the body as a shifting image pinned down by desire. Similarly, Joseph Campbell can speak of the body as the material composite upon which our entire existential experience of dissociation necessarily rests. Of our perceptions of the body-ego, Fliess simply tells us that while the contrast between, say, the hawk overhead and the image of that hawk in our consciousness is already open to epistemological critique, the contrast between our material body and its images (object-representations) in consciousness is even more ambiguous. Jung's recognition of the psyche as the substrate of all our knowing is pertinent here, for we are definitely moving into psychic space. Of the sensory spheres, one engages in *exteroception* directly by looking at one's body, indirectly or by looking in a mirror. It is striking that even exteroception can challenge static assumptions of the body image— in photo-finish shots of athletic bodies stretched out like cheetahs or in the classic photographic studies of human locomotion by Muybridge. Exteroception pertains to all stimuli impinging on the organism from without—sight, touch, smell, sound, taste—and is thus comparable to Jung's sensation function. But there is always something that cannot be seen in this way, though I scarcely refer to simply catching a glimpse of the back of one's head. (There actually is serious cosmological theory that maintains that one *would* see the back of one's head, could one only see far enough!) The next two avenues of perception turn away from sharp literal images and into the complexity and depth indicated very precisely by the saying of Jesus in the Gnostic *Gospel of Thomas*:

> When you see your likeness, you rejoice. But when you see your
> images which came into being before you, and which neither
> die nor become manifest, how much will you have to bear![14]

Proprioception refers to one's awareness of stimuli produced *within* the body by movement and tensions within its tissues. Here Reich is loosening muscular spasms—but also finding *memory*. Neither mere physiology nor only sensation, this is a shifting to intuition and the intuitive perception of things as holistic imaginal gestalts. One "engages" in *enteroception* through an awareness of hunger or equivalent functions: "[I]f I am hungry, my stomach feels empty, if satiated it feels full; but the enteroceptively perceived 'stomach' has only a faint resemblance to the anatomical organ."[15] Sexual arousal and orgasm, asphyxia and urgent breathing, stinging in the eyes and tearing, cramped physical confinement and flailing represent additional examples. Here the ambiguity and disparity of perceptive results between enteroception and the actual anatomical organs involved is most evident, and here the necessity for a symbolic or imaginal approach arises. All three sensory spheres contribute to our awareness of the body-ego. In the body-ego *organ* and *function* are thus experienced in consciously specific but anatomically generalized feeling-toned wholes: to gulp, to cum, to catch one's breath, to sob, to explode. Each is based on the generalization of organs or organ systems and functions. This pertains also to the definition of the psychosexual zones, i.e., oral, anal, and genital. All are conspicuous for the specific orifices involved, but are also part of the general radiation of the sexual libido as described in Freud's *Three Essays*. The resulting body image is intuitively organized and intuitively discerned—perpetually shifting and close to vital processes.

Fliess further observes that the three sensory spheres (exteroception, proprioception, enteroception) are *fusion points with the outside world*, and adds a vivid example that highlights the protean representations of the body-ego in consciousness:

> It is at these points [the sensory spheres] that the two environments, body and the outside world, adhere to each other and are mutually requisite to each other. The existence of these particular parts of the body-ego is dependent upon the perception of the outside world. My visual sphere [for example] is represented only by the objects I see; in total darkness it is not represented at all; and in complete quiet the auditory sphere does not exist in the body-ego.[16]

Erich Neumann offers a reinforcing observation regarding the "two environments" of body and world that also echoes Freud: "*All* body openings—eyes, ears, nose, mouth (navel), rectum, genital zone—as well as the skin, have, as places of exchange between inside and outside, a numinous accent for early man."[17] Fliess comes at last to speak of the body-ego's manifest "psychic quality," noting "that its parts are ... in a perpetual state of oscillation between being descriptively unconscious and becoming descriptively conscious."[18] It is clear that Fliess is describing something psychic and intermediary to both body and world. But his theoretical roots do not penetrate deeply enough. Neither religion nor "the numinous" are viable categories for him. But dreams, fantasies, and visionary experience are also pre-eminent enteroceptive (intuitive) means by which experiential holism is represented. A central question must thus remain, beyond rationality but completely open: To what degree are "particular parts" of the body-ego *not* dependent upon perceptions of the flesh or the outside world?

In psychoanalytic thought the origin and essential condition of the body-ego is one of *primary narcissism*, that phase of the oral stage in which the ego has differentiated itself neither from the body and its instincts nor from the mother. Adrift in the uterine mother and turned in on itself, then mirrored by the mother externally and awakened to the second environment over which she presides—the body-ego and the mother imago will later be called "the unconscious." But do note a crucial fact: that which appears to the mundane ego as inner and outer environments remains forever one in the seamless mirroring vessel of the soul. The ancient Egyptian creation myth of Nut and Nu represents this concisely. Nut is a pervasively feminine fluid matrix streaming with stars, in which and from which a germinal masculine element (Nu) arises on its "inner" trajectory as the *psychic* sun ("object representation" = archetypal image). Narcissus, son of the blue nymph Leiriope, is similarly encircled as a child by the flowing stream of a river god. These images of psychic origins also have their place at life's conclusion: the inner lid of Egyptian sarcophagi typically feature the blue-skinned goddess (Nut) stretching out over the departed, just as images of the Virgin of Guadalupe with her own star-struck *tilma* are employed today in Mexico for the same reassuring purpose. *The mother imago is the perennial compliment of the body-ego and vice versa—the primal root of psyche's fundamental androgyny.*

Our three sensory spheres—whose reflective activity manifests images of the body-ego and thus of ourselves—perpetually mirror the accumulating imagery, resonant echoes, and consciousness of a living rhythm in which and from which narcissism turns inside out to discover the world. Perforce we recall the Orphic Phanes, a cosmic analogue to

Nu and Narcissus and possessive of distinct solar qualities. As "first born" hatched from an egg, a cave dweller with Night (who displays herself in triad), as double-sexed, creaturely and golden-winged, a "coming of light" who appears with all manner of beasts, bearing within "the honored seeds of the gods"—Phanes is the stuff of both narcissism, body-ego, and individuation. Thus, Jung can speak of the ego as a relatively constant personification of the unconscious, because the ego is associatively rooted in the body-ego, and the body-ego is nothing less than an image of the Self, whatever its variations of form. A pertinent personal dream emerged at this point in this writing that suggests how the subtleties discussed appear in the living psychic process:

I stand immediately outside a narrow cave opening at the base of a forested hillside. The cave recedes into velvety darkness behind me. I look out on a large enchanted garden. Wildflowers and shrubbery are everywhere amidst the tree trunks. Songbirds, hummingbirds, and butterflies flit through arching strands of gooseberries, raspberries, and bougainvillea. I realize that I am naked. Suddenly a dignified swarthy Persian man appears at my side and wraps me in a beautiful dark robe with myriad little circular mirrors sewn into it with golden thread.

The archetypal mother-anima figures here as both the receding darkness of the cave and the enchanting garden ringed round with living images. The scene has a feeling of ritual rebirth about it, of seeing with one's most original eyes. Consider how data from all perceptual spheres may contribute to the dream, while the extraordinary mirror-covered robe provided by the Persian bodes of deepening perceptions of the body-ego, and indeed the whole unconscious.

Psychoanalysis consistently neglects the deep *telos* of psychic life as well as its *initiatory* intents and purposes beyond adult sexuality or orgastic potency. The theoretical shortcoming again results from a categorical rejection of archetypal and religious understanding. While ceaselessly discussing "object representations," psychoanalysis knows nothing about *the anima*. The problem lies in the restriction psychoanalysis imposes on our objects of desire through its reduction of psychic life to physiology, its extremely one-sided personalistic understanding of the mother-child dyad, and its limited notions of projection generally. Following a description of the body-ego, Fliess betrays this theoretical strain through an ungainly compounding of terms. He posits a "pleasure-physiologic-body-ego." Its parts "lend themselves to a partial or total displacement;" its "extension or projection ... into the object world is much more frequent and extensive than that of the body-ego," its "disparity between anatomical organs and functions" is far greater and given to "fantastic elaboration."[19] This extension into the object world implies a global psychic field that may be imagined in terms of the hermetic engraving of the anima circled by myriad lumina that is included among our illustrations (see Fig. 1). Fleiss rightly observes that the piqued sexual energies and anomalous projective identifications of the body-ego in sexually abused individuals may be extravagant, but his limited physiologically based theory cannot accommodate psyche's expansion into the transpersonal. The anima is *the* primordial projective factor. Both mystical Judaism and Gnosticism recognize a feminine emanation indwelling the world, i.e., the Shekhinah, Sophia (Wisdom, Holy Spirit). Like Maya, spinner of imaginal forms and *inspiratrix* of discriminating knowledge, this feminine being belongs not to the mother alone but to the archetype of the anima. Here again what appears as mother-bound narcissism on an infantile level turns itself inside out to emerge creatively as Phanes, son of Night, germinal counterpart to the anima. Marie-Louise von Franz comments to the effect that whether a man compulsively peeks up women's skirts on the tram or lights a candle to the Virgin in the local cathedral, he is seeking essentially the same emotional experience. Thus, the elusive object of desire is ultimately unrestricted by personalism or biography.

Freud and Jung parted ways over their conflicting views on the nature of libido. While Freud, Reich, and to a great extent Fliess retain a sexual notion of the libido, Jung speaks of a free psychic energy. Both perspectives are important to a discussion of sexuality and the religious imagination. But Jung recalls of his time in psychoanalytic circles that he never wearied of insisting that sex not be taken too literally, but in a wider sense. A broad range of sexual images will be introduced, but however "spiritual" their aspect, they need always to be considered in relation to the body. Jung speaks of the necessity to "reconcile ourselves to the mysterious truth that the spirit is the life of the body seen from within, and the body the outward manifestation of the spirit—the two being really one ...."[20] The question of *telos* remains one with living processes. Jung's notion of libido includes this as a heuristic principle:

> I see the real value of the concept of libido not in its sexual
> definition but in its energic view, thanks to which we are in the
> possession of an extremely valuable heuristic principle. We are
> also indebted to the energic point of view for dynamic images
> and correlations which are of inestimable value to us in the chaos
> of the psychic world.[21]

The energic point of view sees psychic energy intimately correlated
with the physiological apparatus, but free and applicable to all psychic
spheres. This includes what has been termed "the religious function
of the psyche," though the term "function" carries an unfortunate
mechanistic and positivist nuance. Life itself is the touchstone for the
truth of the spirit. A rich sense of the actual look, feel, and emotional
attitude of that proposition is conveyed by art historian H. A.
Groenewegen-Frankfort in relation to Cretan art:

> Cretan art ignored the terrifying distance between the human
> and the transcendent which may tempt man to seek a refuge in
> abstraction and to create a form for the significant remote from
> time and space; it equally ignored the glory and futility of single
> human acts, time-bound, space-bound. In Crete artists did not
> give substance to the world of the dead through an abstract of
> the world of the living, nor did they immortalize proud deeds
> or state a humble claim for divine attention in the temples of
> the gods. Here and here alone ... the human bid for timelessness
> was disregarded in the most complete acceptance of the grace of
> life the world has ever known. For life means movement and
> the beauty of movement was woven in the intricate web of living
> forms which we call "scenes of nature"; was revealed in human-
> bodies acting their serious games, inspired by a transcendent
> presence, acting in freedom and restraint, unpurposeful as cyclic
> time itself.[22]

Jung emphasizes that his conception of the unconscious leaves the
entire question of "above" and "below" open, and was well aware of
the mystical impression created by speaking of psychic energy. But
rather than bounding off into ever more convoluted expressions in the
manner of the 19th-century mechanist, Jung immediately capitulates
that psychic energy is indeed an X-factor, like "instinct," "spirit," or
"matter." All are simply *nomina*—god-words, root-fantasies, time-
honored and collectively agreed-upon expressions that indicate

experiential realities, but remain in themselves as difficult to define as the quantum probabilities of physics or the infinitesimal strands of string theory in contemporary cosmology. Jung's devotion to the intermediary *psychic* space is an affirmation that neither psyche nor life can be reduced to matter/instinct or spirit/mind:

> Just as in its lower reaches, the psyche loses itself in the organic material substrate, so in its upper reaches it resolves itself into a "spiritual" form about which we know as little as we do about the functional basis of instinct.[23]

Jung thus wrote a book on *the transformation of the symbols of psychic energy*, recognizing that living images and their dynamic correlations constitute the prime datum of experience. Amidst the early struggles of psychoanalysis to define the instincts (from a unitary drive to a theoretical morass of partial drives), Jung specifies five. Hunger, sex, and the need for activity are to be expected. But his inclusion of *reflection* and *creativity* would be unthinkable without jettisoning the old biologism. Psychologically as well as religiously, this leads to an open confession of *mystery*. Recall Reich's arousal of memory through tactile stimulation and the holistic gestalts of Fliess's enteroceptive perception. From our reflections on the body-ego, a provocative fact emerges. Given the myriad organ representations that are associated to the ego, and our awareness that consciousness and memory appear even on the cellular level, the specific number of human instincts *remains* both unitary and illimitable. Forthcoming enteroceptive (intuitive) descriptions of the human form—organ by organ and *soul by soul*—present nothing less than the archetypal fantasies on which the whole psychoanalytic conundrum of quantifying the instincts hangs.

A further point of departure appears in Jung's early work as an experimental psychologist, his paper from 1906, "Association, Dream, and Hysterical Symptom." Knowing that specific complex reactions in subjects of his word association experiment were confirmed by psychogalvanic measurement of innervations in the skin and musculature, Jung persuasively demonstrates that precisely the same emotional themes appear repeatedly in the imagery of their *dreams*! The ego appears to shine more brightly than other complexes owing to its concrete orientation and literal identifications with the external world, but other luminous psychic contents are perpetually flickering at this ego's fringe. Jung observes:

> [T]he light of consciousness has many degrees of brightness and the ego-complex many gradations of emphasis. On the animal and primitive level there is a mere "luminosity," differing hardly at all from the glancing fragments of a dissociated ego. Here, as on an infantile level, consciousness is not a unity, being as yet uncentered by a firmly-knit ego-complex, and just flickering into life here and there wherever outer or inner events, instincts, and affects happen to call it awake.[24]

These disparate bits of consciousness are highly precise in their patterning of behavior and their generation of psychic imagery and, like the body-ego (*psychosoma*), lie in a state of deep *participation mystique* with nature and world.

The primitive, the animal, as well as the child were all celebrated as Dionysus in antiquity, a god of the body-soul if ever there was one. But the understanding of Dionysus is almost invariably distorted for those of Christian upbringing. Jung was the son of a Swiss Reformed pastor just as Nietzsche was the son of a Lutheran pastor. Both men speak of a Dionysus who, in reality, more closely resembles the dark Wotan, the frenzied oracular god of Teutonic lore. In his masterful "Dionysus in Jung's Writings," Hillman explores Jung's relation to Nietzsche, and to Wotan as well as Dionysus, significantly expanding our understanding of the luminosity and glancing fragments aforementioned. He sees an inverse relationship between the presence of Nietzsche in Jung's consciousness and the absence of Dionysus. It is "as if the more deeply Jung entered into Nietzsche, the more he was dissuaded from Dionysus."[25] Hillman thus proceeds to contrast two conceptions of Dionysus in Jung's work. The first is largely informed by Jung's highly complex reaction to the explosive philosopher poet. We know from Jung's *Memories, Dreams, Reflections* that in moments of tremendous inner upheaval, Jung had been disturbed by thoughts of Nietzsche's tragic fate. But where Nietzsche speaks of Dionysus, Jung sees Wotan in the hinterland. Jung emphasizes especially the philosopher's late madness and self-identification with Dionysus as Zagreus (the "dismembered"), describing this first Dionysus as the "abyss of dissolution, where all human distinctions are merged in the animal divinity of the primordial psyche—a blissful and terrible experience."[26] The statement has a cautionary, if not an overtly moralistic, tone. Focused on the exemplary individuation process presented by Jung in *Psychology and Alchemy*, Hillman then cites one particular dream from the series where Jung refers to various animal images as carrying "the Dionysian element." The dream displays a powerful regressive current and a threat of dismemberment, but abruptly comes to its *lysis* with a voice saying "everything must be ruled by the light." Precisely *which* light? Hillman asks, as his essay comes to the central point:

> Jung concludes that the *nekyia* [regressive descent] is now reversing and that the light refers to that "of the discerning conscious mind." The chapter ends with the "active interpretation of the intellect" and "symbols of the self." Immediately thereafter, we turn to the study of the mandala while pictures accompanying the text turn from horrid images of human shapes to abstract contemplative forms.[27]

Owing to the contamination of both Nietzsche's and Jung's conception of Dionysus by Wotan, Hillman sees Dionysus being misinterpreted. In the dream series, it is as if the mandala is held up to ward off Dionysus in the manner of a cross held up to ward off the Devil. Thus, the imminent dismemberment experience of the dream is averted.

Turning to the second Dionysus (now relatively freed from Nietzsche and Wotan), Hillman sees Jung's conception of the god acquiring broader significance where Jung says, "The classical world thought of this pneuma as Dionysus, particularly the suffering Dionysus Zagreus, whose divine substance is distributed throughout the whole of nature."[28] The god and his dispersal via recurring dismemberment represent the universal principle of the one and the many. Hillman notes that:

> In Aion (*CW* 9ii, 158n) dismemberment is again placed against the background of the Neoplatonic Dionysus: "The divine powers imprisoned in bodies are nothing other than Dionysus dispersed in matter."

Here both psychologists reckon with the dispersal of *lumina* we have encountered repeatedly in this exploration of the ego's ambiguity, the body-ego of psychoanalysis, and the shimmering image of Phanes (Dionysus as creator) in Orphic mythology. Consider their subtle psychosomatic perceptions vis-à-vis the abstract and rigid tenets of patriarchal sexual morality or the pervasively Apollonian purview of Ezekiel, Philo, Paul, or Augustine. From the latter perspective two irreconcilable halves of one whole remain in a state of perpetual antipathy:

> The movement between the first and second view of dismemberment compares with crossing a psychic border *between seeing the God from within his cosmos and seeing him from outside.*[29]

Kerényi affirms this realization of archetypal specificity with the observation: "Speaking mythologically, each God is the source of a world that without him remains invisible, but with him reveals itself in its own light, and this world passes beyond the world-picture of natural science."[30] Recall the rending opposites we encounter in the split worldview of patriarchy—an ascetic and transcendental impulse exemplified by Paul or by Augustine's Manichaeism on the one hand, and Christian heretics who resort to the wildly instinctual *transdescendence* of the libertine on the other, exemplified by subterranean chambers, orgy, and those ultimately extinguished points of light in the darkness. Both seek to control the living body (and that of women) but surrender soulful reflection to the degree of their own extremism. The rending opposites indicated are described by Sartre: "According to Baudelaire's conception, man ... is the clash of two opposing movements which are both centrifugal and of which one is directed upwards and the other downwards. They are movements without driving power, mere spouts—two forms of transcendence which, to borrow a distinction of Jean Wahl's, we might call *transcendence* and *transdescendence.*"[31] Hillman's reference to inevitable dismemberment and, even more, to the beheading of an "old king" with its dissolution of central control (the passing of patriarchy), is clear in what follows—and pertinent as well to the tension between the legalism of Atonement and the psychosomatic "At-one-ment" we seek all along:

> If we leave the "malady" of Nietzsche as our model for dismemberment, we may also leave the view of it as only rending by opposites and violent enantiodromia. Instead we may understand the violence in a new light. If we take our clues from

Jung's exploration of the theme in alchemy [see Jung's "The Visions of Zosimos," CW 9i], dismemberment refers to a psychological process that requires a body metaphor. The process of division is presented as a horrifying torture. If, however, dismemberment is ruled by the archetypal dominant of Dionysus, then the process, while beheading or dissolving the central control of the old king, may be at the same time activating the pneuma that is distributed throughout the materializations of our complexes. The background of the second Dionysus offers new insight into the rending pain of self-division, especially of bodily experience.

Jung reminds us that Dionysus was called the divided one. His dismemberment was evidence of his divisibility into parts. In each part he lived as the pneuma dispersed in matter. Bits of Dionysian spirit are like sparks shining in the terra foetida, or the rotten stench of the decaying body as it dissociates into pieces. We experience this process in psychosomatic symptoms, in hysterical conversions, in specific sado-masochistic perversions, in cancer fantasies, in fears of aging, in horror of pollution, or in disintegrative conditions that have a body focus. This experience has its other side. The dismemberment of central control is at the same time the resurrection of the natural light of archetypal consciousness distributed in each organ.

Concluding then:

From this perspective of dismemberment, our rending can be understood as the particular kind of renewal presented by Dionysus. This renewal describes itself by means of a body metaphor. The renewal that goes by way of dismemberment is not a re-assembly of parts into another organization. It is not a movement from integration to disintegration to re-integration. Perhaps, it is better to envision this renewal not as a process at all. Rather, the crucial experience would be an awareness of parts as parts distinct from each other, dismembered, each with its own light, a state in which the body becomes aware of itself as a composite of differences. The scintillae of which Jung speaks in regard to the multiple consciousness of the psyche may be experienced as embedded in physical expressions. The distribution of Dionysus through matter may be compared with the distribution of consciousness through members, organs and zones.[32]

While Jung often employs the circular mandala as an image of human wholeness, in a discussion of regression to the archetypal Mother and her Divine Child, Jung also cites the "anthropoid psyche" as its goal—the original image of incarnate wholeness.[33] Imagery of the Self, of the whole human being, may emerge *geometrically or as a body imago*. Hillman projects an aesthetic and intuitive eye into the "anthropoid" body, discerning the archetypal light of consciousness in each organ. The fantasy of wholeness is thus freed from the static geometric forms of Jung's mandala as the progressive goal of individuation, and so is Dionysus. In antique Orphic ritual, Dionysus is born, crowned, and sacrificed almost immediately. He undergoes transformations as frenetic and stark as those of the self-sacrificing and perpetuating *anthroparion* (dwarf) in the Visions of Zosimos to which Hillman refers. The mandala may be his crown, his moment, but this glory is fleeting. Hillman's closing thoughts on dismembering and re-membering are thus particularly striking: "Perhaps, it is better to envision this renewal not as a process at all." Not only does this resonate with the timeless quality of myth, it strongly suggests that we may never be more whole or more conscious than we are right now!

Hillman explores the archetypal light together with disturbing organic imagery of illness, age, and dissolution. Otto also speaks of "wild and demonic forms" of numinous experience—the "grisly horror and shuddering" that appears on a Dionysian level. Jung sees regression to the anthropoid psyche as a *nekyia* (ancient expression for ritualized descent) leading to the "prenatal" level. Indeed the birth process itself is the grand paradigm of initiation that transpires on a Dionysian level. Here the work of psychiatrist Stanislav Grof offers us a dynamic extension of the process and non-process described described by Hillman.

Grof devoted thirty years of research to the exploration of regressive psychedelic experience and somatic memory. His explorations beyond "ego-death" to a remarkable array of deep psychosomatic experiences represent a veritable sequel to Jung's *Symbols of Transformation*, particularly given Jung's discussion of a descent to the "realm of the Mothers" and the "divine child" awaiting his conscious realization. Grof describes four Basic Perinatal Matrices (BPM) that correlate with the universal matrices of experience, which Grof designates as "systems of condensed experience" (COEX systems). These may be understood as archetypal and transpersonal experiences in their broadest experiential application. The perinatal phases are: I. undisturbed uterine life; II. the onset of biological delivery prior to dilation; III. slow stressful movement through the birth canal; and IV. breach and emergence. These are *not etiological or causal,* as the literalism and reductionism of developmentalism would seek to persuade us, *but palpable metaphors—correlates of similarly structured life experiences that are not necessarily related in linear time.* Consider, for example, how the "one-, two-, three-, to four" progression of the matrices parallels fairytale or ritual sequences, or again, the ubiquitous pattern of status-disequilibrium-crisis-renewed status.

In adult regressive experience, all these matrices involve personal, psychosomatic, archetypal-visionary, and even cosmic equivalents of the perinatal phases. Basic Perinatal Matrix I represents the "original state of symbiosis with the maternal organism at the time of intrauterine existence."[34] It tallies experientially with the oceanic expansiveness of sea or space, "good mother" experiences, loving harmony, mystical union, visions of Heaven or Paradise, ease and optimism, etc. BPM II brings the experience of being steadily encroached upon, like the proverbial hero trapped in a chamber whose walls begin to contract: cosmic engulfment, "bad mother" experiences, guilt and inferiority, suffocation, no exit, prison, Hell, absurdity, existentialism, etc. BPM III is a phase of especially piqued psychosomatic arousal. The birth passage subjects a fetus to 50-100 pounds of pressure on its skull and body. Grof accordingly stresses the fusion here of victimization, aggression, and global arousal:

> The most important of these are the elements of titanic fight, sadomasochistic experiences, intense sexual arousal, demonic episodes, scatological involvement, and encounter with fire. All these occur in a context of a determined *death-rebirth struggle.*[35]

BPM III tallies with torture, the simultaneity of pleasure and pain, crucifixion, dismemberment, etc. Finally, BPM IV brings a sense of fortuitous escape: the passing of a storm, spring, beautiful lights or peacock colors, rebirth, Phoenix imagery, illumination, etc. Again, one may discern how numerous life situations and processes ("systems of condensed experience") parallel the perinatal processes—from secure adapted states, to ever-renewed challenges, to enhancement of the same coupled with passionate struggle and movement, to more tempered states of renewed adaptation or transformation.

Well known to Jungians, the alchemical "Axiom of Maria Prophetissa"—from One comes the Two that generates the Three which resolves itself in Four (One realized)—runs intuitively parallel to Grof's schema. It is BPM III that indicates most precisely the stuff of Dionysian dismemberment, though different individuals tend to regressively tap into one matrix more readily than others. Together with personal complexes, object-relational history, and one's innate archetypal endowment, perinatal experiences are immediately pertinent to the formation of individual sexual styles—from one individual's delight in tranquil and blissful union, another's inclination to a submissive role, to another's aggressive, orgiastic, or polymorphous disposition, etc.

Grof's research represents a powerful challenge to scientific assumptions about memory. He finds that psychedelic subjects "can relive their biological birth in all its complexity, and sometimes with astonishing objectively verifiable details," which should be scientifically impossible for want of the myelinization of infantile neurons (associated with memory). He observes also that such memories "appear to include the tissues and cells of the body," and furthermore: "The process of reliving one's birth trauma can be associated with psychosomatic re-creation of all the appropriate physiological symptoms."[36] This extends to the reappearance of bruises and birthmarks. One is forced to such extremity in the attempt to trace somatic memory that the very question of psyche's *independence* from the body emerges. Grof observes that as regressive psychedelic experience "extends into the transpersonal realms, the limits of linear causality are stretched ad infinitum."[37] The memories of his subjects include not only episodes of embryonic life, but the moment of conception; aspects of cellular, tissue, and organ consciousness; archetypal images and patterns; memory of former incarnations; consciousness of different animal species with insights into their courtship and breeding—and on to identification with plants or minerals, stellar bodies, the universe at large, etc. Grof is thus forced to dramatic conclusions:

> If one adheres to the old medical model in which a material
> substrate is necessary for memory, the nucleus of a single cell—

the sperm and the ovum—would have to contain not only the information discussed in medical books concerning anatomy, physiology, and biochemistry of the body, constitutional factors, hereditary dispositions of diseases, and parental characteristics, but also complex memories from the lives of our human and animal ancestors, and retrievable detailed information about all the cultures of the world. Since LSD experiences also involve consciousness of plants and inorganic matter down to the molecular, atomic, and subatomic structures, as well as cosmogenetic events and geographical history, one would ultimately have to postulate that the entire universe was somehow coded in the sperm and ovum. At this point, the mystical alternative to the mechanistic worldview appears to be much more appropriate and reasonable.[38]

Bearing these extraordinary insights with us, let's return to the original dispersion of the alchemical *scintillae* that Jung and Hillman describe. As the experiences of Grof's subjects suggest, the field of the soul sparks represents a kind of archetypal cosmic background radiation of psychic existence. I thus refer to the archaic myth (foundational to astrology, Jewish mysticism, Orphism, Gnosticism, and hermetic science generally), where a shattering of an aboriginal vessel of light sees bits of light spread abroad in the darkness. Phanes (coming of light) and Sophia (*anima mundi*) may be seen as premier personifications of this creative field. Consider this starry field's spontaneous appearance in the life crisis of a twenty-year-old California girl, brusquely abandoned by her mother, just past a suicidal crisis, and literally battling with vampires in her dreams. Then this one arose:

I am on the beach with a wonderful friend of mine as a huge truck full of his lively, "really together," and trustworthy friends pulls up. Looking up I see thousands of beautiful galaxies spiraling across the night sky. They sparkle and turn as little connecting lines and subtle geometric forms begin to be generated. Golden bands like arrows move up, down, and across the sky as a gigantic keyhole appears in the middle region. I'm afraid I might be pulled into the hole but then, from another part of the sky, comes an enormous key that slides into the dark keyhole and turns into it tightly. Then I am back at home with a knife, killing vampires quite methodically.

The dream moves the patient beyond the old personalistic psychoanalytic conception of "the primal scene" (the child's vision of the parents copulating) to nothing less than the stuff of creation mythology and an archetypal *coniunctio* of vulva and phallus. Jung's specific identification of the alchemical *scintillae* with the archetypes is crucial here. He compares them with will-o'-the-wisps and fishes' eyes, as we might compare them to fireflies, with a propensity for the formation of complete archetypal images. Like the dreamer's galaxies, the archetypes are "seeds of light broadcast in the chaos." According to Khunrath, the dark starry field represents "the seed plot of the world to come." Jung states that "one such spark is the human mind," holding with Khunrath that there are "fiery sparks of the soul of this world ... the light of nature ... dispersed or sprinkled in and throughout the structures of the great world into all fruits of the elements everywhere."[39] Paracelsus observes, "As the light of nature cannot speak, it buildeth shapes in sleep from the power of the word (of God)."[40] But it is Agrippa von Nettesheim, an alchemist and daring opponent of the witch craze of Frankfurt, who speaks of the archetypal *scintillae* in a way that parallels the creaturely multiple-eyed Phanes as well—filled with seed, for via these *scintillae* "gleams of prophecy come down to the four-footed beasts, the birds, and other living creatures."[41]

Psychologically, we speak of a constellation, the "coming together of stars" of a complex or dream. This spontaneous emergence presents itself on a spectrum from mistakes, word slips, body language, discordant moods, psychosomatic symptoms, and on to the specific assemblage of images and personifications in dreams, fantasy, and imagination. Diseases thus return to being gods. The *Gospel of Thomas* is as simple as it is encouraging here: "Let him who seeks continue seeking until he finds. When he finds, he will become troubled. When he becomes troubled, he will be astonished, and he will rule over the All."[42] As suffering and deepening insight reveals—as "troubled" leads to "astonished"—the particular shape and intention of biographical complexes conform ever more to archetypal images that were vitally alive long before ego-consciousness arose to experience them. As if departing the familiar gravity of one planet to be drawn by the gravitational pull of another, we may muse on the emergence of archetypal images from the deep recesses of inner space.

I recall one personal dream in which I am standing wistfully before the home of my aging widowed mother by night. A voice out of nowhere abruptly informs me: "This is not where your mother lives. This is the home of the Green Virgin!" Looking around, I behold the sun and moon rising together, side by side, from horizon to mid-heaven in a conspicuous *coniunctio solis et lunae.* A huge blue whale filled with stars swims comfortably from between them off across the dome of the sky. Indeed, the psyche challenges the literalism of personal biography with some rather surprising god-parents! Constellations of the disparate lights, the patterning of the *scintillae* into numinous images, clearly mirrors the constellations of the astrological heavens. And just as body and brain respond similarly to images coming from "within" or "without," not being able to distinguish between the two—so the psychic interior presents as a seamless universe. As above, so below. Our examples indicate how psyche challenges the ego's concrete worldview as it slowly generates an amalgam of archetypal field and extended world to create an interior "world-image." The old exclusive opposites, the *res cogitans* and *res extensa* of the Newtonian-Cartesian era, again have a soul between them! The old antagonism gives way to the holistic and inclusive opposites of hermetic epistemology. The reflective soul-vessel expands at the very cusp of Nature's inside and Nature's outside, where microcosm and macrocosm betray their secret symmetry (Fig. 1).

The soul-vessel is beautifully portrayed in the popular film *Immortal Beloved.* The young Beethoven visualizes running away from his abusive father to lie down in a pool glistening with reflecting stars, and floats suspended to strains of the "Ode to Joy." Goethe's story "The New Paris: A Boy's Tale" features the same luminous circumplex in broad daylight, as the puer beholds a circular hermetic garden that he

> ... had never seen before; all with flowers, each division of
> different colours, which likewise low and close to the ground,
> allowed the plan to be easily traced. This delicious sight, which
> I enjoyed in full sunshine, quite riveted my eyes. But I hardly
> knew where I was to set foot; for the serpentine paths were most
> delicately laid with blue sand, which seemed to form upon the earth
> a darker sky, or a sky seen in the water.[43]

Another dream reflects the same luminous venue, associated with the anima:

I am seated by a body of water on a crystal clear night. The sky is filled with stars that reflect in the still water. I watch as my girlfriend dances gracefully dressed in a diaphanous gown like one of the Three Graces in Botticelli's "Allegory of Spring." I watch as stars sparkle around her. Gazing on, I notice that the stars shine right through her.

The same man also dreamt of being seated alone in the front seat of a theater:

As the curtain opens, an elegantly dressed but unknown woman strides gracefully forward and whips a bowling ball at me as if I were the lead pin. I catch the sphere and it floats just above my lap. The sphere is a universe in itself. Stars and galaxies sparkle from the ever deepening layers of its receding inner space.

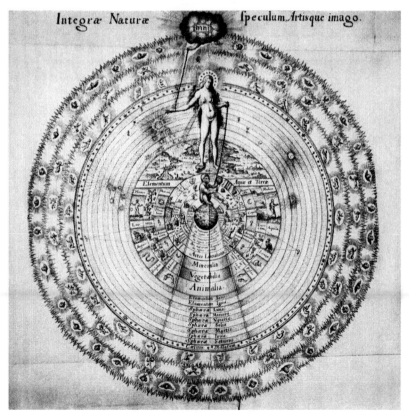

Fig. 1: A portrait of the *Anima Mundi* as the ligament between matter and spirit

In Gnosticism, the dispersed lights appear as *aeons,* the original archetypal principles in the creation of the universe. The aeons represent a particular quality and period of time. Quispel describes an aeon as "sort of half idea and half angel." In Orphism (pagan Greek Gnosis), the multi-eyed divinely seeded Phanes is a comparable figure, just as such subtle androgynous images figure prominently in the mythology of Sophia's descent. Gnosticism itself is rooted in Hebrew Merkabah mysticism, for which Ezekiel's original vision of the Chariot of Yahweh is paradigmatic. A 5th-century Jewish redaction of "The Visions of Ezekiel" records that "Ezekiel sees seven heavens with their seven Merkabahs [chariots] reflected in the water of the Chebar river. This form of speculation about seven Merkabahs [corresponds] to the seven heavens."[44] A saying of Jesus in the *Gospel of Thomas* (2nd century C.E.) is a cameo of mystic phenomenology sufficiently congenial to the Merkabah tradition to be compared to Ezekiel's original vision:

> Jesus said, "The images are manifest to man, but the light in
> them remains concealed in the image of the light of the father.
> He will become manifest, but his image will remain concealed
> by his light."[45]

The psychic images that emerge from the primordial vessel of light are associated with the Hebrew god-imago itself! Some seven hundred years earlier, following the destruction of the first Temple by the Babylonians in 586 B.C.E., Ezekiel was abiding with exiles along the same river Chebar. There he experiences his vision of the Merkabah. The celestial vehicle is surrounded by images of the starry firmament, which appears as "something like a dome, shining like crystal" (Ezekiel 1:22). As the prophet beholds:

> [Above] was something like a throne, in appearance like
> sapphire; and seated above the likeness of a throne was
> something that seemed like a human form. Upward from what
> appeared like the loins I saw something like gleaming amber,
> something that looked like fire enclosed all around; and
> downward from what looked like the loins I saw something
> that looked like fire, and there was a splendor all around. Like
> the bow in a cloud on a rainy day, such was the appearance of
> splendor all around. This was the appearance of the likeness
> of the glory of the Lord. (1:26-28)

Note the five-fold repetition of "something" and the text's language of "appearance" and "likeness." The visionary *phantasma* is so extraordinary as to defy unequivocal earthly reference—its images are elusive, layered in light, and finally inscrutable. At the core of this breathtaking appearance, that which "seemed like a human form" is enveloped in "something that looked like fire." The whole scene appears in numinous splendor as "the glory of the Lord." The virtual coalescence of the human image with divine glory has accordingly been called "Adam the Glory," a figure also called "Man" or "Adamas" in Gnosticism, "Adam Kadmon" in the *Kabbalah,* and the *anthropos* in ancient Greece—all the archetype of the human being, whose essence is God's essence. Psychologically, these are classic images of the Self, with all the ambiguity between the human and divine being so typical of the archetype. The theoretical inference (Self) is underscored by characteristic quaternine imagery: an earlier appearance of four winged creatures and the four wheels of Ezekiel's divine chariot: "Their rims were tall and awesome, for the rims of all four were full of eyes all around" (Ezekiel 1:18). A colorful rainbow, the symbol of a renewed covenant between God and humankind since Noah, also appears in the vision.

Given the ambiguity of human and divine identities, how fantastic might our—or better, *the*—ambit of reflective consciousness actually be? Who or what is looking at Who or hat? This is indeed the numinous *mystery* to which Otto refers in the passage that introduces this chapter. The words of I Corinthians 13:12 (Paul at his best) come to mind: "For we now see in a mirror, dimly, but then we will see face to face. Now I know ony in part; then I will know fully, even as I have been fully known." One draws a breath at such a threshold—the sheer reassuring beauty of it! We are also given a hint that we may ultimately be dealing with an "ocular apparatus" pertinent not only to visionary experience, but to our last breath—to Near Death Experience and a consciousness that looks on as the body is administered injections or electric fibrillation. The theoretical term "the Self" rings hollow n the face of such powerful visionary material, but if any image represents a gravitational pole remote from uninitiated ego-consciousness, it is surely this. Each of the *scintillae* may be conceived as holographically related to every other, just as the archetypes interpenetrate one another. Each is a Monad, a seed-point of a reative consciousness, the coming of light, the *bindu* of Hinduism. Jung relates these individual sparks to the human mind, to complexes, to the self, and to archetypes generally, even as our examples have focused on the *puer*, the anima, and the Self. More than two millennia after the vision of Ezekiel was recorded, Dorn echoes the ancient perception by speaking of a "light of nature" (*lumen naturae*) in relation to "Him to Whom it belongs"—

> … Who deigns to make us his dwelling place. … He has implanted that light in us that we may see in its light the light of Him Who dwells in inaccessible light, and that we may excel His other creatures; in this wise we are made like unto Him, that He has given us a spark of His light. Thus the truth is to be sought not in ourselves, but in the image of God which is within us.[46]

The "spark of His light" carries an additional significance in Gnosticism, where it is specifically correlated with an emergent "call" from the realm of light. It leads the Gnostic to a realization of his spiritual origin and authentic identity, as well as to goals that seem to leave this world, but in fact lie within us. This realization is conveyed by any number of numinous "revealer figures"—actual visionary personages such as the Garden Serpent, Sophia, Christ, Seth, or Norea, who inhabit the Gnostic cosmos. The revelatory call awakens the individual from the "sleep" and "drunkenness" of this world, revolutionizes his view of it, and kindles ardent yearning. Revealer figures might also act as mediums of transport through the seven planetary spheres to the Pleroma (the All). The imaginal venture is never without its dangers, however, as the *Gospel of Mary* and the myth of Sophia's Descent will demonstrate. A figure known as Metatron appears in precisely this role. The example echoes Merkabah mysticism, and describes a rabbi's mystic flight through the seven planetary shells that hold us all with chains of fateful Necessity. Note how intimately the fiery lights are associated with his body:

> As the journey progresses, the dangers become progressively greater. Angels and archons storm against the traveller "in order to drive him out"; a fire which proceeds from his own body threatens to devour him. In the Hebrew Book of Enoch there is an account … of his own metamorphosis into the angel Metatron, when his flesh was transformed into "fiery torches."

> According to the "Greater Hekhaloth," every mystic must
> undergo this transformation, but with the difference that, being
> less worthy than Enoch, he is in danger of being devoured by
> the "fiery torches."[47]

The rabbi's metamorphosis has significant parallels with the human form that appears in the fiery aureole of Ezekiel's original vision. In his shamanic transformation into the angelic medium, the rabbi's very flesh is transformed into "fiery torches" that emerge from his body.

The rabbi's visionary experience displays a highly cultivated ritual intensity, but also has a pedestrian aspect. Every cell in our bodies is a tiny furnace where oxidation transpires continually, a fever in matter, life tilting ever forward on a deep somatic level.

We turn, finally, to the description by Gerhard Dorn of a gradual coalescence of the fiery sparks of the soul into an inner eye:

> Thus little by little [one] will come to see with his mental eyes
> a number of sparks shining day by day and more and more and
> growing into such a great light that thereafter all things needful
> to him will be made known.[48]

Just as billions of cells in the body and countless tiny rods and cones in the retina work in harmony to formulate images of the world, so the archetypal lights of our soul-vessel generate, little by little, day by day, a transformed vision of the world. This "imaginal retina" (our entire archetypal endowment as its rods and cones) is nothing less than the *oculus imagnationis* of alchemy and hermetism, the eye of the imagination born from beyond the dark mirror of the unconscious. My own first memory of childhood rings with my mother's soft laughter as she carries me over a stream of water along a curb where streetlights are reflected in the sparkly current. This discussion is an extension of that original "seeing image."

Elsewhere, a woman much in love with a woman sits one night at the end of a dock over a broad Minnesota lake. Its tranquil surface reflects the starlit sky as their *sacra conversazioni* go on into the night. Capturing that magic in poetry, her final verse gives testament—"That the only ones watching were the angels who gazed through our four eyes." Finally, on the day of concluding this chapter, a psychotherapist client brought the following dream.

I hold an extremely old person in my arms. I'm unable to tell if it is a man or a woman. I separate the long gray hair and then, with a sort of poignant difficulty, I look directly into the person's eyes. Slowly the aged face takes on the aspect of a younger adult man with full vitality, then an even younger aspect of a swashbuckling Errol Flynn type character. As the figure grows still younger, I see only a huge eye looking at me, focused at the center, but soft-edged on its periphery.

The human body presents a unitary image, by whatever consolidation of energies, organ systems, or fleeting images it is comprised or may emit. The whole composite appears in a beautiful passage of pagan Gnostic tradition, the Egyptian *Corpus Hermeticum*:

> Think, my son, how man is formed in the womb; investigate with care the skill shown in that work, and find out what craftsman it is that makes this fair and godlike image. Who is it that traced the circles of the eyes, that has pierced the orifices of the nostrils and ears, and the opening of the mouth? Who is it that has stretched the sinews out and tied them fast, and dug out the channels of the veins? Who is it that has made the bones hard, and covered the flesh with skin? Who is it that has separated the fingers, and shaped the broad surface of the soles of the feet? Who is it that has bored the ducts? Who is it that has shaped the heart into a cone, and joined the sinew to it, that has made the liver broad, and the spleen long, and hallowed out the cavities of the lungs, and made the belly capacious? Who is it that has so fashioned the most honorable parts that all may see them, and concealed the parts that are unseemly? See how many crafts have been employed on one material and how many works of art are enclosed in one compass![49]

Neumann likewise honors the beauty and power of the unitary anthropomorphic form while shifting to an archetypal perspective:

> The Great Goddess as a whole is a symbol of creative life and the parts of her body are not physical organs but numinous symbolic centers of whole spheres of life. For this reason the "self-representation" of the Great Goddess, her display of breasts, belly, or entire naked body, is a form of divine epiphany.[50]

The body is our mother. The father manifests as creative action in and upon body, world, and imagination. We turn accordingly to two fascinating anthropomorphic forms. Both are creator deities, both essentially androgynous, though both possess a phallic nuance as active agents of creation. Of the Polynesian god Tangaroa, a traditional chant proclaims: "Existing alone, he became the universe." He is "light," "germ," "within," "enduring," "wise," and "sacred."[51] Today the wood-carved, round-faced, erect figure (Fig. 2) stands in the British Museum, perpetually in the act of generating gods and men from its body—from ears, eyes, nose, mouth, cheeks, throat, breasts, arms, hips, navel, belly, thighs, and legs. His warm nut-brown surface calls to mind the words of Neumann (also Freud) regarding the numinous accent of the skin and every bodily orifice as a conduit between the inner and outer worlds. Consider how the body of the god and the body of the sculptor mirror each another. Before there was sculpture there was wood, then tree, then earth. It is appropriate that this image is wooden, for wood is mother-stuff, organic, and therefore also *hylic* (material). In Gnostic typology, the *hylikoi* ("wooden ones") were viewed as sensualists, devoid of spirit, though a notion sharply contradicted by this handsome portrayal of the creator.

Strangely enough, our most ancient forebears actually *were*

Fig. 2: An indigenous image of the body as a source of symbols.

plants, albeit the stromatolites that formed shoreline mats and vast reefs in the Precambrian seas—the original self-perpetuating protoplasm of single cells that so fascinated Reich. While the genealogy is amusing, the fact that plants harken back to Earth's transition from a geological existence to life still resonates in the psychic imagery of plants. While elsewhere comparing the "herb of immortality" with the "treasure hard to attain," Jung considers the extension of roots into the inorganic realm in his discussion of tree symbolism: "In psychological terms the self has its roots in the body, indeed in the body's chemical elements."[52] Countless identifications between humankind and plants are celebrated in world mythology. All display affinity with the mysteries of Mother Rite: the tree-births of Attis and Osiris, the return of Persephone in an agrarian context, the proliferation of Dionysian green. Tangaroa is the creator of all the elements of life: sand, rocks, earth, sea, sky, light, and, of course, all of Polynesia. He creates a world and beholds it through our bodies, our eyes.

We turn at last to a portrayal of Phanes on the famous relief at Modena, Italy (Fig. 3). The beautiful full puer figure still carries a lion and two additional zoomorphic faces on his midriff and sides, indicative not only of his supra-solar shining and animal nature, but also his ceaseless transformations and potency. Phanes emerges from between the eggshells he has split above as below, as Time (a serpent) spirals around him. Standing erect and winged, holding a scepter and staff, Phanes is framed in an oval with signs of the zodiac and the four winds appearing at the corners of the relief. A birth is occurring—time and space and existence have come—the androgynous phallic god gives form and life to all created things. Phanes is a living archetypal image whose creation of earth, sky, sun, and moon is an imaginal development, a mythic event referring to the birth of psychic consciousness and a transformed vision of the world. Hidden within the body, slowly emerging, the coming of Phanes' light refers not simply to the sun that we see, but to a *psychic* sun by which we see, as Goethe succinctly hymns:

> Were not the eye to the sun akin
> The sun we never could behold
> Filled not a God's strength us within
> How could the divine hold us enthralled.[53]

More often than not, any perception of so subtle a being as Phanes springs from stark and undignified suffering of the soul. The classic shamanic experience of dismemberment in divine illness sees the novice torn apart by demons, who eviscerate him, count his bones, and replace

Fig. 3: The Orphic creator god Phanes bursting from the egg of Night

his living guts with *mana*-charged crystals. This is the stuff of the crucifixion and the glorification of the body on an archaic level—a realization of the subtle body.

Thirty years removed, I may venture the inclusion of the experience that awoke this author to his psychological life. The disquieting dreams had repeated countless times on the cusp of 1973-74: a muscular bird with razor-tipped wings emerges from an egg and cuts itself to pieces; panting black men with furrowed skulls attempt to tear me limb from limb; weeks later I float helplessly towards an enormous minute-steak grinder in midair as a witch cackles on through the night. Toes first, my body is instantly transformed into flailing strips and sheets of bloody tissue unraveling in space, each with hundreds of tiny shiny cysts on them. One night the phrase "Time is Energy" repeatedly pounds in my mind. It takes two months before the following dream (almost instantly) quells the storm:

To the somber strains of an Albinoni Adagio I slowly float clockwise around a vast stepped pyramid composed of cinder block. Towering hundreds of feet in the air, its flat square deck is precisely inscribed with astrological and occult symbols along channels cut in alignment with distant points on the horizon, planets, and stars. A human form some thirty feet tall stands at the center of this plateau, reminiscent of the bronze statue of Thomas Jefferson in his Washington monument. The form is composed of a subtle matter wrapped in etheric shells from cloudy white, to sky blue, to silver, to gold at the core. Then suddenly I am walking along a sidewalk, where a long-haired college kid in my old satin jacket attempts to shoot me with a sudden burst of automatic weapon fire before roaring off round the corner in a taxicab.

Egos die, personas change, old garments are stripped away to reveal new ones, but scarcely without abandonment and fear. Alas, a preparedness to suffer, to throw one's whole life on the scale, as Jung often reiterates, is a prerequisite to discovering one's *real* work in the world. As the cosmic gives way to the pedestrian, here on the sidewalk, as it were, one may recall the famous observation of St. Augustine, *inter urinam et faeces nascimur* ("we are born between urine and feces"). Still, humankind's perennial sense of kinship with the divine comes shining through.

Truth
is the swell of a breath
and the vision closed eyes see:
the palpable mystery of the person.

—Octavio Paz

CHAPTER FIVE

Syzygy Tango: A Picaresque
of Dreams

Sex and gender represent not only the most fundamental pair of psychic opposites, but an essential religious mystery as well. Eliade has maintained that gender is *the* religious mystery. One's human identity, the particular quality of one's consciousness, indeed the whole question of the religious dimensions of sexuality, lie first and foremost in the bisexuality of the psyche. This mystery of sex and gender is something alive and dynamic, framed by spirit and matter, continuously making us in its image and presenting psychic images for our reflection. It is secondary only to humankind's relationship with the divine source—indeed, in the final analysis it is indistinguishable from it.

Depth psychologically this bisexuality, psyche's androgynous matrix, expresses itself most fundamentally in the intrapsychic dynamism between anima and animus known as the syzygy. Syzygy refers to anima and animus in a state of "being yoked together." This is the essential inner relationship, a tandem arrangement, the original "it takes two to tango." The endless dance of the syzygy colors our moods, our perceptions, our entire approach to sex, love, and world. Its oscillations influence how and when we draw upon the masculine or the feminine aspects of our psyches. However essential to our relationship with external objects of our love, persons are secondary here, for we ultimately know what we know only through object representations, within the psyche. This would imply an untenable solipsism ("I alone exist") were the psyche merely personal. But the archetypal, transpersonal, and impersonal nature of the psyche not only demands a retreat from personalism, but affirms the fact that the deepest subjective experience leads also to an unexpected objectivity, the objective psyche. When human beings discover what lies most deeply within us, they may also behold one another from essentially the same place—this is the mystery of the body of Christ, the body of Dionysus, or the body of Sophia.

The myriad images that may express the syzygy are built up through the lifelong mirroring of one's innate archetypal endowment with accumulating experiences of persons and world—particularly the indelible impressions of parents, siblings, lovers, and guides. Through innumerable struggles of love the syzygy works to differentiate and bring to awareness both the feminine and the masculine aspects of the personality. Then again, images of the syzygy may arise directly from their archetypal source with a startling autonomy and independence from persons we have known. People frequently come into analysis when they are tangled up in confusing romantic and erotic situations. The greater part of analytic work consists of tracing psychic images back to their original intrapsychic source, working to open blockages and assuage the wounds that so sorely hamper one's self-determination and right relationship with others. Finally, the deepest archetypal experience of anima and animus eludes linear time and process altogether, ushering one into a state of liminality. There the syzygy, as a sacred marriage (*hieros gamos*) becomes an all-embracing experience of Now! The selfsame power makes any but its own numinous *moment* irrelevant, even nonexistent. Ritual seeks to create these momentary events—the *coniunctio* as a religious experience supreme and above all others. Here the relativity of time, dimension, and magnitude on the scale of psychic values need be recalled. For the syzygy may appear in its cosmic aspect as goddess and god, e.g., Night and Phanes as co-creators in Orphism, Sophia and Yahweh as co-creators in the book of Proverbs, Eros in continual pursuit of Aphrodite in Greek contexts or again, the Great Parents or the exemplary couple. Gnosticism refers to Sophia as the "*syzygos*" of Christ, and to comparable couplings on different cosmic levels. The syzygy of Shiva and Shakti in Tantric ritual is an additional example.

Like many analysts today, I look beyond Jung's original designation of the anima as simply the contrasexual image of the feminine in a man's psyche or the animus as the contrasexual masculine image in a woman's psyche. The question is always one of admixture—especially far-reaching in its implications for gay, lesbian, bisexual, or transgender individuals, but already clearly perceptible in the preferred roles, specific desires, or erotic preoccupations that any individual discovers within themselves along life's pathway. To be sure, an individual is generally more consciously identified with one than the other according to one's given physiology. Both archetypes arise as an amalgam of: (1) one's latent sexual characteristics (or gender-related aspects); (2) one's biographical experience of the opposite sex (or dimensions of one's own sex) and, finally; (3) one's connection with both archetypes as complementary aspects of the syzygy.

Anima and animus are highly contrasting archetypal structures, as we have seen. Each has generated an entire literature. In one context C. G. Jung indicates different aspects of the anima as Eve, Helen, Mary, and Sophia—the maternal, the relational, the purely spiritual, and the all-encompassing feminine. Always retaining her uniquely feminine quality as she who gives birth, the anima is the archetype of life and of psychic life. As such she is the premiere *creatrix* of form and image, a mediator, a guide, a personification of one's emotional attitude towards life. Through an extensive process of suffering and initiation the anima slowly becomes soul. One's unswerving allegiance to her productions is the process of soul-making itself.

Jung's association of the anima with the *eros principle* of relatedness is most generally cogent. But along with Whitmont, Hillman, and others, I embrace an additional differentiation of Jung's original association of eros with the feminine. In the history of Western symbolism the imagery of Eros is either androgynous or masculine! The former reflects Jung's original symmetry (as does the mythic image of bearded Aphrodite as an archaic phallic mother), while the latter recognizes Eros as a masculine energy, albeit in service to the greater feminine. He is her phallic exponent—as serpent, child, hero, lover, king.

The animus is that agent by which the anima is pursued, penetrated, impregnated, differentiated, and finally honored as the crown of creation. Emma Jung similarly employs a number of masculine personifications in her early characterization of the animus. These appear on an ascending spectrum comparable to the aforementioned—male images of power, deed, word, and meaning. Her animus is thus the equivalent of the Greek logos in graduating nuance and level of application. The masculine identity of Eros disrupts Emma Jung's perspective significantly. Most importantly, it tempers the transcendental inclination of logos to disengage from body and seek its own exclusive goals. It also relieves the feminine (more precisely, women) of that old theoretical burden of responsibility for feeling and relatedness. One ponders what contribution Carl Jung's feminine Eros and Emma Jung's "logos only" animus have made to the conspicuous lack of regard for sexuality, sensuality, and aesthetics (Eros and Aphrodite!) in analytical psychology. Jungian psychology claims every conceivable sphere of culture as its rightful turf, but why not these? I recall a startling moment in the famous video series *The Power of Myth* here, where Bill Moyers begins to paraphrase Joseph Campbell: "So, then, the meaning of life is …" only to be abruptly cut off as Campbell bursts back: *"No, no, not the meaning—the experience* of life!" Just as the thinking function is deeply overvalued in our culture, an obsessive concern for meaning needs to be tempered by life itself. Excessive concern for meaning begins to assume the character of a moralistic perspective that holds life at arm's length. Life, however, is simply not subject to moral critique. Our survey of patriarchal sexual morality repeatedly exposes the maladies associated with the much-fabled supremacy of the transcending logos. C. G. and Emma Jung appear to show us, respectively, a feminine eros robbed of its true phallus (Eros himself) and a male animus with no eros! In this light, the embrace of an archetypal psychology that understands "the animus" by way of the phenomenal specificity of Eros, Hermes, Dionysus, Pan, Apollo, or Zeus recommends itself as inherently more useful and reasonable. The animus, in any case, represents phallic, seminal, willful, active, and ideational qualities—at worst a nagging detractor and ruthless critic, at best a versatile guide and creative hermetic partner with whom one may transverse entire psychic realms.

Reminiscent of the divine vivisection that Zeus performs on the androgynous original human of Plato's *Symposium*, Kerényi points out that if one cuts the god Hermes in twain, one finds Eros chasing Psyche. Likewise, we speak simultaneously of the anima and animus as two archetypes, but one syzygy. Jung describes the archetypal tension, a flickering back and forth between the two, and within the One:

It is a remarkable fact that perhaps the majority of cosmogonic gods are of a bisexual nature. The hermaphrodite means nothing less than a union of the strongest and most striking opposites. In the first place this union refers back to a primitive state of mind, a twilight where differences and contrasts were either barely separated or completely merged. With increasing consciousness, however, the opposites draw more and more distinctly and irreconcilably apart. If, therefore, the hermaphrodite were only a product of primitive non-differentiation, we would have to expect that it would soon be eliminated with increasing civilization. This is by no means the case; on the contrary, man's imagination has been preoccupied with this idea over and over again on the high and even the highest levels of culture, as we can see from the late Greek and syncretic philosophy of Gnosticism. The hermaphroditic *rebis* has an important part to play in the natural philosophy of the Middle Ages. And in our own day we hear of Christ's androgyny in Catholic mysticism.[1]

Phanes, Tangaroa, Nut-Nu, and the Gnostic Sophia-Ialdabaoth are excellent examples of the androgynous cosmogonic gods to whom Jung refers. The greater number of dreams to be explored here feature anima and animus in the interactive process of their protracted mutual differentiation. This selection is also intended to highlight sexual imagery of dreams generally. The following personal dream represents a unique glimpse of an androgynous psychic being who might be the *spiritus rector* of our whole anima-animus intrapsychic dance. Few dreams have ever prompted so deep a sense of the autonomous psychic life:

I am crouching in the middle of an open landscape. Small droplets fall on my hands from the air. Upon gazing up I catch sight of a glimmering winged figure hovering some twenty feet above my head. It is metallic but also a living being, colored in silver, turquoise, and pink coral. The being has full light-bluish breasts that drip milk into the air and a prominent erect phallus. The being hovers, whirring in place in a vibrating aura of light. Then it disappears. Actually, I cannot distinguish if the droplets are milk or semen.

Clearly this approximates the hermaphroditic (alchemical) *rebis* to which Jung refers. It is interesting to note that in the Late Middle Ages visions of the Virgin Mary in the sky dripping milk from her breasts were not uncommon. While overtly sexual, the winged androgyne of the dream is no less self-contained than the Virgin and, hovering in the air, a no less spiritual symbol. In the medieval period these two mytho-types might well be discussion points as to whether salvation (consciousness) comes "by nature" or "by grace," for the androgyne is an emphatic natural symbol and the Virgin the very personification of Christian grace. Similarly, in the Vatican Library one finds a fresco image of Christ on the cross with a shattered statue of Mercury lying at his feet. Allegorical in its commentary on Christ's superiority to the pagan god, it may also be taken to represent the conscious and unconscious aspects of the human psyche. For Mercury (Hermes), Dionysus dismembered, or even for Christ himself (as the Host), the shattered god is an image of dismemberment in the sense of Hillman's discussion of the Neoplatonic Dionysus, the pneuma dispersed through all nature. It could then be Mercury as "duplex" or Dionysus as "the divided one" who would compensate for Christ's one-sidedness—and for the absence of any sexual token in Christian iconography.

Jung views the hermaphrodite both retrospectively in the child and as a living archetype. Likewise we contemplate its pertinence to the child, the individuating adult, or the death bed—the whole arching trajectory of life. This is reinforced by Jung's early psychoanalytic observation: "While perceiving in infantile sexuality the beginnings of a future sexual function, I also discern there the seeds of higher spiritual functions ... even in adult life the vestiges of infantile sexuality are the seeds of vital spiritual functions."[2] The winged creature of the preceding personal dream falls in line with Phanes quite precisely, just as it does with the alchemical Mercurius. Typical of many creation mythologies (also a commentary on the perennial ambiguity of the gender of angels) one will note that Gnostic aeons emerge in androgynous pairs in the creation myth of Sophia. Where there is androgyny there is proximity to the psyche's creative core.

An additional qualification of the syzygy as anima-animus or androgyne must be made in proceeding. The "hermaphrodite" refers to actual physiology, while "androgyne" possesses a psychic nuance. Eliade speaks of androgyny in relation to "imitative rites," raising again this question of literalism vis-à-vis the symbolic. In antiquity, one finds cross-dressing in cult rituals as varied as those of Aphrodite, Dionysus, Cybele and Attis, or Priapus; among eunuchs and transvestite hierodules in Near Eastern tradition; and in the merger of Shiva and Parvati as dual-sexed Ardhanarishvara in popular Hinduism. There are episodes of cross-dressing in the heroic life of Heracles and in the *Bacchae* of Euripides, where King Pentheus is delicately groomed by Dionysus to go meet the maenads in female attire. These historical phenomena are clearly pertinent to today's manifestations of transvestitism and transgender sexual identity. An individual and sympathetic perspective must inform any comment here, for the inner necessity of persons moved to cross-dressing, to pharmacological and surgical gender modifications, or full gender reassignment are as multi-determined as they are private. What does remain psychologically at issue is the degree to which deep emotional injury, the demands of an individuation process, or both motivate such experiments. The degree to which the religious instinct is factored into the equation and consciously cultivated is another worthy consideration. Individuals make breathtaking lifetime wagers here. What does it all mean for personality, life, and soul? Is such concretism a ritual matter, a lifestyle choice, or both? Is it a medium of insight or something that precludes deeper insight through a focus on "mere appearances" and the enhancement of sexual possibilities? Eliade, for one, emphasizes the symbolic dimension of androgyny this way:

> [The] hermaphrodite represented in antiquity an ideal condition which men endeavour to achieve spiritually by means of imitative rites; but if a child showed at birth any sign of hermaphroditism, it was killed by its own parents. In other words, the actual anatomical hermaphrodite was considered an aberration of Nature, a sign of the gods' anger, and was consequently destroyed out of hand. Only the ritual androgyne provided a model, because it implied not an augmentation of anatomical organs but, symbolically, the union of the magico-religious powers belonging to both sexes.[3]

A significant number of individuals with pronounced sexual variations have suffered deep object-relational disappointments and distortions through experiences of childhood sexual abuse. The abused teenager who hung himself in full drag at a nearby middle school and Plato's mythic androgyne both come to mind in relation to this theme. As Jung pointed out, androgyny harkens back to the nondifferentiation of early childhood even as it is an archetype in its own right. Fliess discusses distortions in body-ego that result from early sexual injury. Child sexual abuse is by no means always incestuous, but the experience of early sexual abuse does project victims into an incestuous world of especially confusing internalized objects. And literal transgressions of the incest taboo invariably arise in a context of disturbed object relations.

The torn fabric of an inadequate and, even more, an overtly sexualized and destructive relational history leaves the individual unprotected and susceptible to the underlying power of both residual perinatal dynamics and the unmediated play of the archetypes—both threats of a potentially annihilating abyss. This dangerous incestuous situation arises where the crucially important *symbolic* project of building up trustworthy inner objects is sabotaged through being concretized. Consider, for example, the dream of a thoughtful thirty-six-year-old incest survivor, a gay man who was sexually abused by numerous members of a profoundly dysfunctional family:

I am traveling with some guy as we cross a bridge where an old witch with a cane appears with an old werewolf. The werewolf has a bag of herbs with everything he needs inside it. He keeps throwing the bag in the river and she keeps scolding him and repeatedly goes to retrieve the bag for him. Then further along the river I meet a bunch of male companions and an oriental rickshaw driver who gives us passage. In the group is a man I like very much. He is a father. I kiss him, but then he tries to seduce me. From there I can see a ways off a very friendly woman standing in the structure of a new house that is being constructed. I also see a wonderful attractive man about my own age.

The patient immediately recognized in the old witch and werewolf by the bridge the mindless repetition compulsions that characterized his parents' codependent marital malaise. They constitute a persistent detraction from his drive to emotional integrity and relational progress. The group of younger men are simply his generational and preferential ilk, congenial aspects of himself or, via projection, the guys he may commune with in his search for that wonderful attractive man at the construction site. The patient's gay identity is not at issue here, but his sexualized father imago definitely is. "He is a father." His anonymity marks him as an archetypal image, but what might be an inner personification of paternal recognition, affirmation, blessing, or right ordinance would here seduce him instead. Fortunately the dreamer's anima is patiently presiding over future relational possibilities as well as this man's ongoing development in the house that is being constructed. This is the home of the anima and the syzygy. It exemplifies the progressive, prospective, and personality-building dimension of an incest matrix that definitely includes but must surpass the personal parental imagos, as both Jung and Grof have shown us. The imagery and particular quality of anima, animus, and syzygy are typically intermingled with the parental materials early in the analytic process. Given the decisive role that parents play (so decisive that certain schools of psychoanalysis never get beyond them), sexual encroachment by a parent characteristically leads to an especially piqued and variant sexuality. Here a brief digression on the symbolic dimensions of incest and the incest matrix itself is essential.

I have worked with many victims of incest and sexual abuse in private practice and frontline clinical settings. The special insight I bring to treatment and to a discussion of incest concerns the chronically neglected symbolic dimensions of incest. Clinicians who work with sexual abuse typically lack understanding of the intrapsychic phenomena for want of depth psychological education and *extensive work with personal dreams*. Given the fact that psychotherapists are bound by common concerns for the intact personality of young people, I have found it painfully ironic that the very proposition of a symbolic dimension to incest is met with such non-comprehension. No thorough psychological treatment of incest-related problems can afford to neglect what must be explored by returning briefly to Freud and Jung.

Early in his career in the 1890s, Freud's clinical observations led him to recognize the central role of child sexual abuse in the etiology of hysteria, a symptom picture that overlaps with both the current *DSM:IV* diagnosis of Hysterical Personality Disorder and the Post-Traumatic Stress Disorder, which are characteristic for victims of sexual trauma. To the best of my knowledge, it was feminist social worker Florence Rush whose book, *The Best Kept Secret* (1980), first delved seriously into Freud's ill-fated bobbling on the question of actual incest vs. incest fantasies. It was four years later that Jeffrey Masson published *The Assault on Truth: Freud's Suppression of the Seduction Theory*, which addressed this theme from within the psychoanalytic establishment. In her chapter, "A Freudian Cover-Up," Rush says of Freud:

> [Exposure] to repeated and persistent incriminations of fathers by his patients made him uneasy and, never quite comfortable with the seduction theory, he mentioned it publicly only in the year 1896 and not again until much later (1933), when he was able to reassign the abuse to female fantasy and disavow it as erroneous.[4]

She proceeds to quote Freud directly:

> Almost all my women patients told me that they had been seduced by their fathers. I was driven to recognize in the end that these reports were untrue and so came to understand that the hysterical symptoms are derived from phantasies and not from real occurrences.[5]

The remedy for this tragic shift (rightly infuriating for clinicians) was only initiated with the feminist consciousness-raising of the 1960s.

In seeking to grasp the deeper subjective reasons for Freud's turnabout, Rush reviews the correspondence between Freud and his intimate friend in Berlin, Wilhelm Fliess, from 1896 to when Freud changed his mind. Freud was deeply engaged in his own self-analysis in this period, suffered what he terms an "anxiety neurosis," and was confounded by the death of his father. The correspondence with Fliess shows Freud so troubled by the fact that his hysterical patients repeatedly cited the father as the perpetrator that he was disinclined to speak of it publicly. It appears in his own reflections that owing to "the existence of some hysterical features in his brother and several sisters that even his father [was] incriminated."[6] Rush thus points to incestuous problems in Freud's family background and his own conflict as the key factor in his theoretical reversal. The patriarchal and puritanical mores of Viennese society also played their role. In any event, the reality of actual incest was consigned to the inner world of his patients' imagination, where the massive denial of proper society and even of many professionals preferred to keep it hidden.

Freud's tragically one-sided but enormously influential theoretical position not only viewed incest fantasies as generated by the innate polymorphous disposition of the child, but was given motive force by being bound up with Freud's now antiquated mechanistic drive-theory.

Coupled in this way, Freud's theoretic notions only enforced a therapeutic focus on the individual's inner conflicts and drives towards a particular love object, while woefully neglecting the frequent maltreatment of children by allegedly caretaking adults. How suspicious the child became in the process, how culpable victims of abuse, and how untrustworthy the instinctual drives of the child were destined to remain! Developments within psychoanalysis beyond these old formulations by Freud have grown into the field of object relations, where attention to the interactional field between child and parent is incomparably more balanced. While Freud looked to the suspicious id of the child, Alice Miller's theme of parental narcissism represents the other side of the equation—parents' imposition upon children of their own narcissistic needs. The degree of this negative parental influence is something that one monitors almost daily in analytic practice. It is immediately evident in the notorious "little girl anima" that a father projects onto his favorite daughter and in mother's smothering "my little man" head trip, which boys endure as they await initiation into the adult world. This is why both fathers *and* mothers might seriously consider ritually giving away children of *both* sexes at weddings—a more comprehensive renunciation of old incestuous claims.

Early passages in the *Collected Works* show Jung in general acceptance of Freud's ideas on the child's production of seduction fantasies and that famous makeshift, the Oedipus complex, which was fashioned to compensate for Freud's private anxieties. The following passage from 1913 (as the association of the two men was ending), however, reflects Jung's singular care in striking a balance between the reality and the imagination of incest. His words amount to a great divide for considering the imagery of incest regressively in terms of biography or injury, or progressively in terms of individuation and the religious instinct:

> If dream analysis at the beginning of treatment shows that the dreams have an undoubtedly sexual meaning, this meaning is to be taken realistically; that is, it proves that the sexual problems of the patient need to be subjected to a careful review. For instance, if an incest fantasy is clearly shown to be a latent content of the dream, one must subject the patient's infantile relations with his parents and brothers and sisters, as well as his relations with other persons who are fitted to play the role of father or

mother, to a thorough investigation. But if a dream that comes
at a later stage of the analysis has, let us say, an incest fantasy as
its essential meaning—a fantasy that we have reason to consider
disposed of—concrete value should not under all circumstances
be attached to it; it should be regarded as symbolic. The formula
for interpretation is: the unknown meaning of the dream is
expressed, by analogy, through a fantasy of incest. If we did not
get beyond the real value we should keep reducing the patient
to sexuality, and this would arrest the progress of the
development of his personality.[7]

Jung subsequently reasserts, "it would be of little value to consider
the symbolic content only; the concrete aspects must be dealt with
first." Thus he articulates an appropriately balanced clinical perspective
that embraces both the concrete biographical and the symbolic
archetypal sides of the incest question.

Clinically and in relation to the general human propensity for
flight from the body under intolerable duress, the typical dissociative
tendency of incest victims must be addressed in passing. Abuse victims
suffer criminal acts beyond their control, and typically fly self-
protectively off into fantasy places outside the body—into the
wallpaper, patterns on the ceiling, a picture on the bedroom wall, or
into another state of consciousness altogether in an attempt to escape
the helplessness and depersonalization of the abuse. These spontaneous
fantasies, however dissociative, are too important and too spontaneous
a production of the individual's psyche to be understood merely as
escapism. In reality they help define the airy and aerial dimension of
the psyche, its upper hemisphere, as it were. The specific content of
fantasy must be respected and explored from the outset.

I recall a fifteen-year-old boy who had been exposed to extremely
sadistic experiences of sexual abuse and domestic violence. Deeply
withdrawn, but still well disposed to treatment, the first statement
the boy made was that he wanted to visit all of the planets during his
lifetime. He could not speak directly of his inner states or of the abuse.
Our first three months in therapy consisted almost solely of his drawing
UFOs and different species of extraterrestrial beings surrounded by
strange hieroglyphs, which I would seek to answer by drawing, as we
generated a shared vocabulary. He slowly began to tell his story. When
he turned sixteen, I presented him with a globe of the Earth I'd found

in a nearby secondhand toy store, to his substantial satisfaction. The last few sessions I worked with him he had markedly improved at school and was suddenly knowledgeable of and indignant about what the World Trade Organization means for working people in Latin America. He had returned to Earth.

The dream of a man in his thirties captures a range of key elements as well as the general dynamics of the incest matrix, where regressive forces work in tandem with progressive ones. The fact that he had no history of sexual abuse only underscores the general emotional patterns that sexual abuse so sorely exacerbates:

I am walking at dawn in a place I don't recognize. Suddenly I come across a huge circular pit with tooth-like projections around the sides of the interior. I fall into it, but somehow manage to stay in the center so that I don't get cut by the teeth. The tunnel changes directions, though I am still falling, and the next image is swords rather than teeth protruding from the sides. I manage to make it through. The tunnel levels out and narrows, but I have to crawl, avoiding pits and other obstructions.

At one point I needed my ash staff to get across a large abyss, and it simply appeared. I almost lost the staff a few times (it was important to keep with me). Finally I crawl into an area where I can walk upright, and there I find a large pile of crystal-like objects that are transparent except for their dark cloudy centers. I stuff my pockets with these objects and keep going.

Next a huge penis comes sliding up the tunnel towards me. I am afraid of being crushed, so I back out of the way and sit in a corner. Now I know where I am and what's happening, so I prop my staff between the two walls next to me to keep from being squashed by muscular contractions. After the penis leaves I must decide what to do next. Without coming to any conclusions, I suddenly scoop up some semen and eat it along with one of the crystal objects that I've found. I start growing very fast and begin heading headfirst towards the exit.

Echoes of Grof's Basic Perinatal Matrices II and III appear with singular clarity in this imagery of descent, the *vagina dentata*, and the staff employed to create space between the parental imagos. A stark primal scene, but by extension this is also suggestive of the archetypal World Parents who must be separated like the half shells of Phanes's egg. Given the fundamental bisexuality of the psyche, it is interesting to note that regressed subjects who reexperience perinatal processes in Grof's research are as likely to visualize the contracting uterus as a murderous *masculine* entity as a feminine one, i.e., in archetypal images of Saturn or Moloch as well as the witch or the Goddess Kali. The perinatal imagery with which the dream is suffused also suggests that parental intercourse may have extended well into the pregnancy. It is clear that the muscular spasms of intercourse and those of the birth process (the bereavement process as well?) are intimately related. The dream arose as the patient was grieving the loss of a marriage, suffering through a wide range of constricting emotions and attempting to take a stand against the wounding ideation of inferiority. As the dream so clearly demonstrates, this amounts to an experience of the stuff of masculine initiation. Amplification by way of parallel ritual and mythical examples only reinforces the proposition.

Already encountered in the shamanic initiate's experience of visceral replacement, mineral crystals are understood as bits of solidified light from the aerial vault of the celestial sphere. In his seminal essay "Spirit, Light, and Seed," Eliade opens a series of cross-cultural manifestations of the Solar Archetype with Prajapati, the Vedic creator god, presented as a "Golden Embryo," a sacred seed: "The Brahmanas explicitly consider the *semen virile* a solar epiphany. 'When the human father thus emits him as seed into the womb, it is really the Sun that emits him as seed into the womb.'"[8] Amidst numerous examples of the spirit-light-seed equation offered by Eliade, one derives from the Desanas, a people of Colombian Amazonia, where the *paye* (shaman) is described:

> The soul of the *paye* is compared to a fire whose light penetrates the obscurity and makes everything visible, similar to that of the Sun. A *paye* does not have power without the knowledge that is given by the light, for "he is part of the Sun's light." Like the solar light, the light of the shaman's soul is gold-yellow; in other words, it "represents the fertilizing virtues of the Sun." Every *paye* wears, suspended from his neck, a cylinder made from yellow or white quartz, called "Sun's phallus." Moreover, any quartz or crystal represents the *semen virile*.[9]

Eliade states that "all types of light experiences have this factor in common: they bring a man out of his profane universe or historical situation, and project him into a universe different in quality, an entirely different world, transcendent and holy."[10] Of the Desanas he says in summary:

> Consequently, there is an intimate connection between solar light, holiness, creativity, and sex. All religious ideas, personages, and activities bear also a sexual signification. The reason for this hierophanic pansexualism may be looked for in the identification of solar light and solar warmth with the origin and perpetuation of cosmic and human life.[11]

He concludes his paper with a discussion of the visionary states that the shamans experience upon ingesting botanicals:

> In as much as the sun's light is conceived as a divine, procreative *semen virile*, it is understandable that the ecstatic iridescent visions provoked by the hallucinogenic plant *yage* have been compared with the sex act. The Tucanos [of the Desanas' language group] say that during coition man is "suffocated" and "sees visions." According to a myth, the *yage*-Woman was impregnated through the eyes. As a matter of fact, the equivalence eyes = vagina is familiar to the Tucanos. The verb "to fertilize" derives from the roots "to see" and "to deposit."[12]

The supernatural *yage*-Woman (like Night the mother of Phanes, or the Virgin Mary) is known to have given birth to a child who had "the form of light: he was human, yet he was Light." The effect of taking the *yage* is interpreted by Eliade as:

> regressus to the cosmic womb, that is, to the primeval moment when Sun-Father began the creation. In fact, the visions recapitulate the theogony and cosmogony: the participants see how Sun-Father created the divine beings, the world, and man and how the tribal culture, the social institutions, and the ethical norms were founded.[13]

One of these is the prohibition against incest, giving both society and the individual their right order. We see once more the deep commonality between creation mythology and the mystery of both the syzygy (*yage*-Woman and Sun-Father) and the individuation process. Our earlier reflections on the dispersion of psyche's multiple luminosities (*scintillae*) through the body may also be recalled. For shamanic initiation is not simply a process *from* the carnal body *to* the crystalline and spiritual, but the profound insight, granted to the few, that no real disparity ever actually exists between the two! The crystals of the dream also resemble cells, they are transparent except for their cloudy centers. The dreamer's report of suddenly scooping up the paternal semen and eating it together with the crystals underscores that the experience is ritually significant. With the aid of his father's phallus and seed and his own ash staff and crystals the sacrament of the neophyte's second birth is speedily induced. Psyche simply prompts it in accord with its own archetypal way—where sexual and spiritual imagery are one.

A repetitive dream of childhood demonstrates just how early in life the personal anima may appear on the scene. It recurred any number of times when this male patient was five to seven years of age and once more in late adolescence:

I am sitting on the toilet in my parents' bathroom when the door is opened by a little blonde sister with long hair in a white nightgown with blue ribbons. She looks at me and giggles, before walking across the room and turning on the water faucet. I awaken having wet the bed.

The dream dates from the first years of school, when private bodily matters are steadily constrained by the persona and where relational matters extend beyond the family to the public arena in new and individual ways. The last repetition recalled by the dreamer resulted in nocturnal emission rather than simple incontinence! The water faucet reflects not only the boy's perception of an obvious penis-faucet equation, but represents a first little shift from the concrete to the imaginal—water, like semen, a flow of spontaneous fantasy over which the anima presides. The urine-semen equation appears in innumerable folklore and mythical contexts as a fructifying agent. Here the male dream-ego meets the sister anima counterpart in a dyad of differentiation that moves within the androgynous current. In Goethe's "The New Paris: A Boy's Tale," from which the earlier vignette of a hermetic "as above so below" garden derives, we find a scene with charming similarity to this dream of childhood. The puer dreamer appears in a more dignified setting than his parents' bathroom, but remains both closely related to the parental dyad and open to the challenge of a surprisingly familiar visitor:

> On the night before Whit Sunday, not long since, I dreamed
> that I stood before a mirror, engaged with the new summer
> clothes which my dear parents had given me for the holiday.
> The dress consisted, as you know, of shoes of polished leather,
> with large silver buckles, fine cotton stockings, black nether
> garments of serge, and a green baracan with gold buttons. The
> waistcoat of gold cloth was cut out of my father's bridal
> waistcoat. My hair had been frizzled and powdered, and my
> curls stuck out from my hair like little wings; but I could not
> finish dressing myself, because I kept confusing the different
> articles, the first always falling off as soon as I was about to
> put on the next.[14]

The surprise moment in a dream, the ego's confusion with
inexplicable errors, or such a sense of trickery coming from an
autonomous agency are all part and parcel of the ego's experience of
the unconscious. While rejoicing in his youthful elegance, the attire
his parents have provided him is by no means the sole measure of the
child. He has an identity of his own to discover. The boy's waistcoat
is a token of the parental syzygy. But with his coiffure specifically
winged, his mirror a testament to self-reflection, and the dream's
appearance at Pentecost, the spirited visitor who suddenly appears
amidst the confusion speaks to the real essence of this precocious boy's
nascent personality:

> In this dilemma, a young and handsome man came to me, and
> greeted my in the friendliest manner, "O! You are welcome!" said I,
> "I am glad to see you here." "Do you know me, then?" replied he,
> smiling. "Why not?" was my no less smiling answer; "you are
> Mercury—I have often enough seen you represented in
> engravings." "I am indeed," replied he; "and am sent to you by the
> gods on an important errand. Do you see these three apples?"[15]

The story then employs elements from the Judgement of Paris and
his fateful choice from among Athena, Hera, and Aphrodite. The
dreamy puer is fascinated by three tiny nymphs that dance on his
fingertips before he finally enters the alchemical garden
aforementioned to deal with three beautiful young women. The
appearance of the three female familiars of Mercury in the dream, like
threefold imagery in general, always anticipates fresh psychic
developments, just as a triangle cannot fail in pointing somewhere.

The dreams considered thus far reflect many basic features of our ambivalent incest matrix: parental imagos both personal and archetypal, the intrapsychic tandem of the anima-animus dyad working to differentiate the personality, etc. Here Robert Stein's classic observations from *Incest and Human Love* significantly extend our appreciation of primary relational dyads, both within the family and the psyche itself, as archetypal phenomena, each with its own mystery. Note that such dream figures as the little blonde sister or the seductive father of the abuse above are the spontaneous and original creations of their respective dreams—not unlike the sudden appearance of Goethe's Mercury and those fascinating anima companions. Stein explains:

> The archetype is the depository of all human experience right from its earliest beginnings. Not, indeed, a dead deposit, a sort of abandoned rubbish heap, but a living system of reactions and aptitudes that determine the individual's life in invisible ways. ...
>
> Within the family situation there exists the potential for the following archetypal constellations—Mother-Father, Mother-Son, Mother-Daughter, Father-Son, Father-Daughter, Brother-Sister, Brother-Brother, Sister-Sister. What this means is that a child is capable of experiencing all these archetypal combinations, regardless of his or her sex. While these archetypes refer to internal images, they are initially released by and experienced in relationship to an external object (mother, father, sibling).[16]

Stein articulates the pertinence of archetypal theory to both family systems theory and object relations theory very deftly. He is psychological in the truest sense, for these outer and inner theoretic perspectives are essentially mirror images of one another. Family systems theory is object relations theory turned inside out and vice versa. Where such ostensibly opposite theoretical perspectives are split off from one another, or worse, where incest is conceived merely in regressive, personalistic, or biographical terms; or worst of all, where an individual's innate capacity for symbol formation and individuation is ignored—we are still engaged, as James Hillman notes, in a kind of "micro-sociology." All the relational dyads ultimately pertain to far more than human relationships with significant persons in our lives. As a system of reactions and aptitudes they pertain to whole spheres of any individual's psychic life, to the differentiation of personality, even *to different aspects of initiation*. We are obviously all mirrors to one another, but the precise way in which the imagery of these relationships is shaped by the archetypes and the imagination remains the decisive factor psychologically.

The concrete acting-out of incest may take place between seven of these eight essential familial dyads. My work with teenage sex offenders and their families has included virtually every combination, each with its destructive impact. While the so-called "identified patient" in a family system may be the victim of he or she who acts out incest concretely, any number of *emotionally incestuous* binds and intergenerational transgressions are typically being played out as well. The result for an individual family member may be an impediment, a wounding, or the overt destruction of a personality. Any concrete enactment or emotionally excessive incestuous bind subverts the symbolic integrity and intentionality of the Incest Archetype as an individuating force. Jung can accordingly observe of this progressive aspect that:

> Incest symbolizes union with one's own being, it means individuation or becoming a self, and because this is so vitally important, it exerts an unholy fascination—not, perhaps, as crude reality, but certainly as a psychic process controlled by the unconscious.[17]

Given the enormous power of parents, with their potential narcissistic invasions and ambivalent emotions or (shifting to the intrapsychic) of internalized parental imagos that are simply too laced with trickery to be confronted or escaped, a special implication for individuation may arise from *sibling* dyads. I have encountered any number of situations where not only sex, but extremely intimate emotional bonds have served, as it were, to keep siblings afloat in an otherwise intolerable family. (One notes in passing that siblings are genetically more akin to one another that they are to either biological parent.) Sisters and brothers share the same generation, they represent the earliest and most intimate human likeness to one another with that fundamental exception of gender, and they are therefore often prototypical for early constellations of the anima and the animus in siblings. But as Stein indicates and we have observed, the archetype of sister and brother (or other familial dyad) can pop up completely on its own! It is no accident that the most primary gendered personages in the art and literature of alchemy are portrayed as an incestuous brother-sister pair. Such soul-stuff is beautifully reflected in the following dream, whose imagery parallels the transformative hermetic baths of alchemy, Stein's incest matrix at its most elemental, and indicates as well how gendered elements within the personality are differentiated though ceaseless male-female interactions, conjunctions, and disjunctions. The dreamer's *soul* sister (anima) appears here as both a part of and not part of his own body. Initially startled awake by a dramatic occurrence involving "two grand golden women" before falling back asleep, the dreamer provides us a fine example of the archetypal feminine (her *doubling* a harbinger of emergent psychic materials) presiding over gender itself:

I am naked with a group of people in a clear rectangular swimming pool. Our bodies are clean and beautiful and we are all in a mood as liquid as the water around us. Everyone is engaged in erotic play with one another. I float upside down (we can breath above or below the water) in an inverted "69" position with a lovely woman. I kiss and lick her lower body—her thighs, vagina, and ass with complete abandon. There is a bluish hue in the air. I feel the gentle lapping of waves against me from the movements of others. Everyone's body is milky white and blue. My body feels wonderful and I languish serenely in the pleasure of it. Then I stand lightly beside the pool in a curving posture, my skin milky white. I have the body of a woman as much as my own. I slowly slip the top of my bathing suit up over my woman's breasts. Everything is so beautiful, serene, pure!

Whether experienced in images that reflect family experience or in purely archetypal images and emotions, the numinosity of the archetype may inspire fascination, awe, devotion, terror, ecstasy, or a remarkable sense of peace. A review of Stein's family dyads from a mythical, religious, and ritual perspective further illustrates the depth of fascination germane to each dyad: the mystery of the Mother-Son dyad in Christianity or the rites of Cybele and Attis; the Mother-Daughter dyad in the Eleusinian Mysteries of Demeter and Persephone; the Father-Son dyad in Christianity or in Roman Mithraism (where initiates move through seven grades of initiation from Mercury, the puer, to Saturn, the old man); the Father-Daughter dyad in the myths of Zeus and Athena or Agamemnon and Iphigenia; the Brother-Brother dyads of Egypt, the Old Testament, or Greek heroic mythology; Sister-Sister dyads celebrated in the cult of Artemis, in Amazon lore, or among the women of Lesbos, etc. Summarizing these notes on the Incest Archetype, we turn finally to the dream of a thirty-five-year-old man that captures the syzygy with extraordinary clarity. The royal pair is archetypally "just so," unhinged from family and biography, and progressively supportive of the individuation process. The dream's initial sequence is suggestive as well of the emotional life-and-death issues that one will be called upon to confront in any real psychological opus:

I find myself deep under the earth in a chamber in which a huge metal furnace stands open. Inside in its fierce orange flames I see the corpse of an old man baking away, not turning to blackened ashes but to a chalky white and brittle state. I am given a small ritual shovel and tap off the old man's jawbone, teeth, and fragments of his upper ribs. I then transfer these to a small manger made of freshly cut evergreen branches. Only then do I notice that the chamber is encircled by tall stately women in long gowns. I then walk through a passageway to a much larger and brighter adjoining chamber around a huge oval subterranean pool. I am amazed to see beside the pool a pair of impressive thrones: a gold one surmounted by an illustrious king and a silver one with a stately queen upon it. The king is fishing— casting his line in again and again until he pulls a big iridescent fish from the water and flings it adroitly to me. It is wriggling in my hands with such intensity that I awake.

The circular chamber in the earth, the flaming furnace, the manger, the ring of female attendants, and the subterranean oval pool mark this dream as archetypally related to both Mother mysteries, ancient practices of ritual incubation, as well as to alchemy. One recalls that Demeter held the mortal child Demophoon in a fire each night to render him immortal, but was interrupted by the boy's mortal parents. Jaw, teeth, and the upper ribs (pneumatic cavity) represent what is most enduring in humankind; their placement in a manger clearly anticipating a rebirth. The dream leads to the conspicuous token of an individual life proffered and affirmed—the lively iridescent fish, presented and presided over by the King and Queen syzygy, the personifications of authentic inner ordinance, devotion, and wholeness.

Patriarchal sexual morality views procreation solely as a means to practical increase, the production of new members of the tribe, kingdom, or state, the fulfillment of a civic obligation. It speaks of eros only negatively, shutting out every aspect of eros spare that which accomplishes this external collective goal. The individual soul is left out of account, along with the significance of procreation for the inner life. In the *Symposium*, Socrates describes the instruction given him by his mysterious teacher, Diotima, concerning all the phenomena connected with love. She explains that when men display their ardent desires most worthily, "The function is that of procreation in what is beautiful," that "such procreation can be either physical or spiritual," and furthermore: "There is something divine about the whole matter; in procreation and bringing to birth the mortal creature is endowed with a touch of immortality."[18] While recourse to a female partner and physical offspring is traditionally considered an avenue to immortality, Socrates turns quickly to the subject of "procreativity of soul," a similarly ever renewing process. This becomes the primary theme of the work:

> Now, why is procreation the object of love? Because procreation is the nearest thing to perpetuity and immortality that a mortal being can attain. If, as we agreed, the aim of love is the perpetual possession of the good, it necessarily follows that it must desire immortality together with the good, and the argument leads us to the inevitable conclusion that love is love of immortality as well as of the good.[19]

The most basic impulse to immortality cited is seen in the continual reproduction of animals and birds, but the discussion grows ever more human, psychological, and process oriented:

> Even during the period for which any living being is said to live and to retain his identity—as a man, for example, is called the same man from boyhood to old age—he does not in fact retain the same attributes, although he is called the same person; he is always becoming a new being and undergoing a process of loss and reparation, which affects his hair, his flesh, his bones, his blood, and his whole body. And not only his body, but his soul as well. No man's character, habits, opinions, desires, pleasures, pains, and fears remain always the same; new ones come into existence and old ones disappear.[20]

This theme of perpetual process and the parallelism of body and soul might be answered today by somatic environmentalist Stanley Keleman, who observes that "if you destroy now you materialize, you in fact destroy your whole life. Because the message of somatic reality is in fact to materialize, to take shape, to take a particular shape."[21] The body's continual material self-replacement extends for Socrates also to pieces of knowledge that may be known, forgotten, remembered, and replaced. New impressions continually work to give one's knowledge the same appearance of uninterrupted constancy that the body presents:

> It is in this way that everything mortal is preserved; not by remaining ever the same, which is the prerogative of divinity, but by undergoing a process in which the losses caused by age are repaired by new acquisitions of a similar kind.[22]

No hasty transcendentalism or Apollonian flight from the life processes appears here, perhaps especially because Eros (finally personified by homely Socrates himself) is imagined from the very beginning *as a spirit intermediary to humankind and the immortal gods, and participating in both natures.* He thus grants us our claim. For immortality may be experienced within the changes and transformations of life itself, particularly against the backdrop of the ambiguous nature of *time* in the psyche. "The body dies; the body's beauty lives."[23] With this prologue on love, beauty, procreation, immortality, and continual renewal, we may turn to a pair of dreams from a thirty-year-old man in analytic process. The first dream opens with the dreamer's own experience of Eros and Aphrodite as a lively child and a lovely stripper before moving on to celebrate the procreativity of soul with the imagery of childbirth. It challenges any patriarchal notion that sex, desire, and beauty are somehow incompatible with thoughtful maternity.

I am sitting in a strip joint where a powerfully erotic stripper is dancing completely naked on stage and titillating one and all. Then I notice a lovely naked boy, who reminds me of my son and of me at about three. He's on stage gleefully and very courteously dancing in rhythm with the stripper, wishing so much to be connected with her.

Then with others in a car: We stop along a great river in the desert. Gazing off to the right I see the most mysterious and beautiful oblong island in the middle of the current. It is a magical place, tightly bound by profuse green plant growth with luxuriant palm trees growing at its center.

Then I find myself sitting attentively next to a young woman who is in the last phase of giving birth and doing nicely. I hold her hand firmly with both hands. The last major contraction pushes the child out. Closing my eyes for a moment, I meditate on how excruciating this must have been for her and the child. A doctor is in attendance as I look at the baby and compliment her, "You did just fine! It's a lively boy-child."

The dream is a striking indication that what was once celebrated as beautiful and numinous in the erotic life of the soul lives on today in our culture's profuse sex industry. At the same time such inner reflections demonstrate that this soul-stuff can be realized through insight, imagination, and heart. The specific dream experience prompted a feeling of enormous affection for the gleeful child on the part of the dreamer (and for the stripper as well!) Gazing at the beautiful dancer leads on to a perception of brilliant images of the natural world, as if the warm desert landscape were an analogue of the stripper's smooth and supple skin. The island oasis is beautifully sensuous, reminiscent of Eden in its timeless and self-perpetuating green. It calls to mind the *hortus conclusus* motif of alchemy, the virginal garden of the adept (Eden), such as we encounter in Goethe's tale. Elliptical, in-turned, and tightly bound within the river channel, the island image anticipates the ensuing birth process just as it may be taken as a quiet image of the self.

The second dream again involves a highly alluring appearance of the anima, intimations of immortality, the individuating isolation of the desert, and the startling incursion of an unexpected superordinate being:

I am wandering in a vast desert. All is extraordinarily open and still. I then see an unbelievably beautiful young woman lying naked on the sand. A voice tells me that by making love with her I will become one of the "Brotherhood of the Sands." The woman parts her legs and beckons me with her ardent and penetrating gaze. As I kneel before her I catch a glimpse of an animal form on the horizon. My awe increases as I see the creature is a sphinx, padding pleasantly towards us. I see that the sphinx has an erect penis. As it draws closer it seems to become one with the sky itself. As I ease down and couple with the woman, the sphinx's phallus becomes a golden whirlwind that spirals down my throat.

The golden whirlwind approximates the Annunciation even as it echoes the promise of God to Abraham that his children would be "as numerous as the stars of heaven and the sand that is on the seashore" (Genesis 22:17). But the spirit is not only poured out at a highly specific erotic moment, nor only by a ray from on high, but through the agency of a remarkable mythical zoomorphic form, a natural symbol. Particularly as a powerful dream experience, what could more persuasively reflect an inner procreativity of soul? The couples' initial penetration of one another is *ocular*: it appears prominently in the meeting of their equally desirous eyes. The commencement of sexual intercourse between the dreamer and his dazzling female companion is simultaneous to the outpouring of the spirit! Furthermore, all transpires at an archetypal intersection where the anima, as a personification of everything associated with our Birth-Sex-Death equation, couples with the masculine as love partner, her animus, a figure uniquely blessed by the gods at the moment he becomes one with her. This defies any concrete conception of reproduction, and serves as one more example of the psyche's unpredictable, polymorphous, and elaborate means of self-generation. The Sphinx of course is that fateful creature whose riddle Oedipus must solve: "What goes on four legs, then two legs, the three legs?"— looking fatefully on as humankind crawls, then walks upright, then hobbles with a staff to its destiny. The sphinx of the dream is again an archetypal image of the undivided, the primal, and the parental in more ways than one. The dreamer actually commented subsequently that as the phallus became a golden whirlwind it seemed no less like an umbilical cord from the sky. Strictly human categories are threatened. This is a pristine instance of solar hierophany, comparable not only to androgynous Phanes, the first born, the bringer of light, he who bears the honored seed of the gods—but open to amplification by the "Ra of the Horizon" motif in ancient Egypt, where the Sun God emerges from the horizon and climbs steadily to the mid-heaven. Before considering the solar hierophany more thoroughly, let's take an additional dream under our wing, that of another man in his thirties who had recently driven in the country with his best male friend:

Out on a broad meadow along a winding creek with my friend Leroy. It is just at that moment before the sun breaks the horizon. As the sun appears, huge phallic stones rise up from the mud at the water's edge. We stand there admiring them in the fresh morning air.

The ash staff employed by an earlier dreamer in incestuous peril, the golden whirlwind, the huge phallic stones rising from the mud to greet the sun, even the king's fishing pole aforementioned—all possess phallic qualities, however varied their imagery. An exploration of cross-cultural images is illuminating here.

One of Jung's more impressive hints about the reality of the collective unconscious springs from a clinical experience where a schizophrenic patient called him to the window. Moving his head to and fro he spoke of a phallic tube hanging down from the sun, that it is the source of the winds, and likewise that it moves to and fro. Some years later, while studying the newly translated *Mithras Liturgy*, Jung read the following:

> Drawing in breath from the rays, drawing up three times as much as you can, and you will see yourself being lifted up and ascending to the height, so that you seem to be in midair. You will hear nothing either of man or of any other living thing, nor in that hour will you see anything of mortal affairs on earth, but rather you will see all immortal things. For in that day and hour you will see the divine order of the skies: the presiding gods rising in heaven, and others setting. Now the course of the visible gods will appear through the disk of god, my father; and in similar fashion the so-called "pipe," the origin of the ministering winds. For you will see it hanging from the sun's disc like a pipe. You will see the outflow of this object toward the regions westward, boundless as an east wind, if it be assigned to the regions of the East—and the other (viz. the west wind), similarly, toward its own regions. And you will see the gods staring intently at you and rushing at you.[24]

Interesting to note in passing is how precisely this document's threefold inhalation of breath to induce the visionary state parallels the holotropic breath work of Grof. Indeed, controlled hyperventilation, like extensive dream work, meditation, and ritual, may also project one into sacred space. The whole ambiance of our dreams and this mystical epiphany are essentially Egyptian and accordingly syncretistic.

Any man who records his dreams over a period of years will in all likelihood encounter the motif of autofellatio. He may be as surprised by it as the reader may be with this apparent textual discontinuity. But be it associated with the autoeroticism of adolescence or a deep emotional regression, or simply experimented with, the fantasy and the behavior point to a mythic image. A counterpart appears in variations of the creation myth of Atum-Ra of Egypt, where unvarnished body metaphor and creative imagination merge. Recall the syzygy of Nut-*Nu*, the second of which is a masculine attenuation that emerges from the watery matrix, then moves into the sky, first as Khepera, the "self-created" solar scarab.

> When I have come into being, being (itself) came into being.
> … I planned in my own heart, and there came into being a
> multitude of forms of being, the forms of children and the forms
> of their children. I was the one who copulated with my fist, I
> masturbated my hand. Then I spewed with my own mouth; I
> spat out what was Shu, and sputtered out what was Tefnut ….[25]

In an alternate translation, illustrated in a papyrus in the British Museum, the god ejaculates directly into his own mouth. The self-generating circulation of archetypal masculinity and a source of psychic life—all come together in this primordial image of the masculine uroboros. Worth interjecting is the fact that "Schu and Tefnut, both children of Re [Nu], are called "eye-twins," Tefnut being the left eye (moon) and Schu the right eye (sun)."[26] The particular form of an ancestral cult image from distant New Guinea amplifies the Egyptian material very concisely—the merger of body, imagination, and spirit in one masculine image (Fig. 1, next page). Note the marked contrast between the body itself and the figure's headpiece. In the body we see an appendage (indistinguishable as beak, penis, or umbilicus) cycling from lower belly to mouth or face as if altogether one with the biological round of the Great Mother. Simultaneously we see a conical hat carefully gradated to indicate an ascending hierarchy of spiritual states. Crucially, the Egyptian image of Atum-Ra appears as the source of "a multitude of forms of being," corresponding quite precisely to the provocative Greek expression for the engendering word, *logos spermatikos*. Many frank erotic metaphors of Egyptian mythology were carried over into Gnostic speculation. They must surely have been familiar to Philo of Alexandria.

Recalling the phallic stones that rise up from the mud at sunrise in the second dream cited, we now reapproach solar hierophany in its lower extension—where the phallus again appears as part of the body, the Mother's sublunary world, and the underworld as well. A haunting

experience of the numinosity of the phallus appears in a childhood dream that Jung recalls from his third or fourth year. His bedtime prayer about Jesus' "taking" children was confusing for the fact that it spoke also of Satan taking children to "devour" them. Jung's growing suspicions about the "dear Lord Jesus" were compounded by seeing Christian pastors, including his father and eight uncles, officiating at funerals—as Jung puts it: "gloomy black men in frock coats, top hats, and shiny black boots who busied themselves with the black box."[27] These perplexing observations as well as expressions of fear and irritation towards Jesuits overheard from his Protestant father lent their dark *mana* to Jung's traumatic sighting of a similarly clad Jesuit priest one day. "I saw a figure in a strangely broad hat and a long black garment coming down from the wood. It looked like a man wearing women's clothes."[28] Jung assumed his women's clothing was a disguise, and was terrified of him.

Fig. 1: Ancestral Figure, New Guinea, Archetype as the sum of generations

Jung accordingly came to ponder how much else of his Christian milieu, its conscious world at least, was also a disguise. At this time in his life a green meadow lay near his family home. Jung finds himself walking there as this dream begins:

> Suddenly I discovered a dark, rectangular, stone-lined hole in the ground. I had never seen it before. I ran forward cautiously and then peered down into it. Then I saw a stone stairway leading down. Hesitantly and fearfully, I descended. At the bottom was a doorway with a round arch, closed off by a green curtain. It was a big, heavy curtain of worked stuff like brocade, and it looked very sumptuous. Curious to see what might be hidden behind, I pushed it aside. I saw before me in the dim light a rectangular chamber about thirty feet long. The ceiling was arched and of hewn stone. The floor was laid with flagstones, and in the center a red carpet ran from the entrance to a low platform. I am not certain, but perhaps a red cushion lay on the seat. It was a magnificent throne, a real king's throne in a fairy tale. Something was standing on it which I thought at first was a tree trunk twelve to fifteen feet high and about one and a half to two feet thick. It was a huge thing, reaching almost to the ceiling. But it was of a curious composition: it was made of skin and naked flesh, and on top there was something like a rounded head with no face and no hair. On the very top of the head was a single eye, gazing motionlessly upward.[29]

An aura of brightness hovered above the rounded head of this being. It seemed that the enormous phallus might crawl after him like a huge worm.

The dream concludes with Jung hearing his mother's voice from up above saying, "Yes, just look at him. That is the man-eater!" While beholding the weird phallus was sufficiently frightening in itself, it was his mother's declaration that this was the "man-eater" that ultimately galvanized Jung's anxiety. With one emphasis (*"That* is the man-eater!") it pointed away from Jesus; in the other ("That is the *man-eater!"*) it implied, through the child's disturbing web of associations, that Jesus, the Jesuit, the dark-clad ministers, and the royal phallus were all of a piece! While these associations are already sufficiently perplexing, Jung's suspicious reaction to the Jesuit's "disguise" in woman's clothes also calls to mind the frequent historical portrayal of the Christian Devil as hermaphroditic. Even in age, Jung takes no small pains to convey and interpret this dream, which haunted him and his relationship with Christianity for decades—particularly upon investigating the theme of cannibalism that underlies the Catholic Mass. The *cella* beneath the earth bore conspicuous relation with the grave in the young Jung's mind, just as the green curtain echoed the green vegetation of the meadow itself. At four years of age Jung would scarcely be aware of the similarity of this chamber to the ritual precincts of any number of ancient mysteries, notably Mithraism, which he would study so extensively. In deep retrospect, Jung states that "through this childhood dream I was initiated into the secrets of the earth."[30] Of the phallus itself:

> I do not know where the anatomically correct phallus can have come from. The interpretation of the *orificium urethrae* as an eye, with the source of light apparently above it, points to the etymology of the word phallus ["shining," "bright"].[31]

He characterizes the phallus as "a subterranean God 'not to be named,'" given its forbidding qualities and sheer numinosity. Similarly, the ancients engaged in little idle banter about abysmal Hades or the chthonic Persephone, and spoke of the Furies as the Eumenides, the "kindly ones." Indeed, Hades himself was known to be highly ambivalent—like the Furies, as *Zeus chthonius,* the bearded underworld serpent, he was known as both Melichios ("honeyed," "easy-to-be-entreated," "gentle") and as the devourerer, *Maimaktes,* "he who rages eager, panting, and thirsting for blood"—clearly the dark side of God.[32] Jung himself recognizes how commonplace it is for children to speak of the "black man" as a typical child's ogre or spook. But he conveys the incredulity of the original moment, the wonder of years, and sustained amazement at cosmic arrangements by recounting his dream vision in *Memories, Dreams, Reflections* as he might murmur quietly to himself:

> [The] fact that *this* was the man-eater, and that *it* was sitting on a golden throne beneath the earth. For my childish imagination it was first of all the king who sat on a throne; then, on a much more beautiful and much higher and much more golden throne far, far away in the blue sky, sat God and Lord Jesus, with golden crowns and white robes. Yet from this same Lord Jesus came the

"Jesuit," in black women's garb, with a broad black hat, down
from the wooded hill. ...
     In the dream I went down into the hole in the earth and found
something very different on a golden throne, something non-
human and underworldly, which gazed fixedly upward and fed
on human flesh.[33]

Jung concludes this account with profound open questions:

Who spoke to me then? Who talked of problems far beyond
my knowledge? Who brought the Above and the Below
together, and laid the foundation for everything that was
to fill the second half of my life with stormiest passion?
Who but that alien guest who came from both above and
from below?[34]

Strikingly, Jung ends up speaking neither of the Lord Jesus nor of
the phallus alone, but of an "alien guest," an unknown divine being that
comes from both above and below—clearly a god-imago quite beyond
the orthodox Christian conception. Recall Rudolf Otto's ultimately
worshipful response to the numinous as "whom or what?—a *mystery*
inexpressible and above all creatures." In the ancient Greek context,
blackness, death, the underworld, green vegetation, and the phallus are
all standard features of the cults involving Dionysus and Hades and a
vegetative and chthonic order of things. But we find Jung also referring
to Christ and God on a "beautiful and much higher and much more
golden throne far, far away in the blue sky." He is a brilliant child here,
imagining the lower and higher order of things in such comprehensive
Gnostic terms—his "alien god" revealing the call of a lifetime. As an adult,
Jung portrays the formidable opposites confronting him in one of his
earliest and most beautiful mandalas (Fig. 2, next page). Its concentric
circles indicate macrocosm and microcosm just as its vertical axis
corresponds with Jung's youthful imaginings in this way: below is
"Abraxas ruler of this world" in the form of a lion-headed serpent whose
head radiates ten golden rays. Atop the axis, on the precise boundary
between the created world and the pleroma (the *potential* world), Jung
portrays none other than Phanes, the golden-winged puer.
     The mystery of the dark phallic god also arises in the dream of
a highly competent thirty-six-year-old female patient, a Catholic and
a virgin, who had spent her life in perpetual caregiving but felt that
her efforts were insufficient. In preceding dreams her pure white room

repeatedly appeared on the second floor of her house, as a sinister male figure stalked her from without. This time the room rests at ground level:

I am in my bedroom when I notice that the door stands a bit open. I am anxious but also curious. Finally I push the door and step out into a dim space. I am shocked to find myself standing before a huge dark-skinned man who wears a pleated skirt—and even more startled to see innumerable male members emerging in every direction from beneath the skirt. He takes my hand gently and leads me down a tunneling hall to a nursery room where he shows me a baby carriage with four chunky babies inside. They need to be changed and fed.

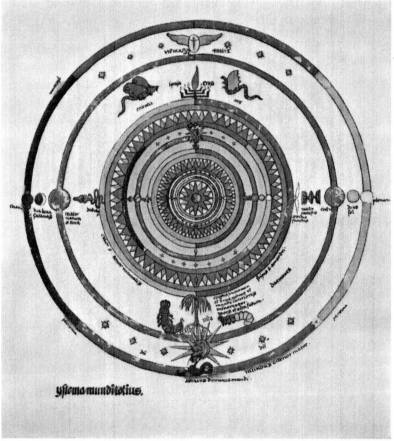

Fig. 2: Mandala of a Modern Man, C. G. Jung

This is an exceedingly gentle and unexpected constellation of the dark phallic animus in an equally gentle woman. It contrasts altogether with Jung's anxiety on encountering the enthroned phallus. The extraordinary anatomical details of the figure, however, more than amply demonstrate why the theoretical designation "animus" pales before the given psychic phenomenon. Few writers speak to this problem more deftly than does Hillman in his classic discussion of sexuality in *The Myth of Analysis*:

> Sexuality changes as the Gods who carry its token—the phallus-penis—change through life's phases. Pan, Priapus, Hermes, Dionysus, Zeus, Apollo, Eros, the Kouroi, Kabeiroi, Sileni, Satyrs, Centaurs—each represents a fantasy pattern through which the instinct can be experienced.[35]

The central image of the dream is black, skirted (androgynous), multiply phallic, and tends four children. In Jungian theoretical terminology it is supportive of the Self (child, quaternity). In archetypal terms it must first and foremost be considered precisely as it presents itself—only then through the figure's affinity with Hades' unseen initiatory context, Hermes as an androgynous but phallic psychopomp, Priapus for the sheer phallic exuberance of the dream, Eros for his sensitivity, recognition, and outstretched hand—then Dionysus, Lord of Souls, who presides over this entire psychic realm. Hillman's statement represents a challenge appropriate to anyone interested in cultivating his or her imagination in the ways of the phallus and the sexual gods. He also points to a proverbial conundrum pertinent to this context:

> The phallus-penis riddle has long troubled psychology, and this trouble will continue because this riddle is an essential mystery of the psyche and not merely a difficult psychological problem. A revelation of this riddle is at the core of initiation and of the mysteries for men and for women—not only in antiquity.[36]

Recall here the dream of the two men friends along a creek at sunrise as stone phalli rise in the mud to greet the sun. The dream imagery indicates the essential vertical axis of the solar hierophany referenced all along. The phalli are planted in moist muddy earth, stand erect, align with the morning sun, and accordingly correspond with both the world axis and its somatic analogue, the spine. This penis-phallus-spine-world axis equation is of fundamental importance in masculine symbolism, where it bespeaks the presence or absence of phallic integrity, uprightness, fortitude, imperturbability, and centeredness—a capacity to hold one's position as a man or a woman. The throng of Greek gods cited by Hillman represents a wide range of specific phallic identities, germinal developments, relational applications, and even cultic contexts. In accord with our psychological focus on the anima-animus syzygy and given the typical tandem arrangements in which a particular phallic element pursues the object of its ardor, it is crucial to carefully assess the phallic image *in relation to the image that mirrors it*. For whether the setup of a dream approximates Hermes pursuing a nymph, Hades carrying off Persephone to the underworld, Paris choosing Aphrodite over Hera and Athena, or Eros intent on Psyche—the specific phallic image becomes immediately more sensible upon considering the anima image with which it is commensurate. Both play their mirroring role in the emotional and psychic situation of the moment. The polytheistic images of the phallus move across the broad earth and into psyche's extended realms. They are pertinent to erotic fantasy, to sexual style, to interpersonal affairs, but reflect finally the dynamic interaction of the intrapsychic elements within the personality itself. At the same time, the phallus may manifest in more essential images of centrality, again surpassing merely sexual meanings. Our mud-phallus-sun dream, for example, possesses a resounding creative and religious significance that has been celebrated in countless historical examples of solar rite. I recall one "minimalist" presentation of the solar hierophany's vertical axis in a dream that harkens immediately to the opening of the creation story of Genesis:

I see a whirlwind descending from the sky where it touches the surface of a vast body of water. The column of wind stirs the water with such force that the water forms a whirling bowl, which continues to round up and around until it forms a clear crystal vessel that contains the whirlwind inside itself. The two are one—the above, the below, and the surrounding.

Once again, psyche appears to be simply showing off how it is structured on an essential level. An entire cluster of intuitive, multiply referent associations rushes in here, all linked to the body, the psyche's play with symbolic analogues, creation mythology, and the structure of essential cosmic forms. The symmetry of the body in its upright posture is arranged around the spine and the world axis in every one of us regardless of gender. As we will see in especially full flower in the chakra system of Hindu tantra, this central axis is a special focus of psychic life and is essentially phallic. Any number of created phenomena—trees, mountains, towers, staffs, tornados, flagpoles, spiral stairways, etc.—mirror this archetypal image continually in a microcosmic-macrocosmic parallelism. It is thus interesting to note the universality of this structuring in the fact that free material bodies of ascending magnitude—planets, solar systems, galaxies, even massive black holes all revolve around a central axial vortex whose gravitational poles harmonize with those of the encircling spherical body. This essential organizing principle appears in the following dreams as it did in that with the mud-phallus-sun equation:

A strange phenomenon is now being tested: the spontaneous appearance of a geyser-like spout of water rising out of the sea in a straight thick column. Surging directly upward with great force to the height of a large crane or skyscraper, the column resembles a great phallus or pole. It comes to exert an irresistible magnetic attraction upon the surrounding islands, which begin to circle the phallic axis.

Coming from below, the watery phallic column is immediately reminiscent of the creation mythology of the Hindu god Vishnu, who churns the world into existence by stirring the cosmic milky ocean. This deed causes all things to be born, including the succession of Vishnu's avatars from primeval fish to tortoise to boar to lion to dwarf and on through Krishna's birth as the divine lover and the Buddha's incarnation, to Vishnu's final appearance as the apocalyptic Kalki. Mark well the appearance of the divinity on increasingly elevated phylogenetic levels in this arcing life trajectory. For in precisely the same way psychic phenomena, including the phallus, characteristically appear along an archetypal spectrum extending from archaic life through lower animal forms, to the human, then to the gods themselves. In lower extension we tend to refer to the archetype as instinct; in its higher extension, to archetype as spirit. Whether we see the Christian Virgin standing on the Serpent or a goddess such as Kali riding on a tiger, we are reminded of the intermediary position of human identity, as well as the uncertain boundaries of the soul. From the same patient who brought the mud-phallus-sun dream comes yet another variation on the phallic world axis:

In a heavy wooden wagon with no top on it. Rebecca is with me—glowing, charged with energy, white-skinned—an indescribably heavenly lover. We make love in every imaginable way in an experience of exceptional beauty. When we climax, however, I somehow see our semen dropping down upon the earth.

Then I witness the ritual installation of a large bearded wooden statue that is alive. This is an ancient god and prophet. He stands at the midpoint between my father's and my only paternal uncle's adjoining properties. The figure gazes knowingly, and transfixed in the earth, as slim red streamers float in the air all around this being.

Personal as this vignette may be, the dream does represent an interesting commentary on androgynous creator gods who nonetheless manifest as phallic. The ballast of that heavy wooden wagon notwithstanding, there is no top on it. The ecstatic sexuality might persuade one that the sky is the limit as the dreamer's phallic desire is answered by the anima with whom he merges. She is described as glowing, white-skinned, and heavenly. While clearly a creative *coniunctio* on this elevated level, the anima-animus syzygy projects its semen downward to the earth. Procreativity of soul follows its own course in broad analogies. For immediately following, and as if erected in response to the unnatural ejaculation, a provocative and emphatically grounded god-prophet is installed at a critical point on Earth. As in their actual life as neighbors, so in the dreamer's psyche, father and uncle personified sharply divergent aspects of the dreamer's own masculinity. The god-prophet accordingly stands directly at that point where the domains of the two older men meet, serving a conspicuous integrative function. He is alive, bearded, wooden, and his erect image is installed in the earth. The red streamers around him indicate an ambiance charged with conflict, passion of blood, while fluttering in the air are veritable banners of the spirit— everything that the god-prophet may assist the dreamer to withstand and embody. The very fact that the living statue is both god and prophet is suggestive again of the threshold between the divine and human. Furthermore, the dream image harkens back in decisive fashion to the most archaic image of the phallic masculine in Greek myth and cult, and sheds light on Jung's experience of the subterranean phallus at the same time.

While incorporated into many classic tales of the Olympian gods (Hesiod, Homer), the phallic deities—most particularly Hermes, Eros, and Dionysus—share common roots in the ancient pre-Olympian and non-heroic traditions of the Great Goddess. This is to say that the phallic gods are indeed more fundamental than patriarchy and serve first and foremost the Great Mother's precedence over the continuity of life. We have already encountered Hermes with three nymphs as his ever-present companions, Eros as both androgynous and as a phallic exponent of the Feminine, and Dionysus as womanish and ever in the company of his maenads. Here the accent falls on the male god with his female retinue. Going back in time, however, these specifically male gods resolve themselves into the phallus as the germinal masculine element essential to the Great Goddess. This is precisely the content and significance of the Goddess (Night) living in a cave with Phanes and "displaying herself in triad: Night, Order, and Justice," of Rhea "compelling man's attention to the oracles of the goddess" by pounding on a brazen drum—and of Night (Fate) as a goddess before whom even Zeus stands in awe.

For all the specificity of Hermes, Eros, or Dionysus, these phallic deities find common root in the archaic image of the herm. The herm was originally a bearded ithyphallic male image carved from fig or grape wood, placed near swamps, springs, fishponds, or elsewhere to indicate the whereabouts of a water source. Similarly the herm might be placed in garden or field as a token and invocation of fertility. This places Hermes in immediate proximity to a crucially important creativity source. In time the herm was refined, fashioned of stone, provided a square columnar base, and used across the landscape as a boundary marker. In contrast to phallic gods who appear in well-nigh perpetual pursuit of their goal, the herm as boundary marker represents an important counterpoint psychologically, as we have seen with our penis-phallus-spine-world axis equation.

Seen as a whole, the phallus, as sexual token, as stature and integrity, and as spirit, represents a comprehensive aspiration for the maturing adult male. Just as a man who is sexually alive, knows what he's about in the world, and is sensitive to the spirit begins actually to approximate what countless women are looking for, so a woman may bring her desire, her emotional integrity, and her imagination more readily and creatively to relationship and to her tasks in the world through the cultivation her own phallic endowment. With this, however, we must move on to explore the mysteries of the phallic herm and the Triple Goddess, for this ancient partnership represents not only a wellspring of sexuality, but a world of numinous experience that patriarchy has done all in its power to obscure.

The herm is most deeply associated with Hermes, the familiar figure of classical mythology who serves as a messenger for the gods, as psychopomp for the soul, and also as the patron of thieves, traders, and sexual opportunists (Fig. 3). By focusing on the herm, however, we concern ourselves with the more secret archaic identity of the god, an identity already formulated prior to the rise of the Olympians, the heroes, and that extroverted world in which Hermes plays so many outwardly directed roles. Kerényi compares Hermes and Eros in some detail, citing ancient sources "which show Hermes in the closest relation to the origins of life and to immortality."[37] The sexual gods and the Great Goddess are inseparable from the living and self-perpetuating world of Becoming. What eternity they possess is contingent on and situated within the given created world. Kerényi observes that:

Fig. 3: Hermes. The phallus both cycles in the biological round and stands erect as World Axis

> Despite the thievery and deceit and shamelessness—and this is probably the most wonderful thing about it—a divine innocence is properly suited to and inherent in it. Hermes has nothing to do with sin and atonement. What he brings with him from the springs of creation is precisely the "innocence of becoming."[38]

This must surely be among the more kindly expressions for a god who is neither moral nor immoral but a natural revelation. Eros is like unto him, with an even greater accent on innocence. It is Plato who cites Poros (poverty) as the father of Eros. Recognizing poverty as a basic existential condition and resourcefulness as a corresponding necessity, Kerényi speaks of Eros as "the Hermes-like God of adventurers." "In many ways he shares with him a Hermetic range of being."[39] Both Eros and Hermes possess spiritual, psychic, as well as phallic (penile) attributes—as does the deceptively simple image of the herm. These qualities tally with those of Hermes, and serve to explain his thievery, trickery, and quick exploitation of unexpected opportunities. Kerényi cites Eros on the one hand as a divine child whose cultic monument in one locale consists of "a crude stone, compared to which the phallic herms show much greater differentiation," but who is elsewhere praised in the loftiest terms of love. He also notes that even in Hesiod's *Theogony,* a document associated with the rise of the Olympians, Eros is paired with Gaia, figuring there as a procreative force of the first order. Though Gaia is only one form of the Great Goddess with whom he appears, this archaic Eros is now familiar. It is he who emerges from dark primeval Chaos as a world creator, and whose germinal nature we have explored in the more elaborate Orphic image of Phanes. Eros lives in a cave with the Goddess and yet he "comes soaring on his wings, if not literally so in Hesiod, just so accordingly to the primitive mythological account, in the Orphic cosmology." At the archaic earth-level of the herm, Eros and Hermes are deeply kindred. Both gods are puerile and phallic, swift in their movements, winged and expansive— but at the same time they are presented in the upright simplicity of the herm. While there is always something ruthless and completely free-ranging about Hermes, Eros differs in being more specifically drawn into the bonds and entanglement of relationships. Hermes quickly and characteristically eludes them. Each is the other's limitation or advantage. According to Plato, Eros "brings wonderful memory, the luminous understanding of the spirit, but not the cold calculating cleverness of Hermes."[40]

> Looked at from the world of Hermetic possibilities, Eros, despite his comprehensive nature, appears limited—a somewhat more idealistic and less cleverly turned-out, dumber son of Hermes.[41]

Dionysus is no less a god of the phallus, and no less archaic in his roots. He was honored with phallic processions in which Greek men wore his phallic token in exaggerated replicas, just as he was represented ritually by a herm-like circular column, cloaked and accoutered with the god's symbols, and surmounted by his mask. In many ways Dionysus, particularly when paired dynamically with Hades, presides over the whole realm in which not only Eros and Hermes, but Pan, the Satyrs, the Sileni, nymphs, maenads, ghosts, and elemental spirits have their life. Priapus too is congenial to him. Mythologically and ritually Hermes and Eros are congenial with Dionysus. Eros even figures specifically *as* Dionysus in the form of Phanes, as we have seen. In turn, the archetypal similarities between Eros (Phanes) and Hermes are pronounced indeed as they stretch historically forward through the Roman Mercury to the alchemical spirit Mercurius. It is, however, Hermes' trajectory backward in time that will deepen our understanding of both the phallus and the herm in relation to the Great Goddess.

A tantalizing first step in this direction is again provided by Kerényi:

> Hermes is expressly assigned to the Goddesses as their permanent escort (*synopaon*). On the reliefs he is always leading a threesome of them, the smallest choir so to speak, just as he was also coordinated with the three Charities on the Acropolis in Athens. As though he were unveiling a mystery, he leads the earnestly striding threesome up to us, to tell us that it is just these three who allow everything to burst into life in the deeps of the caves, the springs, the roots, the hills.[42]

Whereas the three nymphs appear as mere adjuncts to the male god Hermes late in this mythical trajectory, on this archaic level the situation is essentially reversed. It is clearly a threefold feminine nature that manifests the profusion of life with the aid of the phallic masculine. Behind the earnest play of the nymphs, so often associated with trees, springs, and grottos, stands the grand and formidable image of the Great Goddess as triune. Kerényi stresses the nonclassical and obscured identity of the Triple Goddess:

> The revelation of the Feminine as three distinct figures means only that the original core-knowledge of one Great Goddess with three aspects has been dissolved in classical imagery.[43]

It is precisely "more secret traditions" that shed light on the relationship of Hermes to the Goddess. Kerényi characterizes her triune nature: she consists of "a maidenly being, maidenly not like human brides but like springs and all primal waters, who became a primal mother and then re-appeared once more in her bride-like, maidenly daughter."[44] This parallels the Demeter-Persephone mythologem quite precisely—the Goddess, first as Kore frolicking with the Daughters of Ocean on a open plain; then as Demeter with her long-suffering concern for, and identity with, her daughter in the underworld; then as the re-emergent Kore-Persephone, who is reunited with Demeter in the unending cycle. Examples from alternate pre-Olympian genealogies in Greek myth bring provocative insights of the Hermetic phallus in this goddess context—the first of them being that Hermes was neither a son of Zeus nor part of the Olympian order. In one tale, Hermes is the son of ancient Ouranos and Hemera ("Heaven" and "Bright Day") and "becomes priapically aroused through catching sight of a Goddess." Kerényi affirms that "this mythologem could well be the text for the ithyphallic representation of Hermes, which shows him as the phallus."

> What it relates is a primordial mythological theme of the greatest significance: *it is the first evocation of the purely masculine principle through the feminine.*[45]

Then Kerényi poses a question that speaks directly to the ambiguity seen in Jung's declaration that eros is a feminine principle despite the historical appearance of Eros as androgynous or simply masculine: "Do we know for sure, then, that the primordial mythological Hermes ... was an unequivocally masculine being before this scene was enacted?"[46] The androgyny of Phanes and the archetypal divine child, the mixed gender of many dream images we have reviewed, and the androgyny inherent in Tangaroa and other creator gods rightly fill us with curious anticipation for Kerényi's response. His earlier remark that Hermes cut in two would reveal Eros chasing Psyche returns with the suspense. Kerényi holds that the *opposite* of "unequivocally masculine" is probably the case, and cites Hermes as the *brother* of Aphrodite through Ouranos and Hemera as evidence. Aphrodite shares her mother's lustrous qualities, and was generated by the severed phallus of Ouranos. To Aphrodite's light of day Hermes offers the complement of nocturnal and subterranean light. Another mythologem features Hermes and Aphrodite's *incestuous* production of a son, Hermaphroditos, an androgynous being. The figure appears also in the most ancient Cypriot cult of Aphrodite, the Goddess in her phallic aspect: Aphroditos.

Like Phanes, Hermes has little need of love affairs for the very fact that he contains the feminine aspect in himself. Kerényi states furthermore that this feminine aspect is probably "even the more prominent part before the masculine nature in him became aroused."[47] What goddess arouses this not-unequivocally-masculine phallus to his creative upswing? Night, who displays herself to Phanes in triple form, is not original or sufficiently defined. Who is the primal inspiratrix? Following the pre-Olympian sources Kerényi cites two—Persephone and Artemis—but also "a third, who united these two to form an original trinitarian image."[48] This third is archaic Brimo, a goddess of Northern Greece, praised aloud at culmination of the ritual cycle at Eleusis. "She could be equated with Demeter or Persephone on the one hand or with Artemis-Hecate on the other, since she contained all of these in germ-like form within her."[49] Note how this implosion of differentiated feminine forms into one Great Goddess leads to a vanishing point, an image threshold—a mystery reciprocal to "the honored seed of the gods" born by phallic (if androgynous) Phanes. Legend speaks of Brimo lying with Hermes along the sacred waters of a lake in Thrace:

> There she appears in that elementary sort of maidenliness which does not fear the masculine as something lethally dangerous, but rather challenges, requests, and creates it. Granted, this masculinity is a kind "that had no independent personality behind it but was a mere God-servant of the woman" .... Just as for Hermes the feminine is nothing more than an opportunity, so for the primal woman he was only an impersonal masculine, almost a toy. ... Hermes, the primal lover, is called forth (or brought forth) by the primal woman: he is her own masculine counterpart in the case of the primal Aphrodite, the phallic servant-God in the case of the primal Artemis. ... All these elements of the seminal situation are contained in the tradition: the Great Goddess, the living primal Herm, and as background something about the primal waters, which in mythological language is the arena of becoming.[50]

From the forms of the Great Goddess who arouse the phallus, Kerényi finally cites Hecate, goddess of witches, as rightfully "the most Hermetic" partner of Hermes. Both are winged and intimately acquainted with night and the underworld, both bring wealth to their devotees, both receive similar offerings at new moon, both are guides of the soul. Hecate is commemorated at forked roads by her Hecataia, roadside votive sites reminiscent of the Christian roadside shrines of modern Greece, but placed upon three-cornered pillars. The square-based herms specific to Hermes are a striking counterpoint to the Hecataia, prompting one to wonder if the fourfold herm might commemorate a phallus which, without the Triple Goddess, is most inconsequential. Given these associations, it comes as no surprise that Hecate and Hermes share a relationship with sexuality that is, to say the least, remote from anything sanctioned by any patriarchal sexual morality, be it Olympian or Christian. It has less to do with reproduction than it does with a communion with souls and spirits, with things nocturnal and underworldly. Kerényi speaks only of "a kind of eroticism that one may find crass and vulgar," which provides him a final opportunity to contrast Eros and Hermes:

> On the lofty level of the idealistic, ingenuous Eros, with his passion for self-sacrifice and for reaching out beyond his own life, the union of the phallus, soul, and spirit seems conceivable, but on this low, Hecatean level ...? We must recall that the Hermetic essence, seen in his most ancient representations, may *only to us* appear so low and vulgar, whereas there, where Hecate ruled the world of Northern Greece and Thrace in the form of "Aphrodite Zernythia," it is precisely the crassest that is the holiest and most spiritual.[51]

This penetration to the archaic origins of the herm, and the chthonic dimension of sexuality and religious imagination represented here, anticipates the exploration of Tantric sexual-religious ritual forthcoming in Chapter 6.

Altogether appropriate to the syzygy of Hecate and Hermes, given their nocturnal paths and shared identity as guides, the following dream comes from a married man in his late twenties, who was desperately curious about erotic paths unavailable to him at the time:

*I am being taken on a wild Saturday night adventure through the Niederdorf
[Zürich's red-light district] by a fleeting little figure. He holds my hand as
he leads me in and out of bars and alleyways—scampering here and there.
Finally the little fellow stops and turns toward me. I am shocked to see that
his face is a vulva with bushy eyebrows instead of pubic hair.*

The dreamer's first association to the dream was a childhood
recollection of the American comedian Groucho Marx, with a big cigar
stuck in his mouth, wiggling his bushy eyebrows up and down in a
leering fashion. For all the seriousness of soul-work, we must not forget
that sexuality carries with it humorous, bawdy, burlesque, naked, and
obscene aspects. Hermes is right there with all this—quick, startling,
canny to all the ins and outs of his realm of half-light. Hermes is
shadow, trickster, and guide all at once: perplexing for being ruthless
and cruel in one moment and a gracious gift-giver in another, for being
overtly phallic here and of strangely anomalous gender or of novel
zoomorphic form there—or again, for crawling all the way down the
phylogenetic scale to appear as a star-nosed mole with tiny phalli
around his snout, as a segmented sea cucumber with women's sinuous
hips and multiple breasts, a black serpent with a bearded face, a skeleton
with phalli protruding from its vertebrae, or a saltwater bivalve with
tiny mirrors inside that reflect the sun and moon. All these are natural
revelations that arise at a threshold where our creaturely fabric and
the psyche mysteriously coincide—the psychoid edge of experience
where our deepest perceptions of the creation are rooted. Hermes
accordingly ushers in the experience of liminality wherein collectively
sanctioned notions of order and status are upended—for consciousness'
sake or merely to remind one what it means to be a human being on
an essential level. Culture and moralism may represent many defenses
against nature and life, while Hermes is connected with the whole of
nature while remaining phallus, soul, and spirit. A preeminent natural
symbol, we see in Hermes the *lumen naturae* ("light of nature"). While
not without his relation to salvation "by grace," Hermes (as Mercurius)
is a prime agent of the medieval notion of salvation "by nature." The
dichotomy represents two sides of a deeper whole. Jung observes of
this above and below:

> Worth noting is the duality of soul caused by the presence of
> Mercurius: on the one hand the immortal *anima rationalis* given

by God to man, which distinguishes him from animals; on the other hand the mercurial life-soul, which to all appearances is connected to the *inflatio* or *inspiratio* of the Holy Spirit. This fundamental duality forms the psychological basis of the two sources of illumination.[52]

Mercurius (like Hermes) is the very ligament, the living networker who binds this upper and lower together, a spirit of untamed nature— the *anima media natura,* from whom a full identification with the *anima mundi* is a mere nuance away (Fig. 4, next page). This protean masculine being shifts suddenly into equally expansive feminine and anima identifications, such as we have seen with the soul-vessel mentioned before, and to which we will return in our discussion of Magdalen and Sophia. Mercurius (like Hermes) is closely aligned with the mother-son incest matrix and represents the continuous cohabitation of gendered opposites, anima and animus as syzygy. The ambiguous partnership appears similarly in an alchemical image of Alexandrian origin where "Aphrodite appears with a vessel from the mouth of which she pours a ceaseless stream of quicksilver."[53] "Mercurius truly consists of the most extreme opposites; on one hand, he is undoubtedly akin to the godhead; on the other. he is found in sewers. Rosinus (Zosimos) even calls him the *terminus ani.*"[54] Jung readily associates Mercurius and Hermes as kindred luminous gods of revelation, light bringers comparable to the Christian Lucifer, the Roman Diana Lucifera, or Goethe's Mephistopheles, "the spirit which ever worketh evil but engenders good." Jung observes, "Although the *lumen naturae,* as originally bestowed by God upon his creatures, is not by nature ungodly, its essence was nevertheless thought to be abysmal, since the *ignis mercurialis* was also connected with the fires of hell."[55] Mercurius (like Hermes) is not outside of God, just as he is not outside of nature:

> Mercurius, the revelatory light of nature, is also hell-fire, which in some miraculous way is none other than a rearrangement of the heavenly, spiritual powers in the lower, chthonic world of matter, thought already in St. Paul's time to be ruled by the devil. Hell-fire, the true energic principle of evil, appears here as the manifest counterpart of the spiritual and good, and as essentially identical with it in substance.[56]

Jung's childhood vision of the subterranean phallus, with its single eye gazing upward and an aura of light surrounding it, falls precisely in line with these reflections on the revelatory light, the *illuminatio* that may emerge from the *psychosoma* and the chthonic world.

Fig. 4: Mercurius, at once the crown of consciousness and the depth of our bodily fabric

The imagery of the following dream appears at the ground level of the natural world and comes to focus on an image that harbors profuse life like a pomegranate bursting with seeds:

Tunneling under the ground like a gopher I see a variety of animals as I repeatedly surface to look out here and there. I see a black vulture. Then I emerge to find a primitive swamp plant, a kind of spotted fig or strange vagina with arms extending from it. I try to open it, but it implodes reflexively like a sea anemone. Then I cut it in half. It is filled with all manner of colorful living organisms wriggling all about. Poised precisely at ground level beside this pod, I take a picture of the night sky, with the Big Dipper and Milky Way visible in it.

Tunneling like a gopher is a phallic movement of consciousness that corresponds to viewing the world from beneath the surface. The vulture is an image of the Goddess as spirit—her dark chthonic aspect so akin to winged Hecate, Kali, Black Isis, or the Fates. One is impressed by the perception of such cosmic images as the Big Dipper and the Milky Way (world parents) that are possible from this lower perspective. The swampy setting is precisely that in which herms were erected in antiquity, close to the very source of life and pointing above and below. The strange vagina with appendages extending from it carries the psyche's bisexual imagery on a primal level indeed. What appears when it is cut in two bears immediate *pars pro toto* reference to the upper and lower hemispheres of the psyche that frame the entire dream experience. The colorful wriggling organisms likewise mirror the stars of the surrounding soul-vessel even as they retain a germinal and phallic significance.

Akin to the single herm of ancient Greek is the imagery of the Dactyls, who also appear on a primal level as multiple phalli. Originally formed from the fingertips (*daktylos*, "finger") of the Goddess as she leans back on both arms with fingers clenching the soil, they assist with her labor as a group of three or ten or more. In all the stories of the Dactyls they remain servants of the Great Goddess. They represent the most fundamental movement of the creative masculine within a pervasively feminine matrix, appearing as fingers, phalli with feet, tiny hooded men, or as miners and smiths. A patient once brought a dream in which he was given a mysterious brass box filled with countless fingers, all independently alive and wriggling around and through one another like a swarm of caterpillars. Diminutive in size, the dactyls nevertheless embody all-embracing forces. The closely related Kabeiroi of Samothrace in the northeastern Aegean are similarly described and are also herm-like. In the ancient mysteries of the island, they represent nothing less than Demeter, Persephone, Hades, and Hermes themselves.

Turning to the dream of a passionate and intelligent thirty-five-year-old graduate student, we find a woman whose psyche is clearly working the feminine side of the anima-animus equation as she gains a perception of her essential feminine self:

I am standing in a bathtub about to take a shower. A retarded man comes walking into the bathroom and wants to look at me. I notice then that a large powerful woman stands in the tub with me. I tell the guy to get out! Then I turn toward the woman, but where she stood a large oval mirror now stands. I gather myself together and hunch down so as to be fully reflected in the mirror. Enchanted by my reflection, I see myself in essence—as a lean, beautiful, almost glowing nymph. Then I spread my vagina to the mirror and I can see way into myself—then deeper still into what becomes a vast chamber. There is something really ancient about it.

The deflection of the retarded man who intrudes is related to the sexual abuse she suffered at the hands of an abusive alcoholic father. In the wake of such experience the reclamation of one's body and sexuality as one's own is an essential initiative. The large powerful woman who appears in the tub is of obvious importance in mirroring the dream's real substance. The archetypal "body-mother" of the dream is reparative of an inattentive and passive mother experience, just as there were moments when affirmation would issue from the older masculine. A dream emerged in which this woman, an accomplished swimmer, stood at the end of a diving board wearing only a swimsuit and a pair of downward pointing triangular gold earrings. The downward-pointing triangle, a classic symbol of the Great Goddess, is a creation of the dream. At poolside a beloved old coach just stands there beholding the dreamer with the greatest admiration and not a hint of lust or manipulation.

Just as forms of the phallus are all aspects of the archetypal masculine, so nymphs are untamed personifications of the Great Goddess, who may inhabit a grotto, a tree, a spring, etc. The perception of oneself specifically as a nymph may or may not be a perception of one's sexual self. But it definitely does underscore the greater feminine identity to which the dreamer is heir—seeing herself in essence, vital, glowing, and beautifully mirrored. Her vagina is the vagina of the Great Goddess, a reflection of her physical integrity, sexual pride, and expanding psychic interiority. The vast ancient chamber she beholds rightly gives rise to any number of associations, from the cave or grotto, to the initiation chambers of any number of religious traditions, to the encircling star-strewn sphere of the heavens. The cave is always a model of the cosmos itself, and the dreamer carries all this in her own being.

Such reflections on the body and being of a woman are even more elaborately displayed in the following dream of a woman in her mid-twenties. She is the dreamer who cries "Aphrodite!" upon being assailed by a wild shape-shifting spirit with whom she flies through the air. This dream is striking for its reflection of the body image as a whole, and appropriate in that female sexuality is less genitally focused, less overt in its appearance in dreams, and more intimately related to the realm of emotion than is typically the case with men. Contrasting but complementary images of the anima and animus appear in the dream, as well as an original chakra system descending to a Dark Mother deep in the body (Fig. 5). At its outset the dream-ego, a white man, and a black couple are all together. It is the black couple at the dreamer's left who preside over the dream's initiatory aspect:

Fig. 5: Female patient's chakra system

I am in a space capsule, a time capsule, with a white man and a black couple. The white man has his head covered so that gas comes and puts him to sleep. The black couple sits to my left, one on either side of the door. We begin to go very fast. I have a pain in my chest, have trouble breathing, but am nevertheless focused on a book. In it is a woman's body on which geometric symbols are inscribed. In descending order they are: circle, oval, six-pointed star, triangle, crescent (right below the navel with ends pointing up), and a series of three figures seated on square or rectangular blocks lined up horizontally. Each symbol corresponds to a chakra, a letter, and to a part of my body. My task to complete before we arrive is to determine how they all relate.

As we go further back in time I descend to the next lower symbol. The lunar crescent corresponds to the letter U and I thought it was meant to correspond to my urethra. I struggled with the final symbol because there were three to choose from. I thought it was meant to match with the letter V which seemed to correspond to my vulva. Knowing I was running out of time, I choose the figure on the far left because her arm was bent in the shape of a V. She was an Egyptian woman sitting on a cube of stone and holding a skull in one hand while gesturing upward with the other. We were stopping now— I had picked the woman instinctively and would figure out why later on. Looking up from the book I could see the blue sky moving very slowly. As we slow, I realize I had not breathed for a time. We reintegrate with time.

Getting up with the others, I become aware of the black man. He stands near the door with the black woman. I see he has a white crescent moon on his forehead. He is very beautiful, naked to the waist. The woman wonders if we have traveled back to a place and a time where people don't wear clothes. Out of the window I see a group of people crossing a wooden bridge in black robes. It is early spring, chilly but with green grass and full trees. I know the people are witches or pagans and I want to be with them. I realize then we have arrived in England or New England in the time of the witch burnings. I sadly realize the I cannot go with them because we have returned to this time to be nuns, their foe, their opposites.

After staging a play with various characters:

A black woman comes down some stairs holding a package tied in a bundle. She hurries towards a door, but I trip her. If she gets out the door with the package the play must run its course to its predicted end. But if I can stop her at this point there is a chance of changing the end of the play. I think I succeed in stopping her.

The white man's asphyxiation at the outset of the dream indicates his diminishing influence on the dreamer's consciousness as she descends into her inner psychosomatic world with its ambiguous time-space. One may question the degree to which she falls prey to erratic inclinations precisely because he sleeps. But the dreamer does remain lucid and deliberative throughout the initiatory process itself. The black couple accompanies her throughout. One could find no better example of a psychic movement downward as a simultaneous movement backward in time. Movement by way of a time capsule together with the absence of breath has a perinatal ring to it. But the entire dream is patterned as a process of rebirth with its ordering of the dreamer's constituent somatic and psychic parts. We tend to underestimate the degree to which we exist in a state of dissociation simply for having a brain, a heart, and genitals, each with their claim and influence upon the personality. Recall that the dreamer is still recovering from the influence of a psychopathic former lover, in addition to cocaine.

While the descending symbols bear a conspicuous similarity to the chakra diagrams of India, and while each specific symbol might be discussed at length, the dream is an individual creation. I have asked two Jungians noted for their expertise in body work, Marion Woodman and Arnold Mindell, the same pertinent question: "How specifically do you correlate emergent individuals' images in body-work with those of the Eastern chakra systems?" Both place greater emphasis on individual experience of the kind encountered here. The question is pertinent to the dreamer in that her review of the symbolic diagram has the feel of a prospectus—guiding, yes, but also anticipatory of future experiences where the full affective power of these symbols will surely be upon her. A feminine downward-pointing triangle and then a lunar crescent appear just beneath the navel and in association with the urethra. It is scarcely an accident that the beautiful black man of the dream appears with a lunar crescent on his forehead. It marks him as a chthonic masculine counterpart to the dreamer's anesthetized White male companion. The moon is his third eye, the night vision he brings. The black lunar man can see Dionysus from within his realm; his lunar mind is commensurate with the zones of belly, urethra, and vulva—all under the aegis of the moon, classic images of not only the Great Mother but of Dionysus and the Hindu Shiva. He is intimately a part of the instincts and emotions, processes and cycles of these lower spheres of the body. A vase in the Berlin Antiques Museum shows one of the maenads of Dionysus casually urinating into a bowl. Not only is Dionysus archetypally related to all the body's natural fluids, the urethra knows nothing of culture or persona but expresses undeniable spontaneity, an undeniable truth related to self assertion and the creative flow.

Given the proximity of urethra and clitoris ("key"), an even broader range of implications is drawn in. The dreamer's lowest chakra, with its three cubes of stone and the Egyptian woman with the skull demonstratively holding her arm in a V, capture the special attention of the dreamer. She is directed back toward the surface, as it were. As the culminating symbol of the sequence, and given its cubical and human forms, this is none too surprising—of all the symbols these alone are three-dimensional solids. The skull held by the Egyptian woman is the hallmark of the descent's fulfillment, just as her pointing upward indicates that psyche's lower boundary has for now been met, and with it the necessity for a return to the surface world. To the degree the dreamer gains insight into how all the body's physiologic and psychic centers relate to one another, the reclamation of her bodily integrity and sense of self will be enhanced.

In the Indian system, the lowest chakra, *Muladhara*, pertains to fundamental issues of survival; it is also the birth point of the Kundalini energy, which animates the entire body. The appearance of the skull at this low level is a veritable mirror image of the cranium and accordingly locates the entire sphere of the dream's reflections within the microcosm of the dreamer's own body. Clearly the skull is an image of Fate, but as in alchemy, it is also an image of the *rotundum,* the vessel in which consciousness ultimately comes to refinement. In this regard consider the brief dream of an individual far advanced in his psychological work:

I am standing beside a white bridge at the edge of a river on a brilliant day. Sun-bleached skeletons lie below me on the bank as I suddenly hold a perfectly spherical pitcher of crystal. Within it, held tightly symmetrical, I see my own skull in every detail.

Whatever the strength of the dreamer's daily consciousness, the intuitive insight that may spring from the contemplation of the Egyptian woman's skull must be incorporated into her awareness and self-concept. The frequency with which the skull and the vessel appear in portraits of the Catholic Mary Magdalene is noteworthy here. For she embodies the split between virgin nun and sex witch more than any other Christian saint. Here that appealing V-shaped gesture on the part of the woman is articulate. Reminiscent of the logo of Arm and Hammer baking soda, *Mother Jones* magazine, or any number of socialist or labor organizations, it is an essential image of tensile strength, flexibility, and determination.

Finally, an association of the skull to the Triple Goddess of Fate is in order, particularly given her appearance with the threefold solids and the presence of one black lunar representative of the masculine. The descending bodily centers may also be compared with the progressive stripping off of colored gowns from the body of Inanna during her descent to dark Ereshkigal as described by Perera. Inanna is hung helpless on a stake to rot while the cold-eyed chthonic mother stares unflinching at her beautiful catchling from the upper world. But the personal context of the dream is milder and reflects more youthful issues. For all the specificity we find in her chakra system, and for all the dream's focus on women historically split between the meager option of Christian virginity or heretical witchery, we find a puzzling compulsion repetition in the imagery of the recurrent drama. The vulnerability of the anesthetized White man, the archetypal split between virgin and whore, and unresolved mother issues all have something to do with the dreamer's necessity to trip the Black woman with the bundle. One assumes it may be a child, but we are left without any certainty beyond the fact that it is the feminine partner of our chthonic black syzygy that holds the secret.

This picaresque of dreams has traced many an exemplary form and tandem movement of the anima and the animus in the endless dance we call the syzygy. The dynamics of psychic bisexuality exist *in potentia* in the image of the divine child, and come joyfully and painfully into their own through the contingencies of attachment and separation, love and loss. Primary attention has been given to the inner workings of the syzygy. We've considered how consciousness emerges from an androgynous and psychosomatic matrix; how such imagery appears through the influence of such untamed sons of the Great Goddess as Eros, Hermes (Mercurius), and Dionysus; and how this partnership points to future developments of the kind we will explore in our final two chapters. The appearance of the syzygy at any given moment in adulthood is vividly suggested by a final pair of dreams, one decidedly retrograde and the other anticipatory. The first arose in a thirty-five-year-old male partner following the final agonizing breakup of a tumultuous, madly romantic, but ultimately impossible love relationship:

In a dark chamber in a mood of deep intimacy, I am part of what I see and not part of it. In a candlelit space I see myself all wrapped up with Sarah in a tight ball, like when my wife and I used to curl up together to see how little space we could take up. Not sure if it is really Sarah or someone else. I see the two curled up in a kind of ceremonial fashion. The pair are wrapped in a blue silk shawl. The only sounds are the sleepy curling sounds of a fetus in utero.

Prominent is the dream's reflection of symbiotic merger with the former lover so profound as to echo the sounds of a child in the womb. One thinks of the old Egyptian imagery of Isis and Osiris clinging to one another incestuously in their mother's womb. The details—"I am part of what I see and not part of it" and "not sure if it is really Sarah"— already display psyche's efforts to dissolve the projected image of the beloved for the sake of restoring much-needed equilibrium to the personality. The childlike pair as well as the image of the beloved must be embraced in solitude, as contents of the dreamer's own soul. By the time we speak of "what I've learned" from a relationship this process is already at work. Months later, as this dreamer's solitary and initiatory grief slowly gives over to hope springing eternal, this final dream of our series arose:

I am alone in a closed chamber with a lovely woman who I feel I know. She wears a pale blue gown and stands looking into my eyes. I am aware that this is our bridal chamber, also a prison—the stage where everything must take place.

One must rise by that by which one falls.

—Tantric dictum

CHAPTER SIX

Sacred Sexuality in Hindu Tantra

The shivling, a ritual object familiar in popular Hinduism, derives its form and meaning from a legend in which the sages curse Shiva for what they feel to be perverse behavior contrary to the Scriptures (Fig. 1, next page). As a result, Shiva's phallus falls to the ground:

> The phallus burned everything before it; wherever it went, all was consumed. It traveled through the under-world, in heaven and on the earth, never staying in one place. All the worlds and their inhabitants lived in anguish. The sages were struck with dismay.[1]

Failing to recognize this messenger of Heaven as none other than "Shiva of the marvelous forms," the sages turn to the god Brahma for help. Chiding them for their ignorance, Brahma instructs them:

> As long as this phallus is not in a fixed position, no good can come to any of the three worlds. In order to calm its wrath, you must sprinkle the divine sexual organ with holy water, build a pedestal in the form of a vagina and shaft (symbol of the goddess), and install it with prayers, offerings, prostrations, hymns and chants accompanied by musical instruments. Then you shall invoke the god, saying, "You are the source of the universe, the origin of the universe. You are present in everything that exists. The universe is but a form of yourself. O Benevolent One! Calm yourself and protect the world."[2]

Rightly approached in this ritual fashion, Shiva himself declares: "No other being except the Lady of the Mountain may seize hold of my sexual organ. If she takes hold of it, it will immediately become calm."[3] Brahma's instructions are heeded and the god's wildness is assuaged. In a variation on this account the sages dig a yoni-shaped

Fig. 1: Shivling with female worshipper offering flowers to the source-point of Life and Spirit

trench in the earth in which Shiva comes to rest. Ever after an interlocking image of the *lingam* of Shiva and the *yoni* of Parvati, the shivling stands at the transept of Shiva temples (the location of the altar in European cathedrals) and at the center of ritual devotions to Shiva and his consort. Known as "The Lady of the Mountains," Parvati's identity and nature closely follow her role as the wife of Shiva. Like the *yoni* of the legend, Parvati works to draw Shiva into demands of marriage and thus into a broader worldly life, far from the solitude of the mountains. She stands in opposition to the world-denying aspects of Hindu tradition, mitigating the extremes of both Shiva's asceticism and his mania and ecstatic madness. She is cool, moist, watery—a wife, partner, and master student reminiscent of Hera and Aphrodite.

The most powerful divine symbols are always those in which the greatest range of opposites are compacted. Shiva, in his unbounded phallic and fiery appearance, is called Rudra, who lives with the animals in forests and jungles. Yet Shiva is known also as Mahayogi, the great ascetic, who sits in timeless meditation atop the world-mountain, Mount Kailash. Reminiscent of the array of contrasting qualities borne internally by such composite Western figures as Phanes or Mercurius, Sophia or Isis, this "Shiva of the marvelous forms" combines any number of attributes in one mythic identity with myriad powers. Hymns as self-contradictory and resonant as the Gnostics' "The Thunder, Perfect Mind" are raised to him. The ritual shivling itself is the precise image of the spiritual axis that is one with life in each moment, in whatever space—an intersection (+) comparable to that of *zoe* (life) and *phos* (light) aforementioned on whatever scale or dimension it be conceived. The source of all creativity lies at the dynamic core of its vortex.

This core is a monad, a seed point, a drop of Shiva's golden semen represented, as it may be, by a *bindu* on one's forehead, the dot at the center of the downward-pointing triangular Kali *yantra*, or any chakra center's infinitesimal passage off into the implicate order. With reciprocal accent on the feminine, the actual fashioner of living forms, the turning of one's gaze inward is tantamount to looking back through a birth canal cosmic in its scope. The many yantras of Tantric tradition are cosmograms that mirror the psyche's inner dynamism in resonant interlocking geometries, emerging and expanding before an in-turned third eye. Comparable to the *oculus imaginationis* of Western hermetism, this is the ocular apparatus that beholds not only the inner space of soul and world, but the very wellspring of both creation mythology and individuation. Impenetrable by the intellect alone, the gnosis to which such meditations lead one can only be ascertained imaginally and experientially. The Tantric practitioner pursues this insight through a process of sustained and highly elaborate *transpersonal* enteroception, where the given body reveals itself as a microcosm, as a hologram of universal energies and structures, itself a single cell in the cosmic body.

Curious in light of the overt phallic escapades of Shiva, the vagina *and* the "shaft" are called symbols of the *goddess*, though discrete gender designations grow tenuous within this vortex. Tree and world-axis symbolism display a similar shifting back and forth between masculine and feminine identifications. On the masculine side of the equation, Rudra represents Shiva's primordial identity as a wild archer and hunter, as well as the phallus frenzied to the point of imminent threat. The qualities of this male god are generally germane to the lower dimension of Eliade's solar hierophany, while Shiva as Mahayogi may be envisioned more in terms of its axial upper extension. One source spotlights the former quite vividly:

> The Purana legends portray Shiva as a libidinous adolescent, roaming naked in the forest, charming the wives of the proud ascetics, who wish to conjure heaven by their own will power. Shiva humiliates the ascetics, seduces their wives and, scattering his own seed here and there, makes precious stones and holy places appear on earth.[4]

Shiva's kinship with his Western brother, Dionysus, appears in full flower in this unvarnished picture of enchantment and seduction. The phallus moves wildly abroad through the expanse of the three worlds, while simultaneously "the god's sexual organ becomes an immense pillar which transpierces and fills all three worlds."[5] Thus two general aspects of the phallus are indicated: one related to diverse and far-ranging phallic action in and upon the world (like the multiple phallic gods of Greek polytheism), the other, the phallus as herm, fixed upright—a boundary marker, an axis related to both spine and world. Primal wildness and a superordinate ordering principle are thus one in the phallus of Shiva, and both are essential to creation. These are related to the feminine in their respective ways. As we have seen, Parvati, the magnificent wife of Shiva, often appears with him in domestic scenes. Earthquakes are caused by their lovemaking, just as they may argue over the fairness of a game of chess. The image of Parvati, however, darkens and expands as she assumes her identity as the Black Goddess, Kali. The contrast between these personae is similar to that of Inanna and dark Ereshkigal in the Sumerian mythology. In Tantra, however, it is finally Shakti who represents the sublime beauty and power of every feminine aspect as Shiva's partner in ritual.

These gods and goddesses, the ritual practices that honor them, and the history and goals of Hindu Tantra provide a provocative counterpoint to sex and religion in Western traditions, as well as exceptionally beautiful examples of how the world's most developed erotic mysticism celebrates the divine syzygy. Articulating his own modest hope for a broader influence of Tantra in the modern world, historian Arnold Toynbee observes:

> The present adherents of the Judaic monotheistic religions and of [their] post-Christian substitutes ... are, all of them, ex-pantheists. This historical fact suggests that there might be some hope of their reverting to the pantheistic attitude, now that they have become aware of the badness of the consequences of the monotheistic lack of respect for nature.[6]

The roots of Tantra go back to the ancient Indus River civilizations (ca. 3800-1800 B.C.E.) of Mohenjo-Daro and Harappa, the urban centers of a pervasive goddess culture. Horned, ithyphallic, and often portrayed in meditative posture, the male consort and yogi devoted to the goddess anticipates Shiva, just as he parallels the shamanic Horned God of Old Europe and calls Dionysus once more to mind. The ancient traditions of the Indus region lead to the Dravidian culture of India. It existed for a thousand years prior to the arrival of the Aryans of Iran in about 1500 B.C.E., which is to say, before the philosophical literature of the Vedas, before the advent of major dualistic religious orientations, before ascetic traditions, before the caste system, and before Vishnu, Brahma, and Shiva came to form the familiar male triad of popular Hinduism. The Dravidians were animistic and polytheistic in orientation, embedded in the arable but tropical ecology of South and Central India. Some were jungle people; all were intimately at home in the plant and animal world around them. Contrasting sharply with Aryan spiritualists, who were steeped in the Vedas and considered the world to be merely a part of the "web of *Maya*" and thus illusory, the Dravidian was not a philosophically abstracting culture but a mythological and ritual one. The Dravidians were little inclined to dismiss the created world as ephemeral because, for them and Tantric seekers ever since, the created world is fully real— a living manifestation of Sri Devi, the Great Goddess. Goddess religions have little difficulty with matter. They fully validate the body and its instincts (be this hunger, sex, or aggression) as religiously significant. Accordingly, and in contrast to the wispy *Maya* doctrine of the spiritualists, Tantra recognizes the world's reality in the forms and powers of Shakti.

From a Jungian perspective, the distinction between *Maya* and Shakti corresponds to the difference between an abstract *conception* of the anima as mere fantasy activity and the *experience* of the anima as an immediate, palpable, and fateful reality possessing material, psychic, and also spiritual aspects. The famous erotic temple complex of Khajuraho and the scattered circular Yogini temples (stretching from Delhi to Bhubaneshwar), with their sinuous intermingling of plants, animals, humans, and gods, all harken back to old Dravidian values. A highly secretive religious complex, Tantra has its major centers today in Orissa, Bengal, and Bihar. While the Tantrists are actually less at home in temple complexes than in the secrecy of the forest, a private home, or the boneyard, the roots of their purview reach back to the Dravidians and their deep kinship with the natural world. The contemporary *ecological* importance of any religious system sensitive to sexuality, the body, and nature cannot be underestimated, for this represents the primary life-and-death challenge for every human being alive on the planet today:

> The modern conception of ecology may appear as an attempt to return to a true ethic. … It is not only a question of preserving nature for the service of mankind, but rather of rediscovering man's role in nature, as a co-operator in the work of the gods. *A religion which does not respect the indissoluble oneness of creation, and which is not fundamentally ecological, is nothing but a fraud.*[7]

The contrast between the transcendentalism of the Aryan outlook and the earth-connectedness of the Dravidian-Tantric trajectory represents a polarity world-class in its scope, a ubiquitous archetypal setup whose tendency to split apart has decisively touched this entire inquiry. The same Ayran transcendental inclinations, after all, stand behind the patriarchal developments of Olympian Greece. The contrast is vividly reflected by this anecdote from the *Gospel* of the famous Bengali devotee of Kali, Sri Ramakrishna (1836-1886), who dwelt in her ritual center, Dakshineswar, along the Ganges near Calcutta. He is a young man exploring the insights and methods of various gurus. One especially lofty Vedic teacher says to Ramakrishna, "Brahma ... is the only Reality, ever pure, ever illumined, ever free, beyond the limits of time, space, and causation."[8] With more than a touch of ascetic pride, he adds: "That knowledge is shallow by which one sees or hears or knows another."[9] In response, Ramakrishna, though already enchanted by Kali, is sent off puzzling about this "Absolute." The text continues: "Totapuri asked him to withdraw his mind from all objects of the relative world, including the gods and goddesses, and to concentrate on the Absolute." But the task was not easy, even for Ramakrishna. He finds it impossible to take his mind beyond Kali, the Divine Mother of the Universe. The saint speaks in the first person after grappling with the pursuit of Atman (Brahma):

> But in spite of all my attempts I could not altogether cross the realm of name and form and bring my mind to the unconditioned state. I had no difficulty in taking my mind from the objects of the world. But the radiant and too familiar figure of the Blissful Mother, the Embodiment of the essence of Pure Consciousness, appeared before me as a living reality. Her bewitching smile prevented me from passing into the Great Beyond. Again and again I tried, but She stood in my way every time.[10]

In this scene Ramakrishna stands at an essential threshold—that between what Hindu metaphysics distinguishes as *Prakrti*, or Nature in its broadest sense, and *Purusha*, the spiritual Self. *Prakrti* denotes the existence and dynamism of matter and Nature, of all things gendered, procreative, and becoming—the Goddess by whatever name she may be called. This embraces life, the human body, the psyche (or soul), and all phenomenal manifestations extending to the most subtle images accessible to human consciousness. Shakti, often termed *Kali-Shakti*, refers to the immediate effective power of the Feminine in Creation, a specific morphogenetic and evolutionary energy that gives rise to the totality of nature's created forms. This parallels the medieval notion of the light of nature (*lumen naturae*) in European nature philosophy, with an accent on the sublunary, embodied, feminine, and chthonic dimension of spirit. Jung often states that beyond such experiential realities as these only metaphysical assertions can be made. It is, however, a distinguishing feature of Hindu metaphysics that Vedic seekers focused on *Purusha* (*Brahma*) confidently claim the liberty to speak of a transcendent consciousness, a consciousness of Consciousness alone. This implies again a particular vanishing point or channel to the nonmanifest—transcendent spirit and self with a capital S.

Paul's tenet that "what the flesh desires is opposed to the Spirit, and what the Spirit desires is opposed to the flesh" might be considered against this expansive backdrop—the tension of opposites in the Piscean Era of Western astrology as well. But Tantra ignores this classic rift, largely due to the sheer absence of intellectual abstraction in its worldview. This renders such external discursive designations as "aerial" and "chthonic" completely academic, for spirit, consciousness, and light finally represent a unified field phenomenon—though, crucially, one accessed through meticulous attention to the vital, sexual, and religious energies of the *psychosoma*. An immediate parallel to the sparkling *scintillae* of Western alchemy, this symbolism is beautifully reflected in the Mahalinga Mandala, which features in profile a fleshly red shivling in which scores of tiny shivlings appear as an orderly grid of dispersed luminosities (Fig. 2). The body (as microcosm) and sexuality (as ritual medium) are thus central to deep religious experience in the tradition of Hindu Tantra. Archetypal images of sexuality and the gods are rarely so striking as in Tantric temples, paintings, and ritual arts.

No more thrilling an introduction to the sensual and sacred ambiance of the Tantric ritual tradition could be desired than approaching and entering a Yogini temple for the first time. These ceremonial sites were erected between the 9th and the 12th centuries C.E., and represent the most elaborate fixed structures in the history of the traditionally reclusive Tantric cult. Remote circular stone structures, open to the sky in order to mirror it, with niches filled with marvelous sculpted forms of Sri Devi (Great Goddess) around their exterior, an even more enchanting vision meets one's eye in the interior. As if the light of the Goddess were refracted through a prism, sixty-

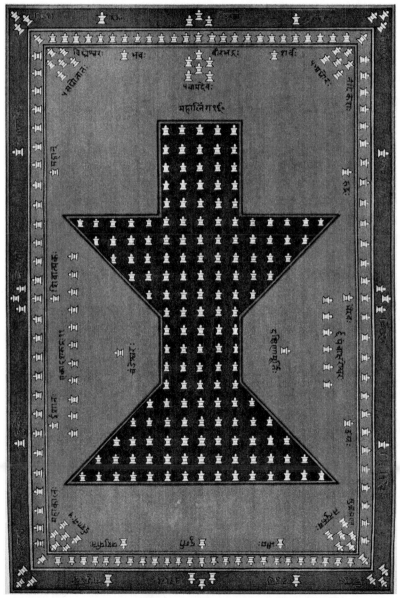

Fig. 2: Shivling mandala opening to reveal a holographic field of germinal luminosities

four or eighty-one enshrined feminine forms meet the eye all around—
these are the yoginis, personifications of the Goddess in her myriad
forms. There are nubile girls dancing as they hold animals aloft; full-
breasted young women beating drums; matronly forms with the head
of a cow, a rabbit, a cobra, or a monster; and aged yoginis whose sunken
breasts are barely distinguishable from their emaciated ribcages. The
yoginis stand in sinuous posture, graced by elaborate pectorals, exotic
headgear and heavy earrings, and wearing jeweled girdles around their
broad hips. The impression of a superabundance of life and the sacred
nature of that life is overwhelming.

Portrayals of Devi in the manuscripts of the medieval *Kaula* school
of Tantra that built these ritual precincts commonly display the
Goddess in a dress with sixty-four of her attributes written upon it.
Then again, a full mandala may appear womb-like upon her belly,
with a specific yogini outlined in each niche of its ambit. In one
example (Fig. 3), the Goddess appears as Durga with a host of weapons
and ritual accoutrements indicative of her exploitation of masculine
energies in her creation and protection of life.

The yoginis of Tantric tradition are each a personification of
Shakti—some individual personifications of the Goddess, others her
attendants and devotees, but all prototypical of Tantric women.
Historical documents display little consistency in regard to their
names. Generally "yogini" refers to a devotee, a sorceress, or a witch—
but also the female celebrant of the Tantric ritual syzygy. As aspects of
Devi, the sixty-four yoginis "were formed from different parts of the
body of Devi herself—from voice, sweat, navel, forehead, cheeks, lips,
ears, toenails, womb and also from her anger."[11] The yoginis may also
fly, taking awesome dominion of the upper air in a manner reminiscent
of European witches, and ushering the Tantric celebrant into the
nocturnal world of the *Kaula marga*, the ritual of union alternately
known as the *Pancha-makara* rite. One document from the original
era of Yogini temple construction conveys this most vividly:

> As abruptly as darkness descends at nightfall, even so, without
> warning did the Mahayoginis appear out of the sky, the earth,
> the depths of the nether regions and the four corners of space.
> They traversed the skies at tremendous speeds causing their locks
> of hair to come undone, and these flowing tresses swept across
> the sky, hampering and angering the other denizens of the aerial

regions. In their hands they held staffs topped with skulls and decorated with myriads of little bells which jingled furiously. ...

Fig. 3: Goddess Durga with Yogini Chakra, as womb, temple precinct, and diverse female forms

The ornamental designs on their cheeks were painted with
blood which was being lapped up by the many snakes adorning
their ears. Hovering over the gruesome human skulls decorating
their heads were vast numbers of giant vultures who obstructed
the rays of the sun.[12]

At the center of the open temple stands a square, covered platform
where first the guru, then the central Shakti of the *Kaula marga* take
their places. Ensconced on this platform a single *male* figure typically
appears, rightly calling to mind the position of Dionysus at the center
of his band of wild, long-haired, orgiastic, snake-garnished maenads.
This is Shiva as *Bhairava*, just as every male ritual celebrant is a *bhairava*,
though the figure is also known as *Ekepada*, "one footed" (Fig. 4). One
could find no more appropriate combination of fundamental masculine
tokens, nor a more telling personification of phallus as world axis than
he. His single foot calls the etymology of Oedipus, "swollen foot," to
mind, along with numerous other associations of the foot and leg as
phallic. Ekepada's prominent erection is echoed by the single leg, the
figure's damaged staff or weapon, and by a tiered conical hat that
precisely parallels that of the ancestral figure from New Guinea,
discussed earlier, as an explicit indication of spiritual hierarchy. Ekepada
is the phallus, no less than Hermes (as archaic herm born through
the feminine) or Phanes (aroused by the Triple-Goddess in the cave of
Night) are phallic, and is thus essential to all the creations of the
Goddess.

Long before the sky darkens on the night of the *Kaula marga*, its
participants commence with elaborate preparations for the rite. First
and foremost, the site of the proceedings must be the most private
and secure available. Tantra is a highly secretive tradition and, today,
far more likely to be enacted in a concealed location rather than in
the old temples, which are largely archaeological sites today. Its
unsuspected devotees are drawn from all castes, and no disrespect,
particularly for women, is countenanced. An extended period of
instruction, moral preparation, and assessment by a presiding guru is
prerequisite for participation. The atmosphere must be soothing and
seasoned with incense. Leis of red and white flowers, oil lamps, symbols
of pertinent deities, ritual receptacles for perfumes and colored chalks,
mats and cushions, and sacramental foods must be carefully prepared
and placed in the precinct in anticipation of an experience of pure

perfection in time. Each participant retreats at nightfall for a period of private purification before appearing at the appointed hour. Then, upon re-assembly, each member holds an oil lamp into the night air to trace the path of the Milky Way, reckoning it as the true outer

Fig. 4: Ekepada, the "one-footed" ithyphallic Tantric deity with headpiece and weaponry

perimeter of the ritual circle. Each kneels with one hand on the earth to pray: "May all the things that I do and all the things I say be done and said with a pure heart."

Entering the inner precinct, the male participant's arbitrary selection of a floral lei from the pile of garlands in the ritual circle determines his Shakti for the night. The presiding guru blesses all the preparations and participants as the ritual moves into an interactive process of somatically-focused invocations. Partners lie outstretched, then upright and face to face as they administer an extensive massage in which each part of the body is blessed and its unique psychic power is invoked. While ritual forms vary, Danielou records this description:

> The head is smeared with ash while invoking Agni, the fire-god; the forehead while invoking the deities of the waters; the ears while invoking the Earth or Shiva; the eyes while evoking the Wind or Rudra; the nostrils while invoking the directions of Space; the neck while invoking the Moon; the shoulders while invoking Shakti (the power of realization); the arms while invoking Dhruva (the pole star, symbol of Constancy); the elbows while invoking Soma, the intoxicating drink; the wrists while invoking Vishnu, the Preserver; the hips while invoking Anala, the interior Fire; the navel while invoking Prajapati, the Lord of the Animals; the testicles while invoking Brahma, the Creator; the thighs while invoking the Nagas, the serpents; the knees while invoking the snake-daughters; the calves and heels while invoking the Vasus (deities of riches); the feet while invoking the daughters of the sages; and the back while invoking Ocean.[13]

Thus the human celebrant progressively comes to realize an ever more intimate and complete relationship with partner, self, and deity. Primary sacramental elements of the ritual of union are exchanged between each partner of the coupled pairs. A classic feature of Tantric ritual consists of partaking in the so-called five "m"s: *matsya* (fish), *mamsa* (meat), *mudra* (parched grain), *madya* (liquor) and, finally, the climactic *maithuna* (sexual intercourse). Also characteristic are oblations and praises offered to one carefully selected woman, who serves as the primary Shakti of the night. In like manner to the Hindu belief that devotional images are merely sculptures until they undergo proper invocation and sanctification, the appointed Shakti thus blessed becomes the actual incarnation of Devi (*Kali-Shakti*) and is worshipped accordingly in a Shakti *puja*. She is generally of exceptional strength, beauty, and spiritual power, far advanced in the cult and often a prostitute (prostitutes being highly respected in Tantric circles).

Each male participant casts a handful of flower petals into the lap of the central Shakti as well as that of his own partner. After a slow and deliberate exchange of touch, multiple invocations are uttered as ash, colored pigment, and perfume are applied, and an extended meditation on the central Shakti ensues. She remains transfixed in trance as individual couples turn to one another, couple sexually in double lotus position, and sink ever more deeply into their identification with the Shiva-Shakti syzygy. This intercourse has nothing to do with physical reproduction. Its aim is rather maximal arousal of the sexual energy and, accordingly, the power of Shakti. The individual shakti and shakta (female and male partners) remain focused on one another in their ever more heightened and ecstatic state:

> Kaula doctrine states that through such *bhoga* (enjoyment) as opposed to *yoga* (renunciation), its followers will achieve a state of bliss that is termed Kula. Kula is defined as a state in which the mind and sight are united, the sense organs lose their individuality and sight merges into the object to be visualized. … In the Kaula ritual circle, each *sadhaka* was to think of himself as Shiva and of his partner as Devi, and in this manner to try to anticipate the bliss of Kula.[14]

In the experiential immediacy of the living mythic image *which each celebrant has become*, mind merges with visionary sight, and the distinction between exteroception and enteroception (outer and inner vision) breaks down, and sight (here one's "seeing image") is holistically one with the vision it beholds. This corresponds on an archaic level with a Latin expression often employed by Jung, the *sacrificium intellectus*. The term indicates no disparagement of the intellect ("doctrine") whatsoever, but rather a conscious devotion of its power and focus to the immediacy of psychic reality. Distinguishing neither subject nor object any longer, the ritual participant is projected into a third place beyond the pale of linear time—into a Janus-faced *tertium non datur*, the experience of the living syzygy in fire and light unsullied by abstract ideation. Physical orgasm and profound spiritual release are inseparable from one another. The climax of the ritual is calculated to transpire at precisely the darkest moment before dawn, whereupon all the ritual celebrants quickly and silently disperse.

The Tantric seeker has recourse to any number of individual meditative techniques and ritual practices, but all are intimately related to the chakra system within his own body and the Kundalini energy that arises from its deepest fabric. While a detailed consideration of all seven wheels of the chakra system of Tantrism would overstep the requirements of our theme, their progression must be noted. Together with their location, these are the Muladhara (perineum), Svadhisthana (belly), Manipura (midriff), Anahata (heart), Visuddha (throat), Ajna (forehead), and the Sahasrara (above the head). Even the uppermost and most subtle of the chakras, the Sahasrara or crown chakra, retains the imagery of gendered opposites in Kali's downward-pointing triangle, however elevated a position the Sahasrara chakra may assume. For it is only through *Prakrti*, under Kali's aegis, but more particularly as the individuating energy of Shakti, that the divine syzygy of Shiva and Shakti becomes real and embodied. She is the active power behind the dynamism of masculine and feminine elements within the individual as between ritual partners. Tantra is thus a striking example of the far-reaching fact that the archetypal feminine almost invariably presides over the mystery of gender itself, while the archetypal masculine inclines towards the abolition of all such qualities. This is particularly evident in mysticism and cosmology. Tantra, Gnosticism, and Orphism all provide evidence for the observation.

Just as Dionysus, Hermes, Phanes, creator deities generally, and the human psyche possess significant bisexual qualities, Shiva may appear in the specialized form of Ardhanarishvara. Popular iconography portrays him dressed in a symmetrical combination of female and male attire, his masculine aspect on the right and feminine aspect on the left. Of Ardhanarishvara it is said, "The divine hermaphrodite divided his body into two halves, the one male, the other female; the male in this female procreated the universe."[15] Noteworthy in light of the stormy Rudra's overt phallicism, a unique feature of Tantric ritual doctrine is the conception that Shiva is relatively passive (though attractive) to the active dynamism of Shakti, who is none other than the generally familiar Kundalini serpent. Pleased with the distinguishing male token as we are, men may be startled by this notion. With deeper inner reflection, however, men would also be startled to discover the degree to which the archetypal Mother and the anima preside over the whole phallic parade. Here in the wake of the ritual of union and with Shiva appearing androgynously, a simple anthropomorphic representation of Shakti is articulate. Clearly a feminine form, an initial impression of her simple phallicism is decisively qualified by the fact that she is *giving birth* to the Kundalini serpent (Fig. 5). This specific image is most immediately related to

Fig. 5: Shakti birthing the Kundalini serpent, with whom she is one and the same

the lowest, or Muladhara, chakra, located at the perineum and genital zone. It represents a distinct parallel to both Phanes being born from an egg and aroused by the Goddess in the cave of Night, and ancient Hermes who, like Eros, represents a phallic masculinity *born through the feminine.*

The lingam of Shiva stands erect and immobile at the base of the spine with the Kundalini serpent coiled around it. The identification of Shakti with the Kundalini serpent is fully comparable to Eve and the Garden Serpent in Gnostic speculation, or is so once the moralistic patina of orthodox Christianity has been removed. This extends to the celestial counterpart of Eve and Adam represented by the Gnostic Sophia and a sevenfold masculine creative partner, not to mention all those Mediterranean goddesses with a snake as their phallic element. In any case, the arousal and ascending movement of Shakti serpent power up through the chakras constitutes the essential activity of the Tantric quest. Her energy radiates through all the masculine and feminine aspects of the *psychosoma.* The radiation of the Kundalini energy up through the body proceeds along two discrete imaginal channels that interweave in double-helix (like the two serpents of Hermes' caduceus) and is immediately pertinent to an unfolding realization of the anima-animus syzygy. The lunar, or *Ida,* channel is associated with the left nostril, while the solar, or *Pingala,* channel is associated with the right. Breath work, meditation on diagrammatic yantras, and the repetition of specific verbal *mantras* (with or without sexual ritual) constitute essential means for evoking and controlling Shakti energy. Ajit Mookerjee describes a ritual attitude wherein "the body is depersonalized and the deity is invited to enter its pure dwelling-place":

> Tantrikas believe that the flesh must be "awakened" from its dormancy. "This gathering up is effected by cosmicizing the body, and treating it as a 'tool' for inner awareness by taming it with yogic rituals, awakening zones of consciousness and activizing its latent subtle energies. ... In the Tantras the relationship of man and cosmos has been reversed, and man himself has 'become' the cosmos. That is, his significance in the cosmic order has been exalted to the extent that he, and his body, are seen as a tool (yantra) of unlimited power, capable of transforming even his baser capacities into eternal values, an

exaltation considered as a moment of power from the realm of
the gods to the realm of man."[16]

Psychologically, and with recourse to a Janus-faced perspective that
sees in the child the essence and future of all Tantric developments,
Mookerjee's observation of sex and childbirth is again noteworthy. He
speaks of "peak experiences," which "can occur when there is deep
emotional resonance and mutual understanding during intercourse,
or during the delivery of a child."[17] Emphasis here is on the mother's
experience. But the implications of the perinatal processes described
by Grof, whom Mookerjee quotes in what follows, return in relation
to ritual sexuality and, with them, the whole question of a newborn's
subjection to material conditions vis-à-vis the cosmic expansiveness
of an adult's numinous experience of sex:

> During sexual intercourse, the partners can experience glimpses
> of cosmic unity and transcend their feelings of individual
> separateness. At the same time, this sexual union can lead to the
> conception of a new individual and send him or her on the way
> toward *isolation from* cosmic consciousness and in the direction
> of increasing individualism and alienation. Similarly, while the
> mother is experiencing cosmic feelings during the delivery of
> her child, the newborn is confronted with the agony of birth
> and trauma of separation. The emotional and physical pain
> involved in this process then becomes the decisive factor
> alienating the new individual *from* undifferentiated cosmic
> consciousness that he or she experienced as a fetus.[18]

The crucial role of the personal mother and attentive care for the
newborn is implicit here, even as the trajectory from the unconscious
complexity of the infant to the reunion of differentiated psychic
opposites in a ritual *coniunctio* reflects but one rhythmic cycle in life's
passionate continuity.

An extraordinary objective observation of the dynamism of this
entire biological round (the Birth-Sex-Death equation) appears in the
dream of a man in his later twenties—a conspicuous constellation of
the dark instinctual Mother:

*It is a cold autumn night as I walk, again as a boy, beside my grandmother
to the house of a very old lady at the end of the block. Once inside the
woman's musty kitchen, gramma and she begin to visit. Standing alone, I*

begin to eye a trapdoor with a little ringed handle recessed in the yellowed linoleum. Suddenly the door slams open with incredible force. The corpse of a black woman is just as suddenly thrown up from the darkness of the storm cellar and sprawls limply across the floor. An uncanny stillness prevails, like the silence before a tornado, before an enormous, extremely muscular, and fanged black woman rises up from below. She seizes the corpse, begins tearing it fiercely with her jaws and—in an instant—disappears beneath the floor as the trap door slams shut!

The dreamer possessed no knowledge of a comparable vision experienced by Ramakrishna as he sat in meditation by the Ganges. From beneath the sacred waters a beautiful pregnant woman emerges and proceeds to birth a pretty child. As she lifts the child into her arms, however, her jaws begin to distend and transform into a gaping maw with which she savagely devours the child, only to disappear again in the current. Ramakrishna's vision speaks directly to the split image of the feminine in biblical Scripture and in a popular Christian icon. The first example appears in the book of Revelation, where a pregnant woman appears with a seven-headed dragon; the latter in any number of Catholic sanctuaries where the Blessed Virgin stands "victorious" atop the Serpent of Eden. The open secret that emerges in Tantra, in certain schools of Gnosticism, in myriad pagan examples, and archetypally as well, is that the Mother and the serpent are one and the same. Might not birth itself be seen as the emergence from one mother for the feeding of another, the fitful mother of experience and all its vicissitudes?

The appearance of the fanged black woman devouring her counterpart in our dream reflects the uroboric aspect of the Terrible Mother (Kali), a continually "devouring" archetypal image ferociously present but more or less turned in on itself. The child born of the Goddess in Ramakrishna's vision suggests one modest and incremental step towards the application of Shakti's power to the purposes of individuation and the religious quest. Whether Shakti is portrayed as birthing a child or a serpent, her energies flow into immediately gendered halves of a whole, from the Muladhara chakra at the base of the spine on upward. Danielou observes: "[The] snake goddess lives in the earth and is the mother of all living beings. The goddess is thus associated with the most fundamental bodily functions, as opposed to the illusory digressions of the brain."[19] From a Muladhara perspective (concerned as it is with sheer survival), the whole Creation is really only food and eater. This consciousness is narrowly focused and embedded in the excretory and sexual region of the body—the zone of instinct and the explosive pleasure principle.

From the earth element of the Muladhara, the ascending sequence of chakras are associated with water, fire, air, ether, and on to that most subtle crown chakra, where the Kundalini Shakti meets Pure Consciousness in the "Lotus of a Thousand Petals." Just as Western alchemical procedures may repeat certain processes over and over, the Tantrika may circulate the Shakti power within his body in accord with the specific requirements of his practice.

Tantra has rightfully been referred to as the religion of the future, for it represents a true marriage of heaven with earth that respects both. The words of Gopi Krishna may thus conclude this chapter on a hopeful and prospective note:

> What I realize beyond the least shadow of a doubt is the fact ... that in the human body there exists an extremely subtle and intricate mechanism located in the sexual region which ... tends to develop the body generation after generation ... for the expression of a higher personality at the end; but when roused to rapid activity, it reacts strongly on the parent organism, effecting ... a marvelous transformation of the nervous system and the brain, resulting in the manifestation of a superior type of consciousness, which will be the common inheritance of man in the distant future.[20]

The Bridal Chamber is the Holy of the Holies.

—*Gospel of Philip*

CHAPTER SEVEN

Gnostic Reflections: Sophia, Magdalen, and the Bridal Chamber

The mystery of the syzygy lies at the core of Gnostic speculation in those ancient systems that are based on the ancient mythology of Sophia and her male consort. Whether we imagine this syzygy psychologically in terms of the inner experience of a single initiate of the bridal chamber, with reference to an exemplary Gnostic partnership (Magdalen and Jesus), or as Sophia and Christ in cosmic union—we confront one essential mystery. The bridal chamber represents the union of disparate gendered elements of childhood meeting on the more differentiated level of reflective adult experience. Crucially, this conjunction simultaneously represents a union with the divine realm, known in Gnosticism as the All, The Entirety, the Treasury of Light, etc. The core dynamism of masculine and feminine thus stands at the threshold of the divine mystery. The ceaseless lifelong dynamism of the anima-animus syzygy, considered in such detail in Chapter 5, anticipates the sacred marriage (*hieros gamos*) all along. It is the consummation and goal of the individuation process as Jung understands it:

> It is a psychological fact that as soon as we touch on these identifications [the Great Mother and her male counterparts] we enter the realm of the syzygies, the paired opposites, where the One is never separated from the Other, its antithesis. It is a field of personal experience which leads directly to the experience of individuation, the attainment of the self.[1]

Gilles Quispel once shared his recollection of a conversation with Jung wherein he felt a bit embarrassed upon explaining the bisexual speculations of one especially important Gnostic sect, the Valentinians, who anticipate meeting their contrasexual partner in a mystical state. Among the Valentinians men and women meet their inner opposite as a revealer figure of the opposite sex. Given the individual's primary gender identity vis-à-vis the sheer psychic autonomy and superordinate qualities of the anima or the animus, the contrasexual figure's appearance as a numinous revealer need no longer be surprising. In any case, Jung reassured Quispel that this did correspond to the psychological facts.

I recall a male patient who suddenly went blind and required emergency surgery to clear his carotid arteries. He reported that in his near-death state, a brilliant female form appeared at his bedside as "the doctor's wife," only to lay her head on his heart in a silent gesture of reassurance. Months later he was still mystified by the indescribable sense of grace that he continued to feel in the wake of the vision. Just as Jung's professional experience confirms Quispel's Gnostic ideas about the contrasexual, another revealing amplification appears in a study of death and dreams by von Franz. Her account is, however, no less pertinent to visionary experiences associated with a psychological ego-death:

> In Persian tradition, every individual who has been incarnated on earth possesses a guardian angel in heaven (often without knowing it)—his *daena*, a daughter of the cosmic Sophia (Spenta Armaiti). This *daena* is his celestial *alter ego*, his *imago animae*, the mirror of his earthly likeness. She is formed from his good deeds, which originate in his active imagination, that is, out of his good thoughts. When a man dies, she appears as a beautiful young girl to meet him at the Chinvat Bridge in the Beyond and accompany him to the other side. She is actually the religious "visionary organ of the soul" itself, "the light it throws and which makes it possible to see." In this sense she is the *religio* of the deceased. ... She is also the "image" which he was destined to become.[2]

Like the post-surgical vision of my patient, this passage does not describe the light of day! The *daena*, the daughter of Sophia met at the threshold of death, is rather a "visionary organ of the soul" that casts its own light—a precise anthropomorphic correlate of the luminous soul-vessel discussed earlier. It must be reiterated that the anima and the animus are *archetypes*, personifications of the collective unconscious that are central agents in the formation of the individual personality. They are more intimately a part of our daily life, specific interactions, and general predisposition than anyone generally imagines, but are also impersonal, even transcendent—existing in an archetypal time-space beyond the ego. Upon entering the Gnostic cosmos, we must accustom ourselves once more to a language of indeterminate dimensions and spiritual hierarchies that refers simultaneously to outer and intrapsychic space. The complexity of Gnosticism, such that even Jung could find it daunting, demands sustained attention to the particular frame of reference in which one moves. For example, in the myth of Demeter-Kore we see Persephone descending from the earth's surface (meadow) to the underworld and back. In the Sumerian myth of Inanna, described by Perera, the goddess descends through seven cosmic levels to dark Ereshkigal and back. But Sophia, the most comprehensive goddess-imago imaginable, descends from the height of a super-celestial realm before the creation of the world. She is lost to "outer darkness" and anticipates an eventual return to her lofty origins. These examples reflect the same pattern of descent and return on the part of a mythical feminine representative of soul.

Von Franz's references to the Persian *daena* as a "mirror of [the visionary's] earthly likeness," as "the *religio* of the deceased," and an image which the deceased is "destined to become" are especially noteworthy here. Not only does the anima represent everything in life that one can never get the better of, Jung's correlation of *religio* ("to tie back, tie up, tie fast") with *reflexio* suggests that the deceased finds in his soul the *summa* of an entire lifetime of religious reflection. The proximity of death, that ultimate compromise of the ego's integrity, only accents the timeless quality of accumulated, luminous, self-representing, and expanding psychic contents. A closely related frame of reference issue arises in the contrast between the exalted Gnostic heavens (with their ascending planetary shells, imprisoning kings, and formidable gates of passage) and the perilous Egyptian underworld, the Tuat, through whose gates the soul of deceased must pass to find its repose. The two are veritable mirror images of one another—as above so below.

Gnosticism is heavenly in its emphasis, but also sees in Sophia the animating spirit of the material elements (air, water, earth, fire) of which this world is composed. The underworld receives less emphasis for the very fact that this earthly plane is already considered a cosmic catastrophe, particularly owing to the separation of human beings by gender. Concerning the height, breadth, and depth of Sophia's cosmic ambit as well as the world-image she conveys as the *anima mundi,* we learn from the earliest sources: "She reaches mightily from one end of the earth to the other, and she orders all things well." (Wisdom of Solomon 8:1) Both the Biblical narrative of world creation of Proverbs 8:22-31 (10th century B.C.E.) and the apocryphal Wisdom of Solomon (7:15-22), written in Alexandria five hundred years later, describe this beautifully. They portray the divine syzygy at work even as they focus on the handiwork, mediating role, and broad nature of feminine Wisdom:

> The Lord created me at the beginning of his work,
>   the first of his acts of long ago.
> Ages ago I was set up,
>   at the first, before the beginning of the earth.
> When there were no depths I was brought forth,
>   when there were no springs abounding with water.
> Before the mountains had been shaped,
>   before the hills, I was brought forth—
> when he had not yet made earth and fields,
>   or the world's first bits of soil.
> When he established the heavens, I was there,
>   when he drew a circle on the face of the deep,
> when he made firm the skies above,
>   when he established the fountains of the deep,
> when he assigned to the sea its limit
>   so that the waters might not transgress his command.
> when he marked out the foundations of the earth,
>   then I was beside him, like a master worker,
> and I was daily his delight,
>   rejoicing before him always,
> rejoicing in his inhabited world
>   and delighting in the human race.

—Proverbs 8:22-31

May God grant me to speak with judgement,
and to have thoughts worthy of what I have received;
for he is the guide even of wisdom
and the corrector of the wise.
For both we and our words are in his hand,
as are all understanding and skill in crafts.
For it is he who gave me unerring knowledge of what exists,
to know the structure of the world and the activity of the
elements;
the beginning and end and middle of times,
the alternations of the solstices and the changes of the seasons,
the cycles of the year and the constellations of the stars,
the nature of animals and the tempers of wild animals,
the powers of spirits and the thoughts of human beings,
the varieties of plants and the virtues of roots;
I learned both what is secret and what is manifest,
for wisdom, the fashioner of all things, taught me.

—Wisdom of Solomon 7:15-22

These Biblical personifications of feminine Wisdom are congenial to Gnostic Sophia speculation with the exception that the traditional notion of God (as Yahweh) undergoes a radical transformation in Gnosticism—from the Father who creates Wisdom to Yahweh as the *son* of Sophia! In the preceding text, Wisdom and Yahweh appear in aboriginal time and work cooperatively to bring forth the world of time, space, and matter. While one with God, it is feminine Wisdom who rejoices in the human race and so intimately connects with us. More particularly as *anima mundi,* Wisdom represents knowledge of all the elemental structures of the world, the specific unfolding of time and events, the specific features of the created world in their astronomical, meteorological, zoological, botanical, and geological essence. She is the whole of life itself and the unerring knowledge of all that exists—a *creatrix* and revealer at once.

From roughly the same period as the second passage quoted above comes an extremely instructive example of ritual experience where ego-death, mysterious instruction by an autonomous feminine voice, and the revelation of a mythic world-image all come together: the visions of one Greek man named Timarchus. His experiences at the Oracle of Trophonius (Hermes) are described by Plutarch and quoted by C. A. Meier in *Ancient Incubation and Modern Psychotherapy.* Timarchus descends into an oracular chamber (cave) where he remains for three days, leading his companions to fear he is dead. He finally emerges to describe a vision of the microcosm he has seen as his soul issues forth from the fetters of his body. Rejoicing as it rises in the pure transparent air, Timarchus first hears a strange whirring, then a sweet voice that accompanies him as he beholds a vast inner landscape with circular fiery islands moving over the depths of a sea. The scintillating landscape elements orient themselves around a vortex that spirals round in the midst of the encompassing firmament, reminiscent of Jacob's ladder (Genesis 28:10-12) or the previous dream of the phallic world axis (Chapter 5). Timarchus then beholds a chasm "strangely terrible and full of utter darkness" expanding into the chthonic depths beneath him. The original text of Plutarch continues:

> Time passed, and an unseen person said to him, "Timarchus, what do you wish to learn?" "Everything," he replied, "for all is wonderful." "We," the voice said, "have little to do with the regions above; they belong to other Gods; but the province of Persephone, which we administer, being one of the four which Styx bounds, you may survey at your will." To his question, "What is Styx?" "A way to Hades," was the reply, "and it passes right opposite, parting the light at its very vertex, but reaching up, as you see, from Hades below; where it touches the light in its revolution it marks off the remotest region of all."[3]

Following Timarchus's appraisal of the upper and lower hemispheres surrounding the world axis, the voice initiates a discussion of life, motion, birth, and death over which "a Fate, daughter of Necessity, presides, and holds the keys." In light of our frequent references to the *scintillae*, it is interesting indeed to note how the confused Timarchus exclaims: "But I see nothing ... save many stars quivering around the gulf, others sinking into it, others again darting up from below." "Then you see the spirits themselves," the voice continues, "though you do not know it."[4]

Here I recall once being asked by a seminar participant to distinguish between spirit and soul. I spontaneously responded that this was largely a question of *density*, for proximity to the body and created things is a pervasive feature of souls. As Gottfried Wilhelm von Leibnitz observes, "Souls in general are the living mirrors or images of the universe of created things."[5] Timarchus's guide goes on to describe the subtle variations in which the human soul (as a spark, or multitudinous sparks) is mingled with the flesh or, alternately, is freed and called spirit "by men who are said to have understanding."[6] Timarchus remains focused on "the stars tossing about, some less, some more, as we see the corks which mark out nets in the sea move over its surface." They are "like the shuttles used in weaving, in entangled and irregular figures, not able to set the motion into a straight line."[7] Recall the dream of the young woman who sees a cosmic keyhole against a background of galaxies:

> Looking up I see thousands of beautiful galaxies spiraling across the night sky. They sparkle and turn as little connecting lines and subtle geometric forms begin to be generated. Golden bands like arrows move up, down, and across the sky as a gigantic keyhole appears in the middle region.

Plutarch even extends his interpretation of this tossing and lack of alignment to include an object-relational note:

> The voice said that those who kept a straight and ordered movement were men whose souls had been well broken in by fair nurture and training and did not allow their irrational part to be too hard and rough.

There are even indications of an awakening of perinatal memory as Timarchus enters and returns from the visionary state:

> Timarchus wished to turn round, he said, and see who the speaker was; but his head again ached violently, as though forcibly compressed, and he could no longer hear or perceive anything passing about him; afterwards, however, he came to by degrees, and saw that he was lying in the cave of Trophonius, near the entrance where he had originally sunk down.[8]

The entire episode has a synchronistic and fateful conclusion. For as the visionary sequence concludes Timarchus is told by his guide, "you shall know more clearly in the third month from this; now begone!"[9] He died in Athens three months later. In this exchange between Timarchus and his guide in Persephone's realm we find a distinct parallel to an individual's meeting of his *daena* in von Franz's Persian example. It is the synchronicity of Persephone's reference to "the third month" and his actual death that underscores the sheer autonomy of this uncanny and prescient knowledge.

In the radically introverted experience of incubation, Timarchus is granted the shimmering vision of *an entire self-contained world-image*—the microcosm or the self, as Jung would describe it. The anima leads him to it, explains it, knows its relation to his fate. In the Gnostic cosmos—as with the examples of archetypal imagery (puer, anima, self in Chapter 4) within a mirroring interior vessel strewn with *scintillae* seen earlier—an identical structure appears. As if tricked by a mirage, Sophia herself (early in the myth of her descent) is so confused by reflections of the Treasury of Light in the lower realms that she is lured *downward* by them. All the archons of the Gnostic cosmos (the "kings" presiding over the planetary shells) are likewise reflections of their celestial prototypes. In any case, the anima builds a bridge between the visionary's former naïve ego-consciousness and the deeper expanses of the psyche. The Persephonean guide is an additional example of the "visionary organ of the soul." For Timarchus she is "the mirror of his earthly likeness" and "the 'image' which he was destined to become." She is kindly Providence and encroaching Fate at once. In summary, the imagery of the anima as the (Persian) *daena*, as "the doctor's wife" of my patient's near-death vision, and as the feminine guide of Timarchus corresponds to a breathtaking anima epiphany (twelve years earlier) to the same man who dreamt of the powerful Black men and the purple-powdered woman beneath Rome:

In a desert landscape, I spy a red stone half-buried in the sand at my feet. Picking it up, I see that it is the sculpted hand of the Hindu god, Shiva, but with seven fingers. I walk down to a small waterhole, step in, but begin to sink. I simply lie back and float motionless to stop it. Women come and draw water. Then I step out of the pool. Walking back to where I found the sculpted hand, I see an elegant glass table on which a lovely meal has been set. A chair is pulled out for me. Taking my place, I look forward only to behold a lithe and radiant fair-skinned woman of unearthly beauty. She looks into my eyes with a tender intimacy and penetration such as I have never experienced before or since!

This deeply reassuring dream vision and each example preceding are all indicative of the mystical ambiance and ultimate harmony of masculine and feminine at the center of the soul and in the Valentinian ritual of the bridal chamber.

Greek, Egyptian, and Persian amplifications are all appropriate to this context, not only given their topical pertinence, but also because all these ancient traditions touched Gnosticism in the Alexandrian milieu in which it flowered. Free elaboration and elaboration on existing traditional lore ("gnosticizing tendencies") are essential features of Gnosticism. Quispel maintains that "never in the history of Western religion has the spirit been so free as in 2nd-century Alexandria."[10] For years the Persian roots of Gnosticism were exaggerated, owing to the radical dualism of some Gnostic systems such as the Manichaeism that Augustine embraced for eleven years. Even before Christian forms of Gnosticism appeared, however, one finds kindred systems both Egyptian (*Corpus Hermeticum*) and Greek (Orphism). But no influence on Gnosticism is more fundamental than mystical Judaism. Alexandria had a large Jewish quarter, and a second Temple built, to the consternation of many devout Jews. This is the city where Philo Judaeus weaves his strands of Judaic, Platonic, and even Eleusinian lore and describes his philosophy as a mystery religion. It is also where the Gnostic teacher Valentinus was educated and taught in the first half of the 2nd century.

While the Gnostics posited many divine images as theological principles, Jung's understanding of the archetypes as multiform living organs of the psyche defies any fixed theological understanding. Rather, they occur as diverse qualities of *experience*. In a late passage, Jung characterizes the anima in a manner immediately pertinent to Gnosticism and reminiscent of Emma Jung's four-tiered description of the animus as well. Jung's examples are contextually bound to Goethe's *Faust*, which he discusses so often:

> Four stages of eroticism were known in the late classical period: Hawwah (Eve), Helen (of Troy), the Virgin Mary, and Sophia. The series is repeated in Goethe's *Faust*: in the figures of Gretchen as the personification of a purely instinctual relationship (Eve); Helen as an anima figure; Mary as the personification of the "heavenly," i.e., Christian or religious, relationship; and the "eternal feminine" as an expression of the alchemical *Sapientia*. As the nomenclature shows, we are dealing with the heterosexual Eros or anima-figure in four stages, and

consequently with four stages of the Eros cult. The first stage—
Hawwah, Eve, earth—is purely biological; woman is equated
with the mother and only represents something to be fertilized.
The second stage is still dominated by the sexual Eros, but on
an aesthetic and romantic level where woman has already
acquired some value as an individual. The third stage raises Eros
to the heights of religious devotion and thus spiritualizes him:
Hawwah has been replaced by spiritual motherhood. Finally,
the fourth stage illustrates something which unexpectedly goes
beyond the almost unsurpassable third stage: *Sapientia.* How
can wisdom transcend the most holy and the most pure?—
Presumably only by virtue of the truth that the less sometimes
means the more. *This stage represents a spiritualization of Helen
and consequently of Eros as such.*[11]

A single correction might be proposed here: the replacement of Helen
of Troy by Mary Magdalen. Magdalen represents a far more developed
example of the anima than does Helen, though Jung could not have
known this for want of Magdalen documents available today. The
conundrum of Jung's theory of Eros as a feminine principle vis-à-vis
Eros as a masculine figure impacts the discussion here again. For what
we actually find above are four different stages *of the anima.* Jung's
images represent "four stages of eroticism" only insofar as each feminine
image mirrors the aspect of Eros that is commensurate to it—the
particular form of desire that each evokes. All these female figures have
in some wise been related to Magdalen. *Sapientia* is, of course, the
Latin expression for Wisdom, for Sophia. The implication of Jung's
final sentence is utterly extraordinary: The central image of desire in
Homer's *Iliad,* Helen of Troy, the lover of Paris and "the face that
launched a thousand ships," may undergo a "spiritualization" that
renders her an equivalent of the Goddess of Wisdom. As "something
which unexpectedly goes beyond the almost unsurpassable third stage"
(Virgin), as something less but more than "the most holy and the most
pure," we encounter in Sophia a feminine image that retains significant
affinity with the most ardently sought lover of the pagan world!
Sapientia must therefore represent an anima image sufficiently
comprehensive to mirror Eros on all levels—the impulse to fertilize;
the personalized desire for romantic, sexual, and aesthetic experience;
and a yearning for the grace of a spiritual mother. Consider it: the

intense erotic passion and the lofty devotion one may feel for a chosen lover are suddenly directly pertinent to the religious quest!

This clearly challenges any orthodox theological contention that erotic desire and sexuality are incompatible with either religion or with the achievement of wisdom. Indeed no better example could be cited than King Solomon himself, the probable author of the creation narrative of Proverbs, he who "loved many foreign women along with the daughter of the Pharaoh: Moabite, Ammonite, Edomite, Sidonian, and Hittite women," and has been a paragon of religious wisdom for centuries (I Kings 11:1). In regard to how Magdalen might serve as a replacement for Helen, this can only be judged by the particulars of Magdalen's biography and identity as we know them from textual sources and popular fantasy as well.

Paradoxically enough, no figure in Christian history is more intimately associated with sex or with Jesus than Mary Magdalen. The very fact that the 14th-century interrogators of Free Spirit John Hartmann could ask their heretical suspect if he believed that Christ had sex with Mary Magdalen after [*sic*] the Resurrection is indicative of the free-ranging eroticism of fantasy that clings to Magdalen throughout the Christian epoch. What this implies regarding medieval assumptions of an erotic relationship between Magdalen and Jesus *during* their life together could, until very recently, only be inferred from equally varied literary and isolated opinion. A popular figure in medieval poetry and drama, "we find Magdalene variously portrayed as a medieval princess, a queen of the courts of love, or the typical stereotyped saint."[12] Accordingly,

> [t]he medieval conception of Mary Magdalene's relationship to her Lord gives us another side of her character. Their love for one another is continually stressed and not always in such platonic terms as we find in the Gospels.[13]

One medieval tale features an outdoorsman named Hilarion out searching for a man wiser than himself, then sitting on a riverbank alone to fish. He meets "a lady beautiful beyond compare, the which for all clothing wore only her own hair golden and exceedingly long." Hilarion asks, "Who art thou, for this forest is haunted by spirits, and I would know whether though art one of such, and of evil intent, as the demon Venus, or a woman like the mother who bore me." Here is the classic contrast between anima and mother. The lady answered, "My name is Magdalene."[14] Magdalen is compared to Venus (Aphrodite), who Magdalen does indeed personify in Christian culture, however much she is expected to repent for it. As a woman wearing only her hair, she might also be compared with St. Mary of the Desert, a reclusive saint of similar austerity and attire. In the lyrics of a 15th-century love song Magdalen speaks of Jesus as a "dere darlyng," "my swete herte, my gostly paramour," "my turtel dove so fresshe of hue," who "beareth both locke and key" and "myne hertes sustenaunce."[15]

Notwithstanding such popular sentiments, we know that not one scrap of Biblical writ confirms Magdalen's identity as either a prostitute or as the bride of Jesus. Magdalen remains the patron saint of sinners and penitents through the medieval period, though this Catholic identity is predicated on precisely the same crisp split between instinct and spirit, whore and virgin, that we have considered from the outset. The institutionalized rumors that Magdalen was a prostitute, or at least a highly sensual *bon vivant*, appears to be just that—banal if perennial instances of patriarchal slander. Indeed, the closer one looks at the historical Magdalen, the more one realizes that Magdalen's identification with Venus and Aphrodite is based almost entirely on rumor and popular fantasy!

The fascination surrounding Magdalen's relationship with Jesus of Nazareth recalls the question posed at the outset of this study: If sexual religious ritual plays so central a role in other religious complexes, what in the broader Christian tradition represents a comparable example of the confluence of sexuality and the religious imagination? Scattered examples from medieval heresy and the witch craze already stand before us, but they are the sporadic experiments of a disenfranchised few. The answer is painfully clear with regard to orthodox Christian tradition (and those situations in analytic work) where tremendous sexual conflict may afflict an individual while that tradition provides no sacred image, no mythology, no ritual, and not even a viable ideological framework for properly exploring such matters. Jesus traditions, however, display tremendous diversity from the beginning. These include forms in which a decisively different Magdalen appears with Jesus at the heart of the Gnostic cosmos. Because Magdalen's identity is so perplexing a combination of Biblical accounts, extracanonical references, popular legends, and pagan associations (not to mention her many portrayals in the arts), one long-established Magdalen site in the South of France is selected here from which to look back in time.

Magdalen is said to have fled to Marseilles, to the coast of Arles (St. Maries de la Mar), or again to Languedoc in the West following the crucifixion. The very profusion of Magdalen lore in the region is persuasive of some historical fact lying in the background. Rising above the rocky landscape of Provence today a towering wall of gray stone meets the pilgrim's eye. Legend holds that Magdalen, an exile from Palestine, once gazed upon these selfsame cliffs, her eyes uplifted to behold the face of her beloved, his eyes, knit brow, and ample beard perceptible in the stone. The impression once rendered the locale hospitable, just as the cave's entrance a hundred yards to the right is said to have offered Magdalen safe haven and meditative seclusion. *The Golden Legend*, an 8th-century collection of saints' lives by Jacobus de Voragine, tells the story of Mary Magdalen's dwelling there for thirty years unbeknownst to anyone:

> There she found neither water nor herb nor tree, whereby she knew that Jesus wished to sustain her with naught but heavenly meats, allowing her no earthly satisfaction. But every day the angels bore her aloft at the seven canonical hours, and with her bodily ears she heard the glorious chants of the heavenly hosts. Then, being filled with this delightful repast, she came down to her grotto, and needed no bodily food.[16]

The Elevation of Magdalen is portrayed by many artists of Catholic tradition, just as Magdalen is depicted in the mouth of this cave with her ointment jar and skull by Goya, Ribera, El Greco, and many others. The rhythm of the saint's daily life moves from the shadowy recesses of her stony grotto to a transcending promontory, then back again, in unending cycles like soul's very own. Precedents of religious seekers dwelling in the caves of the region definitely cancel out any association between grottos and the nymphs in this portrayal of Magdalen at her ascetic extreme. Today the Grotto of Mary Magdalene at St. Baume comes into view slowly through the lacy branches as one ascends along an earthen path lined with gurgling water troughs and small shrines. Far above the cave looms the summit, where a modest single-celled chapel commemorates Magdalen's legendary elevations. Her daily angelic visits call to mind her conversation with angels at the tomb of Jesus. These mystical relations set Magdalen in a characteristic anima role as intermediary between ego-consciousness and the unconscious. That the visitations transpire at the seven canonical hours, and that the *Golden Legend* refers to the scent of beautiful incense remaining in the church where Magdalen dies for seven days, become intuitively provocative. Though she is praised for her sanctity by the Catholics, we may simply note that the Seven Deadly Sins by which any soul was evaluated have traditionally been linked with the seven classic planets—Sloth (Saturn), Gluttony (Jupiter), Wrath (Mars), Lust (Venus), Pride (Sol), Envy (Luna), and Avarice (Mercury). We will come to appreciate their cosmic significance in another light.

All four New Testament Gospels describe the experiences of Mary Magdalen at the tomb of the resurrected Christ. According to Matthew, Mary first encounters an angel at the newly opened tomb and then meets Jesus before the other disciples do. Jesus even instructs her to go and tell the others to meet him in Galilee (28:1-10). Mark records, "Now after he rose early on the first day of the week, he appeared first to Mary Magdalene, from whom he had cast out seven demons" (16:9). It is ironic and revealing that this single verse combines both Magdalen's claim to prime credentials for heading the Roman Catholic Church with the fateful pathology from which she suffered. The role of serving as head of the church rightfully falls to her who first sees the risen Lord: Magdalen, "the apostle to the apostles." The casting out of seven demons by Jesus (mentioned twice in the Gospels) was in all likelihood the first meeting between the two. Luke recounts how Mary's report of the resurrection was received by the apostles as "an idle tale" and not believed (24:10-11). John describes a poignant conversation between the grieving Magdalen and a compassionate gardener whom she suddenly recognizes as her Master (20:1-16). This passage from John is an obvious commentary on the First Adam (gardener) whose Fall is overcome through the self-sacrifice of Jesus, the Second Adam. Magdalen's recognition of Jesus captures a decisive moment. It anticipates the Gnostic bridal chamber ritual as a celebration of the sacred reunion of Sophia and Christ, the central syzygy of Valentinian speculation.

While Magdalen's place in the entourage of Jesus is familiar, the complexity of her nature and the magnitude of her importance are generally underestimated (Fig. 1). For example, despite this passage in Luke, Mary is not typically thought of as a woman of means, with upper-class connections:

> Soon afterwards he went on through cities and villages, proclaiming and bringing good news of the kingdom of God. The twelve were with him, as well as some women who had been cured of evil spirits and infirmities; Mary, called Magdalene, from whom seven demons had gone out, and Joanna, the wife of Herod's steward Chuza, and Susanna, and many others, who provided for them out of their resources. (Luke 8:1-3)

Fig. 1: "Mary Magdalene Approaching the Sepulchre" Giovanni Savoldo

Legend likewise suggests that Magdalen was a woman of considerable wealth. *The Golden Legend* maintains that she was born of parents who were of noble station, and came of royal lineage. Materials from which we might reconstruct an actual biography of Mary Magdalen are as scant as the remains of Migdal (Magdala), her hometown on the northwestern shore of the Lake of Gennesaret near Tiberias. All that remains of Migdal today is a pair of ancient stone grain cisterns set into the earth. We know that Mary possessed sufficient courage to witness the crucifixion (John 19:25), and beheld and conversed with angels at the tomb. She readily appears larger than life. Indeed, the propinquity of Magdalen to so many crucial aspects of Jesus' fate, particularly the tomb and the resurrection, irresistibly calls to mind the revivifying ministrations of Isis upon Osiris.

While reference to Magdalen as a prostitute is conspicuously absent in the Gospels, the confusion is in large measure explained by the fact that a cluster of women and two discrete instances of an anointing of Jesus' feet have frequently been confounded. The Mary who anoints the feet of Jesus at Bethany with "costly perfumes made of pure nard" (John 12:3) is another Mary, the sister of Martha and Lazarus. The "woman in the city, who was a sinner" (Luke 7:37), who anoints the feet of Jesus with tears and ointment, is likewise someone else. And though attempts have been made, any identification of Magdalen with the "woman taken in adultery" (John 8:3) is even more strained.

Through an historical synchronicity in fateful 1945, new documents with deep pertinence to Magdalen came to light. It was then that a 25-year-old herder, Mohammed Ali es Samman, came upon a leather-bound collection of some fifty Coptic manuscripts inside an earthen vessel hidden along a cliff face in the Egyptian desert, where they had remained since the 4th century. Lamentably, this original discovery, comparable in importance only to the discovery of the *Dead Sea Scrolls* at Qumran two years later, was known only to select and proprietary scholars for some thirty years. The Nag Hammadi materials necessitate a complete reappraisal of early Christianity and, like the scrolls, dramatically demonstrate that the original Christian message was a highly visionary one. The Gnostics placed ultimate value on the individual's experience of saving knowledge or *gnosis* ("insight"). Expanding messianic expectations in the Jewish community of Jerusalem characterized the period of the destruction of the Temple by the Romans in 70 C.E. and decisively influenced subsequent Gnostic developments in the following centuries.

Prior to the publication of *The Nag Hammadi Library* in 1978, there was scholarly awareness that Mary Magdalen's identity extended far beyond that of the demure penitent of Catholic tradition. Antti Marjanen's study, *The Woman Jesus Loved,* enumerates the existing sources:

> A new viewpoint to the personage of Mary Magdalene was opened by the discoveries of two new Coptic manuscripts in the course of the eighteenth and the nineteenth century. In them for the first time, the ancient writings *Pistis Sophia,* the *Gospel of Mary,* and the *Sophia of Jesus Christ* were brought to light. All three works were revelation dialogues which showed their readers how some second and third century Christians viewed the risen Lord, his disciples, and his female followers, including Mary Magdalene. Earlier the conception of an extra-canonical Mary Magdalene within Christian tradition was based on three rather brief references of the heresiologists to her connection with some Gnostic groups and on medieval legends. The new texts revealed the existence of another Mary Magdalene tradition.[17]

The *Nag Hammadi Library* introduced four new sources: the *Gospel of Thomas,* the *Gospel of Philip,* the *Dialogue of the Savior,* and the *First Apocalypse of James.* These seven Magdalen texts, together with a description of the creation of the subtle body from the *Apocryphon of John* and the revelatory Sophianic poem, "The Thunder, Perfect Mind," will serve as primary Gnostic documentation of Mary Magdalen's personality, visionary experience, intimacy with Jesus, original teachings, and central role among the disciples. They also shed light on the mythological framework of Gnosticism, the challenges that faced Magdalen as a female spiritual authority, and the particulars of Gnostic ritual. Bear in mind that virtually all these texts originally derive from a period prior to Augustine, prior to the institution of the Apostles' Creed by the Nicean Council of 325, and before the full ascendancy of the Roman Catholic Church.

The fact that Jesus came from an actual family startles even those long since strayed from the faith. Magdalen appears to have enjoyed close relations with the historical family of Jesus—a family of highly observant Jews including at least seven children that stands in marked contrast to the orthodox Holy Family. No less significant is its variance from a basic element of the Apostles' Creed: "And in Jesus Christ, His only Son, our Lord: who was conceived of the Holy Spirit, born of the Virgin Mary ...." Already in Luke 24 we find Magdalen together with Mary the mother of Jesus, who is there called "Mary the mother of James." Magdalen appears again in Mark 16:1 with "Mary the mother of James, and Salome." In a description of the crucifixion in the preceding chapter of Mark, Magdalen appears with "Mary the mother of James the younger and of Joses, and Salome" (15:40). While not including Magdalen, the most telling of all Gospel references to Jesus' family appears with the rejection of Jesus as a prophet by the townspeople of Nazareth, recorded in Mark 6:3 (and almost identically in Matthew 13:55). The verse reads: "Is not this the carpenter, the son of Mary and brother of James and Joses and Judas and Simon, and are not his sisters here with us?" Lost apocryphal gospels, known secondhand through the Church Fathers, also speak of the family of Jesus, and particularly of James, the brother of Jesus who was also a significant spiritual leader. Original texts are as at ease with this familial information, as are the Gnostics:

> In the original accounts—the Gospels as they have come down to us, Paul's letters, and Josephus—no embarrassment whatsoever is evinced about this relationship with Jesus, and James is designated straightforwardly and without qualification as Jesus' brother. There are no questions of the kind that crop up later in the wake of the developing doctrine of the supernatural "Christ" and stories about his supernatural birth, attempting to diminish the relationship. These stories about the birth of "Christ" are, in any event, not referred to by Paul and appear first in the Gospels of Matthew and Luke, thus leading in the second century to embarrassment not just over Jesus' brothers, but the fact of Jesus' family generally, including sisters, fathers, uncles, and mothers. Embarrassment of this kind was exacerbated by the fact that Jesus' brothers ("cousins," as Jerome would later come to see them at the end of the fourth century) were principal personages in Palestine and Jesus' successors there, important in Eastern tradition generally. What exacerbated the problem of their relationship with Jesus even further in the second century was the theological assertion of Mary's "perpetual virginity" and with it the utter impossibility—nay,

inconceivability—that she should have had other children. This even led Jerome's younger contemporary, Augustine, in the fifth century, to the assertion reproduced in Muhammad's Koran in the seventh, that Jesus didn't have a father at all, only a mother![18]

As we know, Augustine would be reassured by the latter contention. In any case, *this* is the holy family with whom Magdalen became an old and intimate friend. She is a companion to both Jesus and Mary in some of the most intimate moments of their lives. Ancient documents consistently portray Magdalen as a diligent student and spiritual seeker in her own right. Her involvement with this influential circle gave Magdalen the education of a lifetime and will forever enhance her credentials as a spiritual authority.

By way of contrast, consider the portrayal of Mary Magdalen as the companion of the traditional Holy Family with Jung's anima concept in mind—the fascinating 16th-century Italian painting "Holy Family with the Magdalene," by Palma Vecchio (Fig. 2). The Virgin gently holds the Christ child with her eyes lowered toward him while John the Baptist stands to her left. Mother Mary is unaware of the provocative interaction transpiring around her. The reclining infant Jesus strains to gaze back over his right shoulder to Joseph and Magdalen, whose eyes mirror one another. The child's focus is

Fig. 2: "Holy Family with Magdalene" Palma Vecchio

unquestionably on these two. Note the dream-like anachronism of the painting: Magdalen is an adult in Jesus' infancy. Joseph's attentive expression coupled with Magdalen's quizzical look and deliberative touching of her perfume vessel prompts an immediate query as to what they may know or understand about Jesus and his mother, or about Jesus' future and fate. In any case, we encounter the two women who play a decisive a role in Jesus' life—his mother and his most personal companion, Mary Magdalen. The opportunity thus arises to pursue one of this study's more essential points—about the syzygy, the mother and the anima in Christian tradition, and about incest. For psychologically the difference between a religious system focused on an incestuous syzygy of mother and son and one based on a syzygy of loving partners of the same generation makes all the difference in the world. Jung's crucial observation that this stage of the anima (the movement of Eros beyond the Virgin Mother to *Sapientia*) represents "a spiritualization of Helen [Magdalen?] and consequently of Eros as such" speaks directly to the psychological point!

Whether a feature of popular devotion or concealed in the more esoteric contexts of its mystics, most religious systems bring specific attention to bear on a special male-female dyad, be this a conspicuous pairing in the god-imago or contrasexual images closer to the individual soul. As we have seen, where these two meet one another is the very nexus of deep mystical experience. Psychologically we know that in order to be satisfying and true this union must be comprehensive and holistic rather than a doctrinal makeshift. Rather than being an "upper syzygy" or a "lower syzygy," it must finally be global, and fully embrace body, soul, and spirit. What we confront in the primary syzygy of Catholicism and Christianity generally is the dyad of Jesus and his mother Mary. Granted, on a refined mystical level the Virgin does recall our First Mother (Eve) and ultimately coalesces in Sophia's nature, as is amply demonstrated in Thomas Schipflinger's classic *Sophia-Maria: A Holistic Vision of Creation*. On the level of popular devotion and daily example, however—as an example of how Christian women (and men) are supposed to be and from a psychological perspective, we are presented with a thirty-three-year-old celibate puer in incestuous union with his mother! The emotional and behavioral consequences of this regressive arrangement are conspicuous in the life of Augustine. Virtually nothing in Christian pedagogy equips an individual to differentiate between the anima and the mother, that first personification of the anima archetype. But in the Holy Family of Palma Vecchio, the artist seems to be contemplating just such a thing.

What does Magdalen or, furthermore, what does Joseph as the earthly masculine of flesh and blood bring to our picture that the Virgin does not? Here a highly pertinent psychological question is just how comprehensive or restricted an image of the mother archetype the Catholic Mary actually presents.

Prominent Biblical materials indicate how Jesus conceived of and negotiated the incest problem. The most fundamental reference is a basic text for Christian weddings. Questioned by Pharisees about divorce, Jesus responds:

> Have you not read that the one who made them at the beginning 'made them male and female,' and said, 'For this reason a man shall leave his father and mother and be joined to his wife, and the two shall become one flesh'? So they are no longer two, but one flesh. Therefore what God has joined together, let no one separate. (Matthew 19:4-6)

Departing one's parents to become one flesh with one's spouse or beloved is clearly the natural course of events for Jesus. Later, when someone mentions that his mother and brothers are at hand and wish to speak to him, Jesus responds, "Who is my mother, and who are my brothers?" Jesus points to his disciples, saying, "Here are my mother and my brothers! For whoever does the will of my Father in heaven is my brother and sister and mother" (Matthew 12:47-50). Uninformed though we may be concerning the emotional tone of the possibly brusque statement, "Who is my mother, and who are my brothers?" the fact that Jesus cites his circle of disciples as fully equivalent indicates an eros function turning well away from the personal to a symbolic equivalent of the mother. This is indicative of the anima at work in the ongoing movement from childhood to community. In the Gospel of John, immediately prior to his death, Jesus looks to Mary, Magdalen, and the others, and subtly disavows his maternal bond by arranging a surrogate son (John) for his mother:

> When Jesus saw his mother and the disciple whom he loved standing beside her, he said to his mother, "Woman, here is your son." Then he said to the disciple, "Here is your mother." And

> from that hour the disciple took her into his own home. (John
> 19:26-27)

That Jesus effects this renunciation *at the moment of his self-sacrifice* is
both archetypally appropriate and provocative. This is the precise
theme of Jung's most fundamental work, *Symbols of Transformation*,
where the hero renounces the personal mother and offers himself to
the archetypal Mother. He gives away all that he has to be reborn
through immersion in the Great Goddess, an inescapable prerequisite
to the birth of psychic consciousness. Finally, and superseding any
Gospel reference to the incest problem, Jesus declares in the Gospel
of Matthew:

> Do not think that I have come to bring peace to the earth; I
> have not come to bring peace, but a sword.
>> For I have come to set a man against his father,
>> and a daughter against her mother,
>> and a daughter-in-law against her mother-in-law;
>> and one's foes will be members of one's own household.
> Whoever loves father or mother more than me is not worthy
> of me; and whoever loves son or daughter more than me is
> not worthy of me; and whosoever does not take up the cross
> and follow me is not worthy of me. Those who find their life
> will lose it, and those who lose their life for my sake will find
> it. (10:34-39)

The terse quality of Jesus' statement recalls his fury with the money
changers at the Temple and, more subtly, the mystery of his
encouraging his disciples (only verses before) to be "wise as serpents
and innocent as doves" (10:16). Jesus addresses the incest problem very
deftly with both its biographical and regressive and its symbolic and
progressive aspects in mind. Magdalen's perfect candidacy for
participation in Jesus' spiritual community further indicates how
appropriate she is as a personal anima. The setup is comparable to Jesus'
famous discussion of rebirth with the Pharisee Nicodemus, whose naïve
concretism is conspicuous in the statement: "How can anyone be born
after they grow old? Can one enter a second time into the mother's
womb and be born?" Jesus answers, "Very truly, I tell you, no one can
enter the kingdom of God without being born of water and Spirit"
(John 3:4-5). Nicodemus struggles to comprehend Jesus' symbolic

statements to such a degree that Jesus puzzles aloud: "Are you a teacher of Israel, and yet you do not understand these things?" (John 3:10).

In all the foregoing, Jesus is completely canny regarding the regressive pull of old emotional loyalties. Earlier in this study a dream was introduced where a whirlwind from on high touches open water to create a spherical vessel of water that contains the whirlwind. This is an image pertinent to the psychological mitosis we observe—to symbolic birth, procreativity of soul, and creation of an interior world-image sprung from water and spirit. Jesus would spurn any personalized, concretized, or literal interpretation of the Mother-Son syzygy, for it represents precisely a situation where "one's foes will be members of one's own household." Jesus renounces it unequivocally. Where the Virgin is imagined as the penultimate feminine image or concretized as an earthly model for Christian women (a fixture in normative Christian culture), opportunities for mutually possessive emotional claims by mother and child, the regressive pull of everyday mother complexes, are rife.

C. G. Jung took no small note of the fact that the Assumption of the Virgin, which holds that Mary the Mother of Jesus was taken up bodily to heaven, was declared doctrinal by the Vatican in 1951. His commentary on this unique development in the collective psyche is pertinent not only to our consideration of Magdalen and the Virgin Mother, but also for its recourse to the kind of pagan parallels we have perforce been referencing. Jung's archetypal approach resembles, and is applied to, the same storehouse of ancient myths and symbols seen in the syncretism of Late Antiquity itself. Mindful of the broader archetypal aspects of the mother complex, he addresses the Assumption of Mary with these words:

> The Christian "Queen of Heaven" has, obviously, shed all her Olympian [sic] qualities except for her brightness, goodness, and eternality; and even her human body, the thing most prone to gross material corruption, has put on an ethereal incorruptibility. The richly varied allegories of the Mother of God have nevertheless retained some connection with her pagan prefigurations in Isis (Io) and Semele. Not only are Isis and the Horus-child iconological exemplars, but the ascension of Semele, the originally mortal mother of Dionysus, likewise anticipates the Assumption of the Blessed Virgin. Further, this son of Semele

is a dying and resurgent god and the youngest of the Olympians. Semele herself seems to have been an earth-goddess, just as the Virgin Mary is the earth from which Christ was born. This being so, the question naturally arises for the psychologist: *what has become of the characteristic relation of the mother-image to the earth, darkness, the abysmal side of the bodily man with his animal passions and instinctual nature, and to "matter" in general?* [19]

The reaction of a highly informed and lively seminar group with whom I shared Jung's "cult of eros" hierarchy (Eve, Helen, Mary, *Sapientia*) in Melbourne, Australia, is telling here. The women of the group spontaneously queried, "Why just Eve? What about *Lilith*!"—the first wife of Adam, who does indeed personify a depth of feminine power and sexuality beyond the Biblical Eve. The inclusion of Lilith in Jung's analysis definitely would represent and facilitate a deeper link between Judeo-Christian materials and the likes of the witch, Persephone, Hecate, or Kali. Such fateful feminine figures are precisely those that strike terror in the heart of patriarchy, but precisely therein lies their neglected transformative and initiatory significance.

Jung proceeds to decry the dead earth of science and technology, of rationalism and materialism—all products of the one-sided development of the thinking function, which brought already to his day the specter of spiritual and nuclear annihilation. (Fate had yet to manifest as our impending global ecological catastrophe.) The declaration of the Assumption might have been intended by the Church as a compensation for the rampant materialism of the age. Mary the Mother of Jesus might indeed represent the opposites of matter and spirit unified through the Assumption, but this is a highly tenuous proposition. Jung also observes that the Assumption is equivocal in its meaning:

> The psychologist inclines to see in the dogma of the Assumption a symbol which, in a sense, anticipates this whole development [the union of matter and spirit]. For him the relationship to earth and to matter is one of the inalienable qualities of the mother archetype. So that when a figure that is conditioned by this archetype is represented as having been taken up into heaven, the realm of the spirit, this indicates a union of earth and heaven, or of matter and spirit....[B]ut this *"spirit" will appear divested of all, or at any rate most, of its known qualities,* just as earthly matter was stripped of its specific characteristics when it staged its entry

into heaven [as Mary]. Nevertheless, the way will gradually be
cleared for a union of the two principles.[20]

This entire investigation represents a clearing of the way to a union
of spirit and matter, in the *psychosoma* of the individual and in our
understanding of the *anima mundi*. Jung stresses that the meaning of
the Assumption is contingent upon the conformance of the Virgin to
the mother archetype, then secondarily upon the adoption of concrete
or symbolic perspective. The former is easily dispensed with, given its
conspicuous accommodation to patriarchy:

> Understood concretely, the Assumption is the absolute opposite
> of materialism. Taken in this sense, it is a counterstroke that does
> nothing to diminish the tension between the opposites, but
> drives it to extremes.[21]

From earth and underworld, from the women's voices I heard in
Melbourne, Jung's interrogative might echo and resound: What *has*
become of the relation of the mother-image to the earth, darkness,
the abysmal side of the bodily man, animal passions, instinctual nature,
and to "matter" in general? This is precisely where Mary Magdalen
and Joseph, as well as Sophia, must take their rightful place in
Christianity today.

Acknowledged or not, the entire edifice of patriarchal Christian
dogma, belief, and practice has now been permanently shaken to its
foundations by the discovery of the *Nag Hammadi Library* and by the
fact that Jesus of Nazareth and Mary Magdalen were Gnostics. These
facts open into another universe, one inconceivable where the Virgin
is held up as the ultimate example of femininity, where the anima *as
such* is left to flounder beneath the rubble of Rome or Jerusalem, where
the Incarnation includes no phallic token, or where popular and highly
sentimentalized images of mother-son incest occlude any appreciation
of the numinosity of erotic love.

A far broader understanding of the greater feminine appears
immediately in a poem from Nag Hammadi, "The Thunder, Perfect
Mind," where Sophia characterizes her nature through the voice of Eve:

> I was sent forth from [the] power,
>> and I have come to those who reflect upon me,
>> and I have been found among those who seek after me.

Look upon me, you (pl.) who reflect upon me,
    and you hearers, hear me.
    You who are waiting for me, take me to yourselves.
And do not banish me from your sight.
    And do not make your voice hate me, nor your hearing.
    Do not be ignorant of me anywhere or any time. Be on
       your guard!
    Do not be ignorant of me.

For I am the first and the last.
I am the honored one and the scorned one.
I am the whore and the holy one.
I am the wife and the virgin.
I am the mother and the daughter.
I am the members of my mother.
I am the barren one
    and many are her sons.
I am she whose wedding is great,
    and I have not taken a husband.
I am the midwife and she who does not bear.
I am the solace of my labor pains.
I am the bride and the bridegroom,
    and it is my husband who begot me.
I am the mother of my father
    and the sister of my husband,
    and he is my offspring.[22]

The mother plays an essential but partial role in this resonant self-revelation. The contradictory statements with which Eve-Sophia describes her identity are not only indicative of the range of qualities ("the members of my mother") that comprise her sacred image; but suggestive of the enormous conflicts that a woman or man will inevitably experience in any deep confrontation with the unconscious. Yet again, and in harmony with the spirit of the poem, they suggest a mysterious coincidence of opposites beneath this veil of language, such as one associates with extraordinary insight and equilibrium in a given personality.

The anima always presides over the syzygy. A challenging cluster of images confronts us in the last five lines of the poem. There the feminine voice identities herself as both bride *and* bridegroom, recalling the conundrum of Eros as an independent masculine figure or as a phallic exponent of the Mother. The ambiguity of the speaker's self-identifications is piqued by reference to literally impossible and conspicuously incestuous intra-familial relationships. No better answer to the problem could be desired than what Robert Stein has taught us. He speaks of the potential for the archetypal dyads of Mother-Father, Mother-Son, Mother-Daughter, Father-Son, Father-Daughter, Brother-Sister, Brother-Brother, and Sister-Sister to be experienced in the family. Focusing there on the developing child, Stein states, "While these archetypes refer to internal images, they are initially released by and experienced in relationship to an *external* object (mother, father, sibling)."[23] In "The Thunder, Perfect Mind," in Gnostic ritual, and in the ambiance of ultimate concerns that surrounds it, the situation is precisely the reverse: a *release* from concrete identification with external objects—psychologically, as an inventory and integration of one's essential constituent parts, and religiously, for the realization of one's divine origin and goal. The insight and differentiation reflected by the poem bespeak an arduous psychological labor, where not only mother, father, and siblings, but any emotionally significant person becomes sufficiently known that the contrast between person and the psychic contents they represent may be clearly distinguished. This is nothing other than an exploration of projections, a resolution of personal complexes, and the differentiation of both the intrapsychic stuff of narcissism and the social stuff of *participation mystique*. And thus it may finally be rightly understood that "Incest symbolizes union with one's own being, it means individuation or becoming a self."[24]

An additional note on "The Thunder" must be included. Just as the "I am " formula of the poem derives from traditional self-presentations of the Egyptian Goddess Isis, so the poem's image of the incest matrix derives from her ancient mythology. The Egyptian calendar dealt with the discrepancy between the 365-day year and the 360 degrees round the geometric circle by setting five days apart as hallowed. On the successive days Isis, Nepthys, Horus, Set, and Osiris are born. In a time-space all their own, the five are not only central gods of the Egyptian pantheon, but possess an interrelated dynamism readily comparable to the fourfold mandala of the human self, or of Osiris, Lord of the Dead, their quintessence. Osiris and Isis are said to cling incestuously to one another in the womb and to have become husband and wife following their birth. Who is their mother? Isis

herself! Isis indeed represents the most important influence on the
Gnostic Sophia of any ancient figure besides the feminine Wisdom of
Proverbs. A famous epiphany of Isis in Apuleius's 1st-century
picaresque, *Metamorphoses,* begs introduction for the sheer breadth of
its references, and as a spotlight on the pervasive role of the Great
Goddess in Late Antiquity. Appearing on the full face of the moon,
Isis states:

> My name is One, my appearance manifold. In various rites and
> under many names the whole world pays me homage. The
> Phrygians, first of the nations born on earth, call me the Mother
> of the Gods, under the title of Pessinuntica [Cybele]. Those who
> sprang from the soil of Attica call me Cecropian Minerva
> [Athena]. The Cypriot tossing on the waves invokes me as Venus
> of Paphos [Aphrodite]; the Cretan archer as Diana [Artemis] of
> the Nets; the Sicilian in his triple form of speech as Stygian
> Proserpina [Persephone]; the Eleusinians as the ancient goddess
> Ceres [Demeter]; some as Juno, others as Bellona, others as
> Hecate; others again as Rhamnusia; the Ethiopians, the Aryans
> and Egyptians so famous for ancient lore, who are all illumined
> by the morning rays of the infant Sun-God, and worship me
> with the rites that are commonly my own, call me by my real
> name, Queen Isis.[25]

The Isis epiphany reflects the internationalism and religious syncretism
of the Alexandrian milieu. The spectrum of divine feminine forms
includes those forms (in brackets) already discussed in various
contexts—feminine personifications of realms above and below, of
earth and sea, the aerial expanse and the chthonic underworld.

Magdalen cannot be equated with Sophia in the way in which
Jesus is identified with Christ in orthodox tradition, however
powerful the intuitive pull of that association. She is human and
remains so, a paradigm of woman as seeker, companion, and
prophet. For women and for men, Sophia represents soul, both in
an intimately personal sense and an expansive transpersonal sense.
Sophia is also the Holy Spirit and as such indicates the spirit in its
specifically feminine nuance. A parallel to Magdalen and Jesus as
well as a provocative parallel to rumors that Magdalen was a
prostitute appears in the famous story of Simon the Magician and
his own mysterious female companion.

Simon Magus, a Syrian magician and prophet contemporary to the first generation of Apostles (Acts 8:9-24), drew his inspiration from a pre-Christian strand of Egyptian Gnosticism. He is the first teacher historically associated with "Sophia" as such. Like Jesus, Simon claimed special spiritual election, albeit with a flamboyance more immediately reminiscent of certain of the medieval Brethren of the Free Spirit. Simon traveled around with a woman named Helena, whom he had come to know in the brothel in the port city of Tyre where she worked as a prostitute. Her name alone places her in the realm of myth, both that of Homer's *Iliad* and that of Goethe's *Faust*. In the latter, Helena is a model of the anima, as Jung recognized, even as the Faust legend itself may be traced to the paradigmatic arch-heretic of Christian history—none other than Simon himself. Hans Jonas records that "Simon's Helena was also called *Selene* (Moon), which suggests the mythological derivation of the figure from the ancient moon-goddess."[26] Another Gnostic scholar, Kurt Rudolph, further characterizes the Simonian Sophia in relation to Helena and to Gnostic myth and doctrine:

> She is considered to be the mother of all and proceeded from him [the All-Father] as "first thought" (*ennoia*) and descended to the lower regions and created angels and powers. These, in their turn, created the world and kept Helena captive for envy's sake, in order to inflict on her every outrage, so that she could no longer return. Enclosed in a human body, she had to wander throughout the centuries from vessel to vessel in ever changing bodies (also in the body of Helen of Troy) until she ended up in the brothel from which Simon delivered her.[27]

This is a kind of divine anima projection, an all-sustaining emanation and indwelling of God's spirit in the created world comparable to the Shekhinah of mystical Judaism. The archetypal descent and return of the Goddess in this frame of reference conforms to the classic pattern of creation mythologies referenced earlier, where aboriginal formative principles emerge from a luminous One and expand as scintillating bits of light into outer darkness. Sophia appears to Simon as his own Helena, though she is but one embodiment of the unrecognized soul of the world. The perpetual reincarnation of the *anima mundi* in the transient female forms underscores the psychosomatic significance of Sophia as well as her intimacy with all things created. She is materially embedded in our Birth-Sex-Death equation as *zoe*, but is also a creature of *phos*, light-spirit. Simon's psychic inflation, such that he would claim to rescue a prostitute, strikes one as presumptuous on a human level, but little of the true character of the pair is known. One might recall Jung's dream in *Memories, Dreams, Reflections* where Elijah appears with Salome on his arm. Dramatic oposites are presented; a noteworthy spirit-man and a classic image of the anima meeting with as much possibility for antipathy as for a congenial coupling.

Regarding the All-Father (or its synonyms) and Sophia, it is essential to realize that "All-Father" implies no differentiated gender at all, unless the aeons *emerging from* the One are included. This phenomenal threshold between *Purusha* and *Prakrti* is readily comparable to that we observed in Hindu speculation. The Gnostic god, like Brahma, is beyond all qualities, but its emanations, the aeons with Sophia among them, come in androgynous pairs, each half with its *syzygos*. The classic pattern of creation mythology is elaborated in the mythopoetic speculation of Valentinus, a Gnostic teacher active between 120-160 C.E. who was educated in Alexandria, visited Rome, and lived out his life in Ephesus. His vision begins with Depth and Silence, proceeds through a series of emanations such as Conscience, Truth, Reason, Man, and Communion, etc., but comes to focus on a rank of twelve aeons, which include Sophia as their little sister. Separated from her original partner, Sophia descends into the middle space only to give birth parthenogenetically to a surprising offspring, as it were, from her own residual androgyny. The story joins the traditional creation narratives of the Old Testament, for in Valentinian Gnosticism, Sophia is none other than *the mother of Yahweh!* Referred to by the Gnostics as Ialdabaoth, an anagram suggestive of the Hebrew god as a child of chaos and a result of the fall, he is also known as the Demiurge—a creative being still further qualified as the "Hebdomad" given his sevenfold structure. The seven classical planets, the seven archons ("kings") who preside over the gates of passage on each planetary shell, and even the structures of the human body all reflect this germinal figure.

We will shortly see this sevenfold principle in action in both the original fashioning of the human being as in the ultimate ascension of soul in the *Gospel of Mary*. Gnosticism displays a fierce ambivalence towards the Creation. On one hand it considers the coming into being of the world to be a tragic error while, on the other, the creation of the material world enables the soul to pass through all manner of sensual and moral experiences for the sake of its own education. Sophia's great error consists in her wandering off from her most original *syzygos* on high. Her ultimate desire, paradigmatic of the Gnostic quest, is to recover the lost knowledge of her super-celestial origin in the All-Father (the Pleroma, the Entirety, the Treasury of Light). Sophia suffers every conceivable emotional conflict and rending psychic opposite. She is life and death, consciousness and unconsciousness, knowledge and ignorance—again the living complexity of "The Thunder, Perfect Mind":

> I am shame and boldness.
> I am shameless; I am ashamed.
> I am strength and I am fear.
> I am war and peace.
> Give heed to me.
> I am the one who is disgraced and the great one.
>
> I am the one whom they call Life,
>   and you have called Death.
> I am the one whom they call Law,
>   and you have called Lawlessness.
> I am the one whom you have pursued,
>   and I am the one whom you have seized.
> I am the one whom you have scattered,
>   and you have gathered me together.
> I am the one before whom you have been ashamed,
>   and you have been shameless to me.[28]

With the firmament and planets hung in place, let's consider Sophia's role in the fashioning of virgin Earth, the structure of the human body, as well as the pairing of Sophia and Ialdabaoth itself.

In Proverbs, Wisdom speaks of having existed before even so much as a clod of earth was formed. In a fine example of the Gnostics' elaboration of traditional themes, Sophia becomes one with the whole fabric of the created world. Interacting rhythmically with a series of compassionate messengers sent to her from the upper world, Sophia actually generates matter from out of her conflicting passions:

> This was the origin and essence of the matter from which this world was to be made: from her longing for the bliss of the ideal world the world-soul derives its origin; earth arose from her state

> of despair; water from the agitation caused by her sorrow; air
> from the solidification of her fear; while fire, causing death
> and destruction, was inherent in all these elements, as
> ignorance lay concealed in the three other passions.[29]

From passion comes matter, just as impassioned behavior typically
involves concretism and literal identifications before any psychological
reflection or insight is possible. Sophia's psychic and spiritual substance
lies concealed in all the material elements, just Simon's Helena is a
soul lost in the world. What Sophia suffers is also a major part of her
very identity, as is also the case with each conscious and unconscious
mortal in whom she delights. The vicissitudes of matter and emotion
are precisely what afflict us in states of unconsciousness, just as these
same processes gradually stir us into psychic consciousness. It is little
wonder then that the power of Sophia working through Ialdabaoth
(the sevenfold Demiurge) is responsible for the original assembly of
the human being. A fascinating account from the Gnostic *Apocryphon
of John* describes this fashioning of the "psychic body." It is an elaborate
extension of the Genesis story where Adam is fashioned from the pink
earth of Eden:

> And the powers began. The first, Goodness, created a soul of
> bone; the second, Pronoia, created a soul of sinew; the third,
> Deity, created a soul of flesh; the fourth, Lordship, created a
> soul of marrow; the fifth, Kingdom, created a soul of blood; the
> sixth, Zeal, created a soul of skin; the seventh, Understanding,
> created a soul of hair. And the multitude of angels stood up before
> it. They received from the powers the seven hypostases in order
> to make the joining of the limbs and the joining of the pieces
> and the synthesis of the adornment of each of the members. ...
> And all the angels and demons worked until they had adorned
> the psychic body, but the entire work was inert and motionless
> for a long time.[30]

The refrain "a soul of..." represents an intuitive perception of specific
body parts and their respective psychic aspects—a perfect historical
example of the holistic gestalts of enteroceptive perception described
by Robert Fliess. An alternate version of the *Apocryphon* cites 360 body
parts and 360 angels, an obvious attempt to correlate the human form
with a perfect geometric circle of the sun. The body of Adam is
specifically fashioned by Ialdabaoth, which is also why it is lies

incomplete for a time. Einar Thomassen recognizes the microcosmic nature of this anthropogenesis immediately:

> [T]he first human received the same components as the cosmos itself. He received a material part and a psychic part, contributed by the material and psychic powers of the cosmos respectively, and put together by the Demiurge. The Demiurge was invisibly moved, moreover, by the Logos, who used him as an intermediary and tool for moulding the human creature. Into this creature, however, the Logos inserted a third component coming from himself: the "breath of life," which is a soul of spiritual origin. Thus while he existed in sickness and deficiency because of his material and psychic components, the first human also possessed a capacity for understanding his predicament because of his spiritual soul.[31]

Inspiration by the Logos, whose superior power flows through Sophia from the Treasury of Light, is required for the human being to stand, live, and become complete. Thus human beings are prepared for spiritual consciousness and Christ can eventually take his place as the New Adam. The familiar descent of the dove from heaven at Jesus' baptism is the paradigmatic example of the "spiritual seed" of the Logos being sown in material and psychic Man. And as with the four elements composing the planet, a soul quality is manifest in every material aspect of the human form. The multitude of angels and demons (a combination indicative of Ialdabaoth's lower realm) utilize seven divine powers as the basic organizing principle of the *psychosoma* to which an eighth is added. This completes what the Gnostics call the Ogdoad, an image of wholeness that parallels the quaternary mandalas of Jungian psychology. In the Indian creation mythology of Rudra (Shiva) the universe is also sevenfold in structure (earth, fire, water, air, ether + sun and moon) and also comes to completion as an ogdoad through the action of "mind." Thus human beings realize their identity as the microcosm. They have become consciously aware of their psychic interior! The *chakras* of Hindu physiology as well as the upward movement of Kundalini parallel Gnostic ideas.

In summary, emphasis falls first on the Sophia-Ialdabaoth syzygy, then on a higher Sophia-Logos syzygy which has, in fact, existed in the cosmic background all along. In Sophia we see the anima archetype as not only cosmic in scope, but again in her characteristic role of mediator. She is one with the entire encircling firmament as anima and as soul-vessel. This is again clearly indicative of the tension between the body-imago ("anthropoid psyche") and the mandala as symbols of the Self in Jung's psychology. The individual little souls in the body correspond both to the *scintillae* dispersed through the earth, all nature, and the surrounding firmament as well. The Gnostics associated Ialdabaoth (Yahweh) with the baleful planet Saturn, who figures as both the ruler and devil of this earth. His creation was seen as a mistake, even as an "abortion" from the perspective of the aboriginal One. Albeit for purposes of the spirit's education, the planetary archons imprison souls within the material realm. The God of the Bible is familiar for his saturnine dominion, jealousy, and propensity to wrath. The Gnostics understand these traits as the result of Yahweh's ignorance of the fact that Sophia is his mother, and his own lack of awareness that greater cosmic powers and processes are at work of which he is only a part. This goes a long way in explaining the contempt of patriarchy for the feminine.

The Gnostic Ialdabaoth is frequently visualized as a serpent, a dragon, or another zoomorphic image. In the Biblical twelfth chapter of Revelation a great red dragon appears with a celestial woman. Jung recognizes this as a Gnostic element in the New Testament. It is selected for specific commentary owing to its greater potential familiarity for the reader and for what this may reveal of the Gnostic attitude:

> A great portent appeared in heaven: a woman clothed with the sun, with the moon under her feet, and on her head a crown of twelve stars. She was pregnant and was crying out in birthpangs, in the agony of giving birth. Then another portent appeared in heaven: a great red dragon, with seven heads and ten horns, and seven diadems on his heads. His tail swept down a third of the stars of heaven and threw them to the earth. Then the dragon stood before the woman who was about to bear a child, so that he might devour her child as soon as it was born. And she gave birth to a son, a male child, who is to rule all the nations with a rod of iron. But her child was snatched away and taken to God and to his throne; and the woman fled into the wilderness, where she has a place prepared by God. (12:1-6)

Note how the dragon sweeps stars *down* from the heavens and casts them to earth. This parallels the abysmal vortex in Timarchus's vision of the microcosm at the Oracle of Trophonius. The degree to which individual souls are mingled with the flesh or are capable of rising is indicated there by a "quivering around the gulf" of scintillating stars, some that sink while others dart upward along the world axis. The Gnostic cosmos is again similarly structured. The same gradations in this admixture of flesh and *scintillae* appear along a vertical axis between upper and lower realms in the Greek example, just as the concentration of these light phenomena are related in both instances to speculation on psychological types. (Note: Gnostic philosophy established three types, corresponding to three of the basic psychological functions: thinking, feeling, and sensation. The *pneumatikoi* could be correlated with thinking, the *psychikoi* with feeling, and the *hylikoi* with sensation. The inferior rating of the *psychikoi* was in accord with the spirit of Gnosticism, which, unlike Christianity, insisted on the value of knowledge.)

We witness in Revelation a comparable threshold between the upper and lower spheres that underscores the ambivalence of the soul's intermediary situation. The "Lady in Travail" with her numerous celestial attributes may be understood as an anima image in just this position. Presumably this is the Virgin Mary, but she has also long been interpreted as the Holy Spirit and thus as Sophia. The Lady is transfixed between the most piqued material and spiritual opposites. All the elemental tensions and emotions of childbirth appear in the seven-headed dragon's threat to her nascent child. In accord with the transcendental inclination of orthodox Christianity, the newborn child (doubtless an image of the Messiah) goes up to the celestial regions to the throne of God. This Virgin Birth represents a release and redemption from the purely earthly conditions over which the red dragon presides—for the Gnostics, the sevenfold powers of Ialdabaoth. The child's birth is the birth of a spiritual body. It represents the spiritual completion of the material and psychic body fashioned by the Demiurge, Ialdabaoth—the "Most High" of the Old Testament. The birth of this spiritual body, the essential eighth principle, is the necessary complement to the sevenfold body. Together they form the celebrated Gnostic Ogdoad aforementioned— the completion of the whole human being. Thomassen can now observe of the divine child:

> [He] has been born not from the Most High [Yahweh-Ialdabaoth] alone, as those created in the likeness of Adam were created by the Most High alone, that is, by the Demiurge. Rather, Jesus is the "new man," the one who is from the Holy Spirit <and the most High>, that is, from the Demiurge, in such a way that the Demiurge completes the formation and equipment of his body, but the Holy Spirit provides his essence.[32]

In the canonical Bible and in Gnostic experience we find a common theme. Psychologically, rebirth through the Virgin represents a symbolic process whereby everything concealed in the *psychosoma* that the Demiurge originally created is reflectively gathered in through the action of the Holy Spirit to birth a new creature of light. This is extremely important *as a specific transformative event*. But the very moment any of this is taken concretely or literally—as an actual prophecy of some inevitable historical scenario, for example—everything changes. Taking the mythologem literally would result in an instantaneous disconnect between matter and spirit—a loss of reflection and thus a loss of soul. For the book of Revelation presents us with a *phenomenology of the self*, not a collective program to be fulfilled! The archetypal images and patterns we find in apocalyptic literature represents something to be experienced by and within the individual soul, just as the Elder John, the author of Revelation, grappled with his own transpersonal vision. The experience of apocalypse ("unveiling") invariably entails a tremendous upheaval in one's prevailing worldview, as well as an inclination towards the reversal of all conscious values. We see this in the puer-senex trajectory of the Brethren of the Free Spirit, where an "innocent" and childlike joy in fresh religious developments slowly gives rise to a power hierarchy all its own. Taken literally, who can witness the child of the Virgin rising up to the throne of God to take up a rod of iron (12:5) and wreak vengeance upon the planet and its diverse peoples without disquiet? A cruel enantiodromia is in the making in Revelation. It is no coincidence that Revelation is largely a struggle between the spiritual ideals and pacifism of the Elder John and the shadow—the Beast 666, the numerical value in Hebrew for the Latin expression *Nero redivivus*. This was a collective fantasy of the period in which a return of the dead Emperor Nero to reconquer Rome was anticipated. Recall that apocalyptic anticipation is absolutely central to early Christianity, and remains so today. The fact that Paul spoke of its advent within the lifetime of his auditors not only exemplifies this fact, but correlates mightily with Paul's disparagement of the body, sexuality, and earth. And amidst the banal consumerism of urban America today one may read a bumper sticker on the back of an enormous Cadillac Esplanade: "In case of the Rapture the vehicle is yours!"

Indeed, literalism and concretism are the greater part of madness, just as they indicate a state of inflation, psychological blindness, and the moral torpor of the "saved." The Christ event, celebrated as *the* saving moment of history, came and went without the apocalypse. And Pentecost—the greatest of all indications that the crucifixion did not, magically in itself, effect the salvation of humankind—is suggestive of an ongoing process. Revelation was likely composed in 95 C.E., but still the continuity of earthly life proceeded—just as any number of Christian concretists walked back down from their hilltops in 1000 C.E. when the Kingdom did not come. Even as we know today that visions as exotic as John's may be experienced by countless individuals, a single two-thousand-year-old apocalyptic vision holds sway over the collective Christian imagination. The fact that a tongue of flame comes to rest atop the head of each disciple at Pentecost is so strongly suggestive of the uppermost (*sahasrara*) chakra that it cannot escape comment. This outpouring of the Holy Spirit following the ascension of Jesus, a conspicuous baptism by fire, resonates with the birth and the ascension of the child in Revelation and in turn with the birth of the "spiritual body" as a Gnostic goal. Particularly given that fire is inherent in all the primordial elements sprung from Sophia in Gnostic creation mythology, one might compare the Pentecostal tongues of fire with *sahasrara* phenomena—the fiery crown of the spiritual body whose numinous contents have remained dormant in the *psychosoma* all along.

Unfortunately again, there is little indication that the child of Revelation represents any more substance or coherence with its archetypal roots than the Virgin of Christian patriarchy retains of the mother archetype. The former actually appears distorted, like an angry little Yahweh, a new patriarch or a theocratic dictator brimming with vengeance. Both have been stripped of their specific earthly qualities. But the Lady of Revelation is not taken up to heaven (until 1951!). Rather she flees to the desert to be protected by God.

In Revelation the red dragon also lives on. First the angel Michael casts him out of heaven:

> The great dragon was thrown down, that ancient serpent, who is called Devil and Satan, the deceiver of the whole world—he was thrown down to the earth, and his angels were thrown down with him. (12:9)

The Devil's complete expulsion from heaven would suggest a far more radical dualism than appears, for example, in the opening chapter of Job, where Yahweh and Satan engage in an almost casual conversation concerning Job's fate. Finding himself cast upon the earth, the dragon continues to persecute the Lady who gave birth to the child. In a series of earthly appearances the dragon appears as a leopard with the feet of a bear and the mouth of a lion, and then as a two-horned dragon, before finally appearing as a scarlet beast "full of blasphemous names" (17:3). The Great Whore of Babylon rides upon it, while upon her forehead is written: "Babylon the great, mother of whores and of earth's abominations" (17:3-5). While an historical allegory for Rome (as well as Babylon), one cannot dispense with the psychological understanding of Babylon as an archetypal image of the feminine utterly removed from the Lady who births the heavenly child. However accursed and laden with flamboyant epithets from on high, we have explicit indication that the Whore of Babylon is pertinent to everything related to sexuality, body, and earth. Jung speaks of her like this:

> This mother, then, is not only the mother of all abominations, but the receptacle of all things wicked and unclean. ... Thus the mother becomes the underworld, the City of the Damned. In this primordial image of the woman on the dragon we recognize Echidna, the mother of every hellish horror. Babylon is the symbol of the Terrible Mother, who leads the people into whoredom with her devilish temptations and makes them drunk with her wine.[33]

Jung notes also a 14th-century miniature "which shows the 'woman,' beautiful as the mother of God, standing with the *lower* half of her body in a dragon."[34] Altogether in line with a brand of patriarchal and spiritualistic prejudice we have observed all along, the image of Babylon is so encrusted with negative moral epithets as to be occluded as an essential archetypal image. As we have seen in Ereshkigal, Hecate,

Persephone, and Kali, the Terrible Mother plays a pre-eminent role in initiation, just as we found with Jung's "Realm of the Mothers," where the divine child slumbers awaiting his conscious realization. Erich Neumann speaks of the dark mother this way:

> The symbolism of the Terrible Mother draws its images predominantly from the "inside"; that is to say, the negative elementary character of the Feminine expresses itself in fantastic and chimerical images that do not originate in the outside world. The reason for this is that the Terrible Mother is a symbol for the unconscious. ... The dark half of the black and white egg representing the Archetypal Feminine engenders terrible figures that manifest the black, abysmal side of life and the human psyche.[35]

One cannot embrace the fullness of life without experiencing her at some crucial juncture. Such is the diversity of the feminine, and Sophia encompasses all of it. Given all that is lost where the child of Revelation's ascent to the throne is taken concretely as a triumph over the earth, the earthly red beast begins to appear in another more acceptable light. This seven-headed beast is an equivalent form to the Gnostic Ialdabaoth, son of Sophia. It represents nothing less than the *phallic exponent of the Goddess*. This attribution is also mirrored by Eve and the Serpent, a zoomorphic image of Christ essential to the discrimination of consciousness in Gnostic understanding. Recall that Phanes too is a creator god, an Orphic Greek demiurge born of the egg that Night lays in the middle of space. He also appears on an archaic level as a dragon-like, seminal, creaturely, multi-headed *monstrum compositum* with myriad eyes. The myth of *Amor and Psyche* describes Eros similarly, before Psyche shines her light upon him. One thus notes that in both Orphic myth and the fairy tale of Apuleius this "dragon" also manifests as a shining solar puer and the golden-winged image of Eros familiar in classical mythology—with neither throne nor rod, but rather the creative illumination of love! Thus traditional Biblical and pagan imagery coalesce in an androgynous amalgam such as we see in Hermes *ithyphallos* or the alchemical image of Mercurius, the individuating principles *par excellence*. It is thus no coincidence that androgynous Mercurius figures as the *spiritus rector* of European alchemy. That science was subject to perennial charges of heresy for seeking to continue the *ongoing process* of redemption that the crucifixion had left unaccomplished. The alchemists' concern for the spirit in the stone and in all nature accordingly provides countless metaphors that are applicable to the religious dimensions of sexuality, the *scintillae* and the Light of Nature central among them.

The earthly suffering of Magdalen reflects the cosmic suffering of Sophia, as do the sufferings of all mortals. The English expression "maudlin" derives from Magdalen, given that her portrayals in Christian tradition include every conceivable human emotion. Like Sophia, Magdalen also yearns for the illumination that a spiritual guide may impart. Here our canonical references to Magdalen being afflicted by demons must be considered in relation to the Gnostic world creation and cosmology described. Mary may have first sought Jesus out as her healer. One wonders what moved so daemonically in Mary's psyche before and after she knew Jesus and the discerning capacity for relationship he brought to their healing encounter. In Luke 8:2 "seven demons" are said to have "gone out" of Magdalen. Did Jesus drive out the demons through confession, exorcism, or some external agency? As teacher and companion, he surely encouraged Mary to face her inner world and offered seminal ideas with which to understand it. But one must not suppose that her healing sprang merely from a discursive process. A larger psychosomatic understanding is required. Palsy was an ailment frequently healed by Jesus. Luke speaks of "evil spirits and infirmities" in connection with Magdalen. A basic principle of Jungian psychology holds that the energy needed to heal an illness is concealed within the symptoms themselves. When the ego is stressed by emotional turmoil or severe physical sufferings, the unconscious tends to manifest itself directly to consciousness in symbolic forms. One must thus consider the casting out of Magdalen's demons in terms of an inner transformation, a coming to consciousness of what had been present all along but until now had existed in a pathological state of unconsciousness and somatization. The fundamental healing factor appears to lie in a recognition of the soul's deep reality through a fearless acceptance of both suffering and the psychic experiences that unfold in the process of that suffering. The healing experience must have touched Magdalen's totality at the most subtle and essential level. From her early encounter with Jesus through the development of their intimate relationship, what Mary found in Jesus contributed immeasurably to an ongoing cure.

What the noncanonical Gnostic literature adds to the image of Magdalen is the erotic quality of her bond with Jesus, her difficult relationship with the other disciples, and her own prominence as a visionary. The *Gospel of Philip* is explicit concerning her personal relationship with Jesus:

> And the companion of the [...] Mary Magdalene. [...loved] her more than [all] the disciples [and used to] kiss her [often] on her [...]. The rest of [the disciples...]. They said to him, "Why do you love her more than all of us?" The savior answered and said to them, "Why do I not love you like her? ..."[36]

Translated here as "companion," the original Greek *koinonos* indicates a very intimate friend, a partner in an enterprise. The term may also indicate a lover. The broken text is the primary document of the affection between Magdalen and Jesus. The closeness between the two makes the disciples, all of them male, extremely jealous and bitter. Beyond the affection they shared, this also springs from Jesus' recognition of Mary as possessing a more refined understanding of the light of gnosis than the others, for following without interruption is Jesus' comment to the group:

> When a blind man and one who sees are both together in darkness, they are no different from one another. When the light comes, then he who sees will see the light, and he who is blind will remain in darkness.[37]

Jealousy and a contentious attitude on the part of the male disciples crops up in a variety of Gnostic contexts, such as the *Gospel of Thomas*:

> His disciples said to him, "When will the kingdom come?" [Jesus said,] "It will not come by waiting for it. It will not be a matter of saying 'here it is' or 'there it is.' Rather the kingdom of the father is spread out upon the earth, and men do not see it." Simon Peter said to them, "Let Mary leave us, for women are not worthy of life." Jesus said, "I myself shall lead her in order to make her male, so that she too will become a living spirit resembling you males. For every woman who will make herself male will enter the kingdom of heaven."[38]

The equation of "living spirit" with "male" would strike the modern ear as misogynistic even without the specific directive that Mary be excluded. But this "becoming male" refers to a specific ascetic notion of receiving gnosis. The essential role of women and the feminine in other groups demonstrates that this attitude was not characteristic of Gnosticism as a whole. For example, the teachings of Valentinus affirm the equality of the sexes and feature Sophia in a central and pervasive role.

The *Gospel of Mary* features the sevenfold imagery of Ialdabaoth as an inner experience of Gnostic cosmology. Magdalen and the disciples are gathered together following the crucifixion in a tense and disconcerted mood. The jealous Peter places Mary center stage, saying, "Sister, we know that the Savior loved you more than the rest of women. Tell us the words of the Savior which you remember—which you know (but) we do not, nor have we heard them."[39] The text continues with a powerful vision of Christ, who commends her for her unflinching reception of mystic sight:

> Mary answered and said, "What is hidden from you I will proclaim to you." And she began to speak to them these words: "I," she said, "I saw the Lord in a vision and I said to him, 'Lord, I saw you today in a vision.' He answered and said to me, 'Blessed are you, that you did not waver at the sight of me.'"[40]

The ensuing account of this conversation between Jesus and Magdalen evidences Mary's keen spiritual understanding and her capacity to discuss the intricacies of Gnostic psychology and cosmology. While the peculiar question of whether Jesus and Magdalen had sexual intercourse after the crucifixion (which arose in the interrogation of the radical Free Spirit, John Hartmann in Chapter 3) is left open here, the meeting of the pair is set in a transitional and liminal ambiance. This is a time of tremendous bereavement, but also of potentially profound insights. The visionary reunion thus provides an additional example of the syzygy in action, this time with a woman meeting her contrasexual partner. This affords a ripe opportunity to consider the accumulation of biographical and psychological experience that steadily raises disparate gendered elements within the personality to consciousness and works to differentiate them. Retaining the prostitute component of Magdalen's popular identity for a moment, consider

Magdalen's biographical experience of men and the masculine beyond the wealthy father we assume and the unknown of her possible brother(s): Mary is progressively impacted by an indeterminate series of male patrons as a courtesan and is probably fully informed regarding the dealings of ruthless King Herod's notorious court (via "Joanna, the wife of Herod's steward Chuza"). She endures significant psychosomatic sufferings, presents herself to Jesus as a patient in order to be healed of her daemonic possession, becomes an inspired student of Jesus, and then his most intimate companion. Mary has her mettle tested in contentious interactions with the male disciples, and finally comes to grief with the arrest and public execution by Roman soldiers of the most important person in her life. All this has transpired, when the resurrected Lord appears to her as a triumphant and affirming inner figure. Whether the appearance of Jesus is an objective post-mortem visitation or a personification of Magdalen's animus, the point remains the same. The visionary meeting is the high point of a entire biography of experience for Magdalen, the culmination of her lifelong experience of men and the spiritual product of a long, highly personalized, tumultuous, religiously decisive, and individuating love relationship. Viewed psychologically, the Christ-figure within Mary's psyche definitely possesses the qualities of a positive animus that supports her creative endeavors and affirms her mission in the world. Her standing thus, unwavering, demonstrates that a phallic uprightness and imperturbability of spirit ultimately knows no gender.

The *Gospel of Mary*, its text unfortunately damaged, immediately proceeds to a startling vision of the inner world, Mary's access to which would be difficult to imagine without her being instructed and intimately inspired by Jesus—as a man and as a creative personification of her own spiritual animus. The first principle (prior to "desire" below) is lost, but it is Mary's dispute with desire and ignorance that concerns us in this Gnostic vision of soul ascending in the face of the demiurgic contenders who confront soul:

> And desire [states] that, "I did not see you [i.e., soul] descending, but now I see you ascending. Why do you lie, since you belong to me?" The soul answered and said, "I saw you. You did not see me nor recognize me. I served you as a garment, and you did not know me." When it had said this, it went away rejoicing greatly.

> Again it came to the third power, which is called ignorance.
> [It (the power)] questioned the soul, saying, "Where are you
> going? In wickedness are you bound. But you are bound; do
> not judge!" And the soul said, "Why do you judge me although
> I have not judged? I was bound though I have not bound. I
> was not recognized. ..."

An occasional feature of Gnostic texts, the principles of desire and ignorance are recapitulated in secondary numerical clusters as the vision proceeds—first three (where "darkness" precedes desire and ignorance), and then a fourth power, which takes seven forms:

> The first form is darkness, the second desire, the third ignorance,
> the fourth is the excitement of death, the fifth is the kingdom
> of the flesh, the sixth is the foolish wisdom of the flesh, the
> seventh is wrathful wisdom.[41]

As a whole, these "seven powers of wrath" are once more a typically pejorative Gnostic designation for the demiurgic powers of Ialdabaoth, the sevenfold Hebdomad, a comparative form of which appears as the seven-headed Red Dragon of Revelation. Psychologically, we witness Mary in a dynamic struggle with the autonomous archetypal powers, which might also be thought of as complexes or "partial personalities" on a personal level. The tension is not merely between Mary's ego-consciousness and her inner world but also among a number of autonomous psychic figures, which interact with one another. Mary, Christ, and soul, as well as the seven powers, are all decisive participants. Each figure in the vision possesses its own affective, imaginal, and ideational quality as well as its own measure of dispersed consciousness. Magdalen's vision is thus a vivid example of the psyche as a field of multiple luminosities. The perplexed seven powers press soul with the words, "Whence do you come, slayer of men, or where are you going, conqueror of space?" as Magdalen's vision comes to its lysis. Soul proclaims:

> What binds me has been slain, and what surrounds me has been
> overcome, and my desire has ended, and ignorance has died. In
> a [world] I was released from a world, [and] in a type from a
> heavenly type, and [from] the fetter of oblivion which is
> transient. From this time on I will attain to the rest of time, of
> the season, of the aeon, in silence.[42]

Mary then falls silent before disciples, who are dumbfounded and seek to repudiate these "strange ideas." Andrew takes exception to Mary even as Peter grumbles concerning the Master: "Did he really speak with a woman without our knowledge (and) not openly? Are we to turn about and all listen to her? Did he prefer her to us?"[43] Mary begins to weep at not being believed. At last the group comes to some reconciliation and goes forth to preach.

In summary, the *Gospel of Mary* clearly focuses on soul's free movement in an intermediary space—gravitating upward towards a celestial empyrean in a way that appears to activate a counter-reaction from the lower demiurgic powers of the instinctual sphere, who would assert their respective claims. Such is the archetypal hinterland of what we call psychodynamics. Desire arrogantly confronts soul only to learn that soul cloaks it like a garment of which the wearer is unaware. Consider the blind immediacy of a physical prompting that is intent on concrete gratification. Soul's words suggest that those same energies may be held reflectively within and contemplated as image and awareness. Such active imagination would reveal the fabric of the soul's garment. Next, ignorance boldly confronts soul, only to learn that though it sought to bind soul, soul cannot be bound. Soul's ascending freedom is triumphant. Soul, as the reflective vessel of consciousness *par excellence*, sees beyond the ego and displaces its limited conception of reality. Soul says, "I was not recognized. But I have recognized that the All is being dissolved both the earthly (things) and the heavenly."[44] Clearly, the sudden ascendancy of a perspective based on soul spells death for the old ego and heralds an expansion of consciousness that is far beyond the ken of the seven powers of earthly wrath.

The influence of these seven powers of Ialdabaoth is fundamental to the concretism and literalism of ego that has rejected the unconscious and remained uninitiated by soul. But it would be simplistic to say that the ego is synonymous with the powers, at least without recalling that fundamental psychoanalytic observation that the body is, to begin with, a "body-ego." However pneumatic and ascendant Mary's vision, the powers have a distinct bodily reference. Intuition suggests that they are related to the seven demons that originally afflicted Magdalen and which we have seen in the psychic body fashioned by angels and demons in the *Apocryphon of John*. Most immediately, the angelic/demonic host pertain to the perpetual experiential fluctuations of our organismic awareness and mood. Magdalen's seven demons and the seven powers of her vision may likewise be understood as essential structures that manifest themselves in a variety of ways. They represent a subtle dimension of reality in which psychic or somatic symptoms are fatefully generated or transformed and which any inquiry into spiritual healing would seek to comprehend.

In ancient Gnosticism these bodily things are never created by the ineffable, transcendent All-Father. They are fashioned by the "angels and demons" who serve the Demiurge. Accordingly, in Magdalen's vision soul seeks to ascend from this transient "fetter of oblivion" to the immaterial godhead. At its extremes, such a radical dualism represents a profound challenge to the psychologist, who would welcome the rediscovery of the soul but would seek to reunite the soul with the body and the world. The question is whether the earthly powers in Mary's vision are destined to appear only as wrathful, foolish, dark, and deadly. Here we can only note that *this* particular ascension motif is intimately associated with death, though *whose* soul is rising is left unanswered. In any case, Eliade makes a more optimistic observation of pantheons worldwide that accords more with a Jungian outlook:

> We must not forget that many of the divinities and powers
> of the Earth and the underworld are not necessarily "evil" or
> "demonic." They generally represent autochthonous and even
> local hierophanies that have fallen in rank as a result of
> changes within the pantheon. Sometimes the bipartition
> of gods into celestial and chthonic-infernal is only a
> convenient classification without any pejorative implication
> for the latter.[45]

Pertinent to the foregoing, a distinguishing feature of the Gnostic outlook, and anticipatory of the charged ambiance of the Valentinian bridal chamber, the Gnostics emphasize the necessity of experiencing the Resurrection *while still in this life*: "Those who say they will die first and then rise are in error. If they do not first receive the resurrection while they live, when they die the will receive nothing."[46]

Thus, the religious moment in Gnosticism is archetypal, experiential, and numinous—scarcely something in which one merely believes! Elaine Pagels speaks to the point:

> Gnostic Christians interpret resurrection in various ways. Some
> say that the person who experiences the resurrection does not
> meet Jesus raised physically back to life; rather, he encounters
> Christ on a spiritual level. This may occur in dreams, in ecstatic
> trances, in visions, or in moments of numinous illumination.[47]

The appearance of Christ in the vision of Magdalen is a vivid example
of just such a psychic experience.

Mary is traumatized, a woman in mourning. Her own longing
for recognition and her need of human companionship are apparently
only exacerbated by so grave a loss. The possibility of her regaining
equilibrium is indicated by soul's statement: "The All is being
dissolved, both the earthly (things) and the heavenly," and more
particularly by the statement, "In a world I was released from a world,
[and] in a type from a heavenly type." Depth psychologically this
indicates Magdalen's triumph over concretism and literalism in both
an inner and outer sense. Though fully of the world, her vision features
soul decisively eluding possession by the powers of the world (the
powers of wrath, the archons, etc.). Thus "world" becomes a living
metaphor. Being released "in a type from a heavenly type" is a
reciprocal commentary on being freed from what I term "imaginal
literalism"—that acquisitive propensity to fix images, to snatch them
from the flow of psyche's living current and enshrine them as icons or
idols. This is a first step towards deadly theology. In Eastern traditions
divine images may be embraced provisionally. They emerge with fresh
numinosity, serve their purpose, and fade. For precisely such reasons
a contemporary Gnostic hierophant can offer the eucharistic cup with
the words, "This is the blood of all the slain gods and goddesses from
the beginning of time."[48] Mary finds herself in a state of graceful
centroversion in the *Gospel of Mary*, a detachment of consciousness
resembling Buddhist "mindfulness."

The foregoing rounds out all we actually know of the intimacy
between Mary Magdalen and Jesus. In the face of centuries in which
Magdalen has been rumored to be a former prostitute, it is extremely
ironic that a strict textually based examination reveals nothing of the
kind. Rather than resembling Venus or Aphrodite, the historical
Magdalen is archetypally far more related to Athena, Hestia (the
reflective Greek goddess of the hearth), or even the oracular Pythoness
of Delphi. Of course, even if Magdalen were a prostitute, it would

say absolutely nothing about her access to religious experience. Perhaps the historical Magdalen might thus be left in peace, and spared further distortion by either patriarchy or today's pulp fiction mill. Crucial to ponder, however, is the fact that Christian tradition has, through centuries, elaborated a fabulous myth of the sensual, beautiful, vulnerable sex woman. As a cultural phenomenon, this myth is composed of textual misinterpretation, patriarchal slander, popular legends, and lavish artistic productions. This is itself the strongest possible testament to the vitality and continuity of Venus and Aphrodite no matter what Christian doctrine says against them. The results of our investigation of the historical Magdalen are thus, in certain respects, quite disappointing for anyone interested in the future of Christianity. True, Christian women now possesses a stunning paradigm of spiritual insight and ecclesiastical authority, just as popular appreciation of both Magdalen and Sophia are clearly expanding. Still, the "make her male" of the *Gospel of Thomas* is haunting and cautionary. The question remains as to what degree might everything associated with the popular Venusian and Aphroditic image of Magdalen—the numinosity of the body, sex, erotic love, beauty, and femininity that these represent—be comprehensively embraced, and the moral imperative of confronting the tragic sexual legacy of patriarchy begin.

Turning finally to the bridal chamber of Valentinian Gnosticism, it is the *Gospel of Philip* from which our knowledge of Gnostic ritual derives, the final ancient document to be considered here. Rather than an actual gospel, the damaged text has been described as resembling catechism notes. The following passage immediately demonstrates that the bridal chamber is one aspect of a sequential ritual program:

> The lord [did] everything in a mystery, a baptism and a chrism and a eucharist and a redemption and a bridal chamber.
>   [...] he said, "I came to make [the things below] like the things [above, and the things] outside like those [inside. I came to unite] them in that place." [...] here through [types ...].[49]

The characteristic Gnostic concern for reconciling the above with the below and an understanding of ritual as a play of types and images are already present in this concise introduction. We might consider the entire course taken to this point: from the original psychic androgyny of the child, through extended reflection on the dynamics of the syzygy working to differentiate masculine and feminine elements within the personality, and on to the possibility of a numinous and salvific reunion. One famous passage from the *Gospel of Thomas* suggests that we have indeed come full circle, just as it indicates—in the image of a child of light—so much of the mystery of Gnosis:

> Jesus saw infants being suckled. He said to his disciples, "These infants being suckled are like those who enter the kingdom." They said to him, "Shall we then, as children, enter the kingdom?" Jesus said to them, "When you make the two one, and when you make the inside like the outside and the outside like the inside, and the above like the below, and when you make the male and the female one and the same, so that the male not be male nor the female female; when you fashion eyes in place of an eye, and a hand in place of a hand, and a foot in place of a foot, and a likeness in place of a likeness; then will you enter [the kingdom]."[50]

Psychologically this mystic marriage bespeaks the soothing and integration of all the conflicting opposites within the personality that have been differentiated and refined through the raw experiences of life's forward flow, though we are unsure of how psychological or concerned with "the development of personality" (in the modern sense) the Gnostics actually were. On one hand Gnosticism represents one of the most ardently transcendental religious developments in the history of Western spirituality. The Gnostics, of course, looked upon the created world as the prison house of Ialdabaoth. On the other hand, Quispel can boldly proclaim: "Just forget about all that talk of the otherworldliness of the Gnostics!" The Gnostics lived lives, bore children, and considered sex to be extremely important for their spiritual development. We know little of their sociology. But in any case, Valentinian Gnosticism generally, and the ritual of the bridal chamber in particular, is unique in Christian history for its emphasis on the equality and complementarity of the sexes and for its recognition of gender and the syzygy as a fundamental religious issue. Again, this was a transient development of the 2nd century C.E.

The question of origins and ritual reintegration calls up the family constellation and the child quite automatically. In sharp contrast to the Holy Family orthodox tradition, the Gnostic *Gospel of Philip* is unapologetic about the fact that Jesus has two fathers and two mothers—Joseph and the transcendent All-Father, Mary and all-pervading Sophia (Holy Spirit). This recognition not only introduces a realistic and much-needed earthly dimension to the symbolism of the bridal chamber but, more particularly, explains and validates the works of the Demiurge as foundational to the entire Gnostic quest:

> Joseph the carpenter planted a garden because he needed wood for his trade. It was he who made the cross from the trees which he planted. His own offspring hung on that which he planted. His offspring was Jesus and the planting was the cross.[51]

Thomassen observes that:

> [T]here can hardly be any doubt that Joseph, the wood-worker and father of Jesus, is interpreted by the *Gos. Phil.* as *a type of the Demiurge*. The "wood" represents matter [*hyle*, wood], and the statement that Joseph's seed hung on the tree must therefore refer to the father of Jesus in a material body.[52]

Thus Joseph and Jesus, like Adam and all humankind, possess a body fashioned by the Demiurge Ialdabaoth. Reciprocally, the text never claims that Mary was not made pregnant by Joseph, but simply that she was not defiled by it: "the Saviour himself was not defiled by submitting himself to physical conception and assuming a human body."[53]

A provocative additional element in the *Gospel of Philip* is the belief that Adam and Jesus were both born of "virgins." Adam was fashioned from the virgin earth of Eden, the material fabric from which Sophia is inseparable. She is also the Holy Spirit who, together with the Logos of the transcendent All-Father, creates the *spiritual* body of Jesus. Thus "the Saviour is a spiritual being in a material body."[54] Harmonizing the two is the primary focus of the bridal chamber. The ritual seeks to call forth an illuminating consciousness (*gnosis*) in the initiate, the "spiritual seed" that fosters his or her awareness of a subtle spiritual dimension in the body, aligned with the All-Father even as it harmonizes the material body that the Demiurge originally fashioned in his creative partnership with Sophia:

> The Father of the Entirety united with Sophia and revealed in the bridal chamber, and from the union of the bridegroom and the bride issued the Saviour's body.[55]

The reunion of Sophia with Christ (emissary of the Entirety) is a joyous personal and cosmic event, one sought in the bridal chamber and anticipated in its full manifestation as a culmination of life and greater world process. For this reason one contemporary Gnostic liturgy can say of Christ and Sophia: "He has come for us, but in truth He has come for She who came for us."[56] Sophia is the *anima mundi*, and as such a personification of the soul of all humankind, our planet, and of the Creation itself. Christ's coming for her is his coming to us—an individual, collective, and superordinate reunion of soul and spirit. Magdalen's recognition of Jesus in the kind gardener she encounters in John 20:16 is an earthly reflection of the same moment of realization.

The elements of the bridal chamber mystery naturally include a symbolic repetition of the central moments in the life of Jesus which, in effect, constitutes one redemptive act. Baptism recapitulates the baptism of Jesus by John the Baptist (John 1:32), an event that includes the descent of Sophia as Holy Spirit in the form of a dove to vivify his spiritual body. Anointing (hot oil, chrism = fire) is symbolic of Jesus' triumph over his demiurgic status prior to baptism and resonates with the mystery of Pentecost. The Eucharist is a celebration of the bread of heaven, which Jesus brings to nourish the spiritual body he has generated. A "redemption" is also referenced in the *Gospel of Philip*. It clearly harkens to rebirth, and the re-annointing of Jesus following his baptism, but is not further described as a ritual component. The symbol of the bridal chamber itself is laced with the foregoing elements in overlapping metaphors, but carries special germinal significance for the birth of a spiritual body, which is envisioned as the epiphany of *a divine child of light*. Note how the *Gospel of Philip* comes to focus on a highly particular quality of light in relation to the ritual birth:

> It is from water and fire that the soul and the spirit came into being. It is from water and fire and light that the son of the bridal chamber (came into being). The fire is the chrism, the light is the fire. I am not referring to that fire which has no form, but to the other fire whose form is white, which is bright and beautiful, and which gives to beauty.[57]

Light phenomena of many kinds and various nuances have played a decisive role in this entire investigation. Phanes is the "coming of light" and a bearer of the seeds of the gods. Dionysus appears as the light of archetypal consciousness distributed through the bodily organs, like the medieval "light of nature" and the *scintillae* of the alchemists. A flash of fiery light is synchronous with the culminating vision of the Eleusinian mysteries. Hermes and Eros are associated with fire and light. Jung's enthroned subterranean phallus is surmounted by a single eye and a strange astral light that mirrors the sun's solar phallus (exemplifying the above and below of Eliade's Solar Hierophany). A rabbi in deep mystical identification with the angel Metatron must reckon with fiery torches that emerge from his own body! But the centrality and ambiguity of light—as the natural light of day or the archetypal light of the psyche germane to enteroception, dream, and vision—is most clearly captured by Ezekiel. Recounting his historic vision of the Merkabah, the prophet repeatedly refers to "*something*" like a throne, "*something*" like a human form—like gleaming amber, like fire, like the Glory of the Lord (Ezekiel 1:22). This is the light of numinous visions, which the *Gospel of Thomas* also describes most beautifully:

> The images are manifest to man, but the light in them remains concealed in the image of the light of the Father He will become manifest, but his image will remain concealed by his light.[58]

Kerényi tells us that "each God is a source of a world that without him remains invisible, but with him reveals itself in its own light."[59] In the bridal chamber Sophia and the All-Father bring the spiritual seed of gnosis to bodily man and woman, creatures of flesh and blood who have been carefully prepared by Sophia and Ialdabaoth for the dawning of precisely this light. The Valentinian ritual of the bridal chamber is a drawing together of everything of which the human being is composed: body, soul, and spirit. Like Magdalen's vision of soul ascending, the ritual process anticipates what the Gnostics called the *hypocatastasis,* the cessation of all emanations emerging from the One, and a return of the elements of Creation and all awakened souls to the Treasury of Light. Meanwhile, anyone engaged in serious reflection on life, psyche, and the light of the spirit may take heart and challenge from Jesus' beguilingly simple observation that "the kingdom of the father is spread out upon the earth, and men do not see it."[60]

Epilogue

Just as Goethe could comment that as a moralist he is a monotheist, as an artist a polytheist, and as a naturalist a pantheist; so any creative response to the complexity of lived experience is a highly individual activity to which the mysteries of personality and the psyche are fundamental. Any religious complex, be it a vast global organization, the most indigenous, or an individual avenue of reflection and ritual practice represents a localized attempt to approach a religious mystery common to all humankind. This exploration of sexuality and the religious imagination has accordingly focused on the archetypal dimensions of historical and contemporary psychic materials in order to affirm their universality; trace the imaginal life of the *psychosoma* in its sexual, erotic, and relational aspects; and to consider the human and ecological implications of the patriarchal Christian legacy at this moment in history.

Jung's observation that the instinct to which a culture devotes the greatest attention is a prime source of religious symbolism is fundamental in this entire inquiry. The overt expression and progressive commodification of sex is sufficiently evident everywhere in the culture to require extended comment. The simple facts that sex is a psychosomatic phenomenon, that its patterns closely parallel those of the religious instinct, that soul and body are inseparable from the natural world, that humankind's relationship with Earth stands at a threshold where survival itself is at issue, and that body, sex, and the natural world are alive with divine energies that have been slandered and distorted through the historical excesses of patriarchy—this is the avenue of your author's effort and intention. One's erotic identity, inclination, and imagination are among the most private aspects of life. Insofar as this investigation offers the reader constructive insights and encouragement to embrace the totality of their physical, psychological, and spiritual experience, to discover the relationship of these with one another, and move fearlessly and joyfully on into their own experience of the sacred, its intention will be gratefully fulfilled.

Notes

PREFACE

1. C. G. Jung, *The Collected Works of C. G. Jung*, trans. R. F. C. Hull, ed. H. Read, M. Fordham, G. Adler, Wm. McGuire, 20 vols. (Princeton, NJ: Princeton University Press, 1953-1979), vol. 5, § 718. (Hereafter *CW*.)
2. C. G. Jung, "Flying Saucers: A Modern Myth," *CW* 10, § 652.
3. C. G. Jung, *Memories, Dreams, Reflections*, ed. Aniela Jaffé (New York: Pantheon Books, 1961), pp. 172-173.
4. Octavio Paz, *Conjunctions and Disjunctions*, trans. H. R. Lane (New York: Seaver Books, 1982), p. 14.
5. Carl Kerényi, *Dionysus: Archetypal Image of Indestructible Life*, trans. Ralph Mannheim, 2 vols. (Princeton, NJ: Princeton University Press, 1976), pp. xxxii-xxxvii, passim.

CHAPTER ONE—RELIGION AND SEXUALITY, PSYCHE AND IMAGINATION

1. Benjamin Walker, *Tantrism: Its Secrets and Practices* (Wellingborough, UK: Aquarian Press, 1982), p. 65.
2. Donald F. Sandner, personal communication.
3. *Diagnostic and Statistical Manual of Mental Disorders* (Washington, D.C.: American Psychiatric Association, 1994), p. 685. (Hereafter, *DSM:IV*.)
4. Vern L. Bullough, *Sexual Variance in Society and History* (Chicago, IL: University of Chicago Press, 1976), p. 132.
5. Jung, "Flying Saucers," *CW* 10, § 653.
6. C. G. Jung, "On 'The Tibetan Book of the Great Liberation," *CW* 11, § 769.
7. James M. Robinson, ed., *The Nag Hammadi Library in English*, 3rd ed. (San Francisco, CA: Harper & Row, 1978), p. 150.
8. Friedrich Nietzsche, *The Birth of Tragedy* (1872), trans. Ian C. Johnston. Accessed online at <http://www.mala.bc.ca/~johnstoi/Nietzsche/tragedy_all.htm>.
9. Rudolph Otto, *The Idea of the Holy* (New York: Oxford University Press, 1975), p. 5.
10. *Ibid.*

11. Mircea Eliade, *Patterns in Comparative Religion* (London: Sheed and Ward, 1976), p. 19.

12. C. G. Jung, *Psychological Types*, *CW* 6, § 722.

13. *Ibid.*, § 715.

14. *Ibid.*, § 722.

15. *Ibid.*, § 78. (Emphasis mine.)

16. James Hillman, *The Myth of Analysis: Three Essays in Archetypal Psychology* (New York: Harper & Row, 1972), pp. 63-64. (Emphasis in original.)

17. Robert Graves, *The Greek Myths*, vol. 1 (New York: George Brazillar, Inc., 1957), p. 30.

18. W. K. C. Guthrie, *Orpheus and Greek Religion* (Princeton, NJ: Princeton University Press, 1993), p. 80.

19. Marie-Louise von Franz, *Creation Myths* (Zürich: Spring Publications, 1972), p. 8.

20. James Hillman, *The Thought of the Heart* (Dallas, TX: Spring Publications, Inc., 1981), p. 28.

21. Octavio Paz, *Conjunctions and Disjunctions*, trans. H. R. Lane (New York: Seaver Books, 1982), p. 14.

22. Wallace Stevens, "Peter Quince at the Clavier," *The Palm at the End of the Mind*, ed. by Holly Stevens (New York: Vintage, 1972), p. 10.

23. Virgil, *Aeneid* VI.126-129.

CHAPTER TWO—THE PATRIARCHAL SEXUAL LEGACY

1. James Hillman, *Re-Visioning Psychology* (New York: Harper & Row, 1975), p. 96.

2. Vern L. Bullough, *Sexual Variance in Society and History* (Chicago, IL: University of Chicago Press, 1976), p. 69. (Emphasis mine.)

3. C. G. Jung, "Archetypes of the Collective Unconscious," *CW* 9i, § 59.

4. C. G. Jung, "Concerning the Archetypes and the Anima Concept," *CW* 9i, § 115.

5. Edward C. Whitmont, *Return of the Goddess* (New York: Crossroads, 1983), p. 83.

6. C. G. Jung, *Aion*, *CW* 9ii, § 427. (Emphasis mine.)

7. Whitmont, p. 43. (Emphasis mine.)

8. Walter Zimmerli, *Ezekiel I*, ed. F. M. Cross, K. Baltzer, and J. L. Greenspoon (Philadelphia, PA: Fortress Press, 1979), pp. 37-238.

9. Sylvia Brinton Perera, *Descent to the Goddess* (Toronto: Inner City Books, 1981), p. 59.

10. Bullough, p. 69.

11. *Ibid.*, 169.

12. *Ibid.*

13. Mircea Eliade, *Patterns in Comparative Religion* (London: Sheed and Ward, 1976), p. 147.

14. Bullough, p. 169.
15. *Ibid.*
16. Gilles Quispel, *The Secret Book of Revelation* (New York: McGraw-Hill Co., 1979), p. 35.
17. Peter Brown, *Augustine of Hippo* (Berkeley, CA: University of California Press, 1967), p. 29.
18. *Ibid.*, pp. 28-29.
19. *Ibid.*, p. 29.
20. *Ibid.*
21. *Ibid.*, p. 30.
22. C. G. Jung, "Psychological Aspects of the Mother Archetype," *CW* 9i, § 158.
23. Brown, p. 30.
24. *Ibid.*
25. *Ibid.*
26. *Ibid.*, p. 31.
27. *Ibid.*, p. 30.
28. *Ibid.*, p. 39.
29. *Ibid.*
30. *Ibid.*
31. C. G. Jung, "On the Psychology of the Trickster Figure," *CW* 9i, § 485.
32. Brown, p. 62.
33. *Ibid.*, p. 59.
34. *Ibid.*, p. 47.
35. Augustine of Hippo, *The Confessions of St. Augustine* (New York: Modern Library, Random House, 1949), p. 81.

CHAPTER THREE—MEDIEVAL SEXUAL HERESIES

1. Johann Wolfgang Goethe, *Faust, Part II*, trans. Philip Wayne (London: Penguin Classics, 1973), pp. 108-109.
2. *Ibid.*, p. 105.
3. Howard McConeghey, *Art and Soul* (Putnam, CT: Spring Publications, 2003), p. 7.
4. Walter L. Wakefield, *Heresies of the High Middle Ages* (New York: Columbia University Press, 1969), p. 72.
5. *Ibid.*, p. 99.
6. Norman Cohn, *The Pursuit of the Millenium: Revolutionary Millenarians and Mystical Anarchists of the Middle Ages* (New York: Oxford University Press, 1974), p. 180.
7. Robert E. Lerner, *The Heresy of the Free Spirit in the Later Middle Ages* (Berkeley, CA: University of California Press, 1972), p. 71.
8. *Ibid.*, p. 82.

9.   *Ibid.*, p. 76.
10. *Ibid.*, p. 113.
11. *Ibid.*, p. 114.
12. *Ibid.*, p. 116.
13. *Ibid.*, p. 117.
14. *Ibid.*, p. 118.
15. Cohn, pp. 150-151. (Emphasis mine.)
16. Lerner, p. 187.
17. Cohn, p. 151.
18. Lerner, p. 136.
19. *Ibid.*, pp. 136-137.
20. *Ibid.*, p. 138.
21. Cohn, p. 179.
22. *Ibid.*, p. 180.
23. Jean-Paul Sartre, *Baudelaire*, trans. Martin Turnell (New York: New Directions, 1967), p. 76.
24. Simone de Beauvoir, "Must We Burn Sade," in *The Marquis de Sade* (New York: Grove Press, 1967), p. 28.
25. Wakefield, p. 79.

CHAPTER FOUR—CONDUITS OF THE BODY

1.   C. G. Jung, *Nietzsche's Zarathustra* (Princeton, NJ: Princeton University Press, 1988), p. 85.
2.   Rudolph Otto, *The Idea of the Holy* (New York: Oxford University Press, 1975), pp. 12-13.
3.   Sigmund Freud, *The Future of an Illusion*, Vol. XXI of *The Complete Psychological Works of Sigmund Freud*, ed. James Strachey (London: Hogarth Press and the Institute for Psychoanalysis, 1978), p. 56.
4.   C. G. Jung, *Symbols of Transformation*, *CW* 5, § 508. (Emphasis mine.)
5.   James Hillman, *The Myth of Analysis: Three Essays in Archetypal Psychology* (New York: Harper & Row, 1972), p. 64.
6.   Wilhelm Reich, *The Function of the Orgasm* (New York: Farrar, Straus, and Giroux, 1973), p. 350.
7.   *Ibid.*, p. 300.
8.   *Ibid.*, p. 21.
9.   *Ibid.*, p. 102.
10. *Ibid.*, p. 327.
11. Dylan Thomas, *Collected Poems* (New York: New Directions, 1956), p. 10.
12. C. G. Jung, "The Personification of the Opposites," *Mysterium Coniunctionis*, *CW* 14, § 129. (Emphasis in original.)

13. Robert Fliess, *Ego and Body Ego* (New York: International University Press, 1961), p. 206. (Emphasis mine.)

14. James M. Robinson, ed., *The Nag Hammadi Library in English*, 3rd ed. (San Francisco, CA: Harper & Row, 1978), p. 135.

15. Fliess, p. 207.

16. *Ibid.*, p. 210.

17. Erich Neumann, *The Great Mother: An Analysis of an Archetype*, trans. Ralph Manheim (Princeton, NJ: Princeton University Press, 1974), p. 39.

18. Fliess, p. 210.

19. *Ibid.*, p. 213.

20. C. G. Jung, "The Spiritual Problem of Modern Man," *CW* 10, § 195.

21. C. G. Jung, *Freud and Psychoanalysis*, *CW* 4, § 270.

22. See Carl Kerényi, *Dionysus: Archetypal Image of Indestructible Life*, trans. Ralph Mannheim, 2 vols. (Princeton, NJ: Princeton University Press, 1976), p. 8.

23. Jung, "On the Nature of the Psyche," *CW* 8, § 380.

24. *Ibid.*, § 387.

25. James Hillman, *Facing the Gods* (Dallas, TX: Spring Publications, 1980) p. 94.

26. *Ibid.*, p. 95.

27. *Ibid.*, p. 96.

28. *Ibid.*, p. 97.

29. *Ibid.*, p. 98.

30. Carl Kerényi, *Hermes: Guide of Souls* (Zürich: Spring Publications, 1976), p. 55.

31. Jean-Paul Sartre, *Baudelaire*, trans. Martin Turnell (New York: New Directions, 1967), p. 39.

32. Hillman, *Facing the Gods*, p. 99.

33. C. G. Jung, "The Dual Mother," *CW* 5, § 506.

34. Stanislav Grof, *Beyond the Brain: Birth, Death, and Transcendence in Psychotherapy* (Albany, NY: State University of New York, 1985), p. 102.

35. *Ibid.*, p. 116.

36. *Ibid.* p. 39.

37. *Ibid.*, p. 49.

38. *Ibid.*, p. 50.

39. Jung, *CW* 8, § 388.

40. *Ibid.* § 391.

41. *Ibid.*, § 393.

42. Robinson, p. 16.

43. Johann Wolfgang Goethe, *Autobiography and Annals: Truth and Poetry*, trans. John Oxenford (London, 1881), p. 386.

44. Gerschom Scholem, *Major Trends in Jewish Mysticism* (New York: Schocken Books, 1941), p. 54.

45. Robinson, p. 135.

46. Jung, *CW* 8, § 389.

47. Scholem, pp. 51-52.
48. Jung, *CW* 8, § 389.
49. Walter Scott, ed., *Hermetica*, vol. 1 (Boston, MA: Shambhala, 1985), pp. 161-162.
50. Neumann, p. 128.
51. Joseph Campbell, *The Way of the Animal Powers* (San Francisco, CA: Harper & Row, 1983), p. 15.
52. C. G. Jung, "The Spirit Mercurius," *CW* 13, § 242.
53. Goethe, p. 130.

CHAPTER FIVE—SYZYGY TANGO: A PICARESQUE OF DREAMS

1. C. G. Jung, "The Psychology of the Child Archetype," *CW* 9i, § 292.
2. C. G. Jung, "Psychic Conflicts in a Child," *CW* 17, p. 5.
3. Mircea Eliade, *The Two and the One* (Chicago, IL: University of Chicago, 1979), p. 100.
4. Florence Rush, *The Best Kept Secret* (Englewood Cliffs, NJ: Prentice-Hall, 1980), p. 83.
5. *Ibid.*
6. *Ibid.*, p. 9.
7. C. G. Jung, "General Aspects of Psychoanalysis, *CW* 4, § 550.
8. Mircea Eliade, *Occultism, Witchcraft, and Cultural Fashions* (Chicago, IL: University of Chicago Press, 1976), p. 95.
9. *Ibid.*, p. 116.
10. *Ibid.*, p. 94.
11. *Ibid.*, p. 116.
12. *Ibid.*
13. *Ibid.*, p. 117.
14. Johann Wolfgang Goethe, "The New Paris: A Boy's Tale," in *Autobiography and Annals: Truth and Poetry*, trans. John Oxenford (London, 1881), p. 41.
15. *Ibid.*, p. 37.
16. Robert Stein, *Incest and Human Love* (Dallas, TX: Spring Publications, 1973), p. xv.
17. C. G. Jung, "The Psychology of the Transference," *CW* 16, § 218.
18. Plato, *The Symposium*, trans. Walter Hamilton (Harmondsworth, UK: Penguin Books, Ltd., 1980), p. 86.
19. *Ibid.*, p. 87.
20. *Ibid.*, p. 89.
21. Stanley Keleman, *Somatic Reality* (Berkeley, CA: Center Press, 1979), p. 82.
22. Plato, p. 89.

23. Wallace Stevens, *The Palm at the End of the Mind*, ed. by Holly Stevens (New York: Vintage, 1972), p. 10.

24. Marvin W. Meyer, ed., *The Ancient Mysteries: A Sourcebook* (San Francisco, CA: Harper & Row, 1987), p. 214.

25. Bullough, p. 62.

26. A. R. Pope, *The Eros Aspect of the Eye* (Zürich: C. G. Jung Institute, 1968), p. 13.

27. C. G. Jung, *Memories, Dreams, Reflections*, ed. Aniela Jaffé (New York: Pantheon Books, 1961), p. 9.

28. *Ibid.*, p. 11.

29. *Ibid.*, pp. 11-12.

30. *Ibid.*, p. 15.

31. *Ibid.*, p. 13.

32. Jane Ellen Harrison, *Prolegomena to the Study of Greek Religion* (London: Merlin Press, 1962), p. 17.

33. Jung, *Memories, Dreams, Reflections*, p. 14.

34. *Ibid.*, p. 15.

35. James Hillman, *The Myth of Analysis: Three Essays in Archetypal Psychology* (New York: Harper & Row, 1972), p. 64.

36. *Ibid.*, p. 63.

37. Carl Kerényi, *Hermes: Guide of Souls* (Zürich: Spring Publications, 1976), p. 51.

38. *Ibid.*, p. 52.

39. *Ibid.*, pp. 57-58.

40. *Ibid.*, p. 58.

41. *Ibid.*, p. 59.

42. *Ibid.*, pp. 60-61.

43. *Ibid.*, p. 61.

44. *Ibid.*

45. *Ibid.*, p. 62. (Emphasis mine.)

46. *Ibid.*

47. *Ibid.*, p. 63.

48. *Ibid.*

49. *Ibid.*

50. *Ibid.*, pp. 63-64.

51. *Ibid.*, p. 65. (Emphasis mine.)

52. C. G. Jung, "The Spirit Mercurius," *CW* 13, § 263.

53. *Ibid.*, § 265.

54. *Ibid.*, § 269.

55. *Ibid.*, § 256.

56. *Ibid.*, § 257.

CHAPTER SIX—SACRED SEXUALITY IN HINDU TANTRA

1. Alain Danielou, *Shiva and Dionysus*, trans. K. F. Hurry (New York: Inner Traditions International, 1984), p. 62.
2. *Ibid.*, pp. 62-63.
3. *Ibid.*
4. *Ibid.*, pp. 54-55.
5. *Ibid.*, p. 62.
6. Quoted in Danielou, p. 9.
7. *Ibid.*, p. 54. (Emphasis mine.)
8. Ramakrishna, *The Gospel of Sri Ramakrishna*, trans. Swami Nikhilananda (New York: Ramakrishna-Vivekananda Center, 1984), p. 28.
9. *Ibid.*, pp. 28-29.
10. *Ibid.*, p. 29.
11. Vidya Dehejia, *Yogini Cult and Temple* (New Delhi: National Museum, 1986), p. 22.
12. *Ibid.*, pp. 26-27.
13. Danielou, pp. 188-189.
14. *Ibid.*, p. 32.
15. *Ibid.*, p. 64.
16. Ajit Mookerjee, *Kundalini: The Arousal of the Inner Energy* (New York: Destiny Books, 1982), pp. 31-32.
17. *Ibid.*, p. 64.
18. *Ibid.* (Emphasis in original.)
19. Danielou, p. 121.
20. Gopi Krishna, *Kundalini: The Evolutionary Energy in Man* (Boston, MA: Shambala, 1987), pp. 175-176.

CHAPTER SEVEN—GNOSTIC REFLECTIONS: SOPHIA, MAGDALEN, AND THE BRIDAL CHAMBER

1. C. G. Jung, "Psychological Aspects of the Mother Archetype," *CW* 9i, § 194.
2. Marie-Louise von Franz, *On Dreams and Death*, trans. Emmanuel Xipolitas Kennedy and Vernon Brooks (Boston, MA: Shambhala, 1987), p. 50.
3. Cited in C. A. Meier, *Ancient Incubation and Modern Psychotherapy*, trans. Monica Curtis (Evanston, IL: Northwestern University Press, 1967), pp. 103-104.
4. *Ibid.*, p. 104.
5. Cited in C. G. Jung, "Synchronicity: An Acausal Connecting Principle," *CW* 8, § 937.
6. Meier, p. 105.
7. *Ibid.*

8. *Ibid.*, p. 107.
9. *Ibid.*, p. 116.
10. Personal communication.
11. C. G. Jung, "Psychology of the Transference," *CW* 16, § 361. (Emphasis mine.)
12. Helen Meredith Garth, *Saint Mary Magdalene in Medieval Literature* (Baltimore, MD: Johns Hopkins University Press, 1950), p. 16.
13. *Ibid.*, p. 68.
14. *Ibid.*, pp. 23-24.
15. *Ibid.*, p. 68.
16. Jacobus de Voragine, *The Golden Legend* (New York: Arno Press, 1969), pp. 360-361.
17. Antti Marjanen, *The Woman Jesus Loved: Mary Magdalene in the Nag Hammadi Library and Related Documents* (Helsinki: University of Helsinki, 1995), p. 3.
18. Robert Eisenman, *James the Brother of Jesus* (New York: Penguin Books, 1997), pp. xxvii-xxviii.
19. C. G. Jung, "Psychological Aspects of the Mother Archetype," *The Archetypes and the Collective Unconscious, CW* 9i, § 195. (Emphasis mine.)
20. *Ibid.*, § 195. (Emphasis mine.)
21. *Ibid.*, § 196.
22. James M. Robinson, ed., *The Nag Hammadi Library in English*, 3rd ed. (San Francisco, CA: Harper & Row, 1978), p. 297.
23. Robert Stein, *Incest and Human Love* (Dallas, TX: Spring Publications, 1973), p. xv. (Emphasis mine.)
24. Jung, *CW* 16, § 419.
25. Apuleius, *Metamorphoses*, trans. Harold Berman (privately published, 1930, copy #302 of 900), p. 271.
26. Hans Jonas, *The Gnostic Religion* (Boston, MA: Beacon Press, 1963), pp. 108-109.
27. Kurt Rudolph, *Gnosis: The Nature and History of Gnosticism*, trans. R. McLachlan Wilson (San Francisco, CA: Harper & Row, 1987), pp. 294-295.
28. Robinson, pp. 298-299.
29. Gilles Quispel, "The Original Doctrine of Valentinus," *Vigiliae Christianae* 1, no. 1 (January 1947): 61-63.
30. Birger A. Pearson, *Gnosticism, Judaism, and Egyptian Christianity* (Minneapolis, MN: Fortress Press, 1990), p. 32.
31. Einar Thomassen, *The Spiritual Seed: The Church of the Valentinians* (Leiden: Brill, 2006), p. 50.
32. *Ibid.*, p. 44.
33. Jung, *CW* 5, § 315.
34. *Ibid.*, § 315, n. 12.
35. Erich Neumann, *The Great Mother: An Analysis of an Archetype*, trans. Ralph Manheim (Princeton, NJ: Princeton University Press, 1974), pp. 148-149.

36. Robinson, p. 148.
37. *Ibid.*
38. *Ibid.*, p. 138.
39. *Ibid.*, p. 525.
40. *Ibid.*
41. *Ibid.*, p. 526.
42. *Ibid.*, pp. 525-526.
43. *Ibid.* p. 526.
44. *Ibid.*
45. Mircea Eliade, *Shamanism: Archaic Techniques of Ecstasy* (Princeton, NJ: Princeton University Press, 1974), p. 186.
46. From the *Gospel of Philip*, Robinson, p. 153.
47. Elaine Pagels, *The Gnostic Gospels* (New York: Vintage Books, 1979), p. 5.
48. Rosamonde Miller of the Ecclesia Gnostica Mysteriorum (Church of Gnosis, Palo Alto, California), personal communication.
49. Robinson, p. 150.
50. *Ibid.*, p. 129.
51. *Ibid.*, p. 153.
52. Thomassen, p. 91.
53. *Ibid.*, p. 93.
54. *Ibid.*
55. *Ibid.*
56. Rosamonde Miller of the Ecclesia Gnostic Mysteriorum, personal communication.
57. Robinson, p. 150.
58. *Ibid.*, p. 135.
59. Carl Kerényi, *Hermes: Guide of Souls* (Zürich: Spring Publications, 1976), p. 55.
60. Robinson, p. 138.

Index

SPRING JOURNAL BOOKS

The book publishing imprint of *Spring Journal,*
the oldest Jungian psychology journal in the world

STUDIES IN ARCHETYPAL PSYCHOLOGY SERIES
Series Editor: Greg Mogenson

Collected English Papers, Wolfgang Giegerich
   Vol. 1: *The Neurosis of Psychology: Primary Papers Towards a Critical
   Psychology,* ISBN 978-1-882670-42-6, 284 pp., $20.00
   Vol. 2: *Technology and the Soul: From the Nuclear Bomb to the World
   Wide Web,* ISBN 978-1-882670-43-4, 356 pp., $25.00
   Vol. 3: *Soul-Violence* ISBN 978-1-882670-44-2
   Vol. 4: *The Soul Always Thinks* ISBN 978-1-882670-45-0

Dialectics & Analytical Psychology: The El Capitan Canyon Seminar,
   Wolfgang Giegerich, David L. Miller, and Greg Mogenson, ISBN
   978-1-882670-92-2, 136 pp., $20.00

*Northern Gnosis: Thor, Baldr, and the Volsungs in the Thought of Freud
   and Jung,* Greg Mogenson, ISBN 978-1-882670-90-6, 140 pp.,
   $20.00

Raids on the Unthinkable: Freudian and Jungian Psychoanalyses, Paul
   Kugler, ISBN 978-1-882670-91-4, 160 pp., $20.00

The Essentials of Style: A Handbook for Seeing and Being Seen, Benjamin
   Sells, ISBN 978-1-882670-68-X, 141 pp., $21.95

The Wounded Researcher: A Depth Psychological Approach to Research,
   Robert Romanyshyn, ISBN 978-1-882670-47-5, 360 pp., $24.95

*The Sunken Quest, the Wasted Fisher, the Pregnant Fish: Postmodern
   Reflections on Depth Psychology,* Ronald Schenk, ISBN 978-1-
   882670-48-5, $20.00

Fire in the Stone: The Alchemy of Desire, Stanton Marlan, ed., ISBN 978-1-882670-49-9, 176 pp., $22.95

After Prophecy: Imagination, Incarnation, and the Unity of the Prophetic Tradition, Tom Cheetham, ISBN 978-1-882670-81-9, 183 pp., $22.95

HONORING DAVID L. MILLER

Disturbances in the Field: Essays in Honor of David L. Miller, Christine Downing, ed., ISBN 978-1-882670-37-X, 318 pp., $23.95

THE DAVID L. MILLER TRILOGY

Three Faces of God: Traces of the Trinity in Literature and Life, David L. Miller, ISBN 978-1-882670-94-9, 197 pp., $20.00

Christs: Meditations on Archetypal Images in Christian Theology, David L. Miller, ISBN 978-1-882670-93-0, 249 pp., $20.00

Hells and Holy Ghosts: A Theopoetics of Christian Belief, David L. Miller, ISBN 978-1-882670-99-3, 238 pp., $20.00

THE ELECTRA SERIES

Electra: Tracing a Feminine Myth through the Western Imagination, Nancy Cater, ISBN 978-1-882670-98-1, 137 pp., $20.00

Fathers' Daughters: Breaking the Ties That Bind, Maureen Murdock, ISBN 978-1-882670-31-0, 258 pp., $20.00

Daughters of Saturn: From Father's Daughter to Creative Woman, Patricia Reis, ISBN 978-1-882670-32-9, 361 pp., $23.95

Women's Mysteries: Twoard a Poetics of Gender, Christine Downing, ISBN 978-1-882670-99-XX, 237 pp., $20.00

Gods in Our Midst: Mythological Images of the Masculine—A Woman's View, Christine Downing, ISBN 978-1-882670-28-0, 152 pp., $20.00

Journey through Menopause: A Personal Rite of Passage, Christine Downing, ISBN 978-1-882670-33-7, 172 pp., $20.00

Psyche's Sisters: Reimagining the Meaning of Sisterhood, Christine Downing, ISBN 978-1-882670-74-1, 177 pp., $20.00

Portrait of the Blue Lady: The Character of Melancholy, Lyn Cowan, ISBN 978-1-882670-96-5, 314 pp., $23.95

MORE SPRING JOURNAL BOOKS

Field, Form, and Fate: Patterns in Mind, Nature, and Psyche, Michael Conforti, ISBN 978-1-882670-40-X, 181 pp., $20.00

Dark Voices: The Genesis of Roy Hart Theatre, Noah Pikes, ISBN 978-1-882670-19-1, 155 pp., $20.00

The World Turned Inside Out: Henry Corbin and Islamic Mysticism, Tom Cheetham, ISBN 978-1-882670-24-8, 210 pp., $20.00

Teachers of Myth: Interviews on Educational and Psychological Uses of Myth with Adolescents, Maren Tonder Hansen, ISBN 978-1-882670-89-2, 73 pp., $15.95

Following the Reindeer Woman: Path of Peace and Harmony, Linda Schierse Leonard, ISBN 978-1-882670-95-7, 229 pp., $20.00

An Oedipus—The Untold Story: A Ghostly Mythodrama in One Act, Armando Nascimento Rosa, ISBN 978-1-882670-38-8, 103 pp., $20.00

The Dreaming Way: Dreamwork and Art for Remembering and Recovery, Patricia Reis and Susan Snow, ISBN 978-1-882670-46-9, 174 pp. $24.95

Living with Jung: "Enterviews" with Jungian Analysts, Volume 1, Robert and Janis Henderson, ISBN 978-1-882670-35-3, 225 pp., $21.95.

Terraspychology: Re-engaging the Soul of Place, Craig Chalquist, ISBN978-1-882670-65-5, 162 pp., $21.95.

Psyche and the Sacred: Spirituality beyond Religion, Lionel Corbet, ISBN978-1-882670-34-5, 288 pp., $23.95.

Brothers and Sisters: Discovering the Psychology of Companionship, Lara Newton, ISBN 978-1-882670-70-1, 214 pp., $23.95.

Evocations of Absence: Multidisciplinary Perspectives on Void States, ed. by Paul W. Ashton, ISBN 978-1-882670-75-8, 214 pp., $22.95.

Clio's Circle: Entering The Imaginal World of Historians, Ruth Meyer, ISBN 978-1-882670-70-3, 325 pp., $23.95.

Mortally Wounded: Stories of Soul Pain, Death, and Healing, Michael Kearney, ISBN 978-1-882670-79-6, 157 pp., $19.95.

HOW TO ORDER:

Mail: Spring Journal Books, 627 Ursulines Street # 7, New Orleans, Louisiana 70116, USA
Tel.: (504) 524-5117; **Website:** www.springjournalandbooks.com